Book design by Alice Connew
Images used under license from Shutterstock.com
Cover design by Elizabeth Taylor
Editing by Dovile Subaciute

ISBN 978-1-5272-6198-3

I SHOULD KNOW THIS

An array of information for the aspiring mind

Foreword

This book is intended to be a useful source of knowledge on a vast array of topics, and compiled into hard copy to make the information contained within accessible.

The colour format by chapter is intended to make it user friendly, so that this book can be revisited again and again, with the contents page telegraphing all relevant areas and themes for ease of reference.

The hope with this book is that will inspire learning and further education. It is not targeted at any specific age group – as one should never stop learning.

"Education is the most empowering force in the world. It creates knowledge, builds confidence, and breaks down barriers to opportunity. For children, it is their key to open the door to a better life."
Helle Thorning-Schmidt

We hope that this book will assist in the quest for knowledge and enlightenment, providing a foundation of useful information to inspire further learning.

"As our circle of knowledge expands, so does the circumference of darkness surrounding it."
Albert Einstein

The greatest gift we believe we can give is choice, and that comes from education. If this book can help with even just a small part of that journey for our readers, then we will be delighted.

(It is also an excellent source of material for pub quizzes, trivial pursuit and the like – be it for questions or answers).

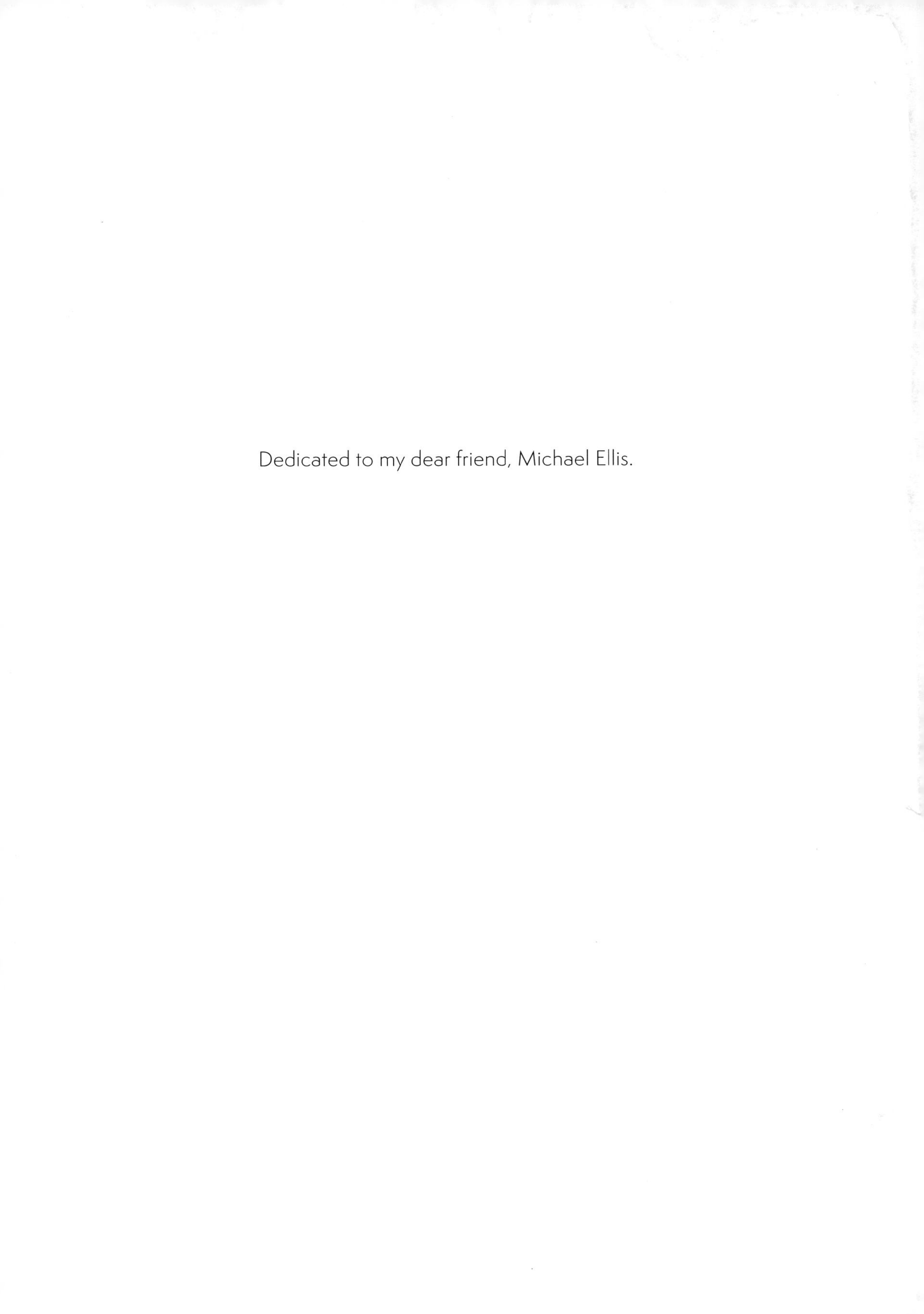

Dedicated to my dear friend, Michael Ellis.

Contents

Science and Nature........cont'd

4. Entertainment..........173

5. Sports..........211

Sports..........cont'd

6. General Knowledge.......251

Geography

Country info – Europe

FLAGS	COUNTRIES	CAPITAL CITIES	POPULATION	LAND MASS KM²
	Albania	Tirana	2,877,797	27,400
	Andorra	Andorra la Vella	77,265	470
	Austria	Vienna	9,006,398	82,409
	Azerbaijan	Baku	10,121,303	82,658

FLAGS	COUNTRIES	CAPITAL CITIES	POPULATION	LAND MASS KM²
	Belarus	Minsk	9,449,323	202,910
	Belgium	Brussels	11,589,623	30,280
	Bosnis and Herzegovina	Sarajevo	3,280,819	51,000
	Bulgaria	Sofia	6,948,445	108,560
	Croatia	Zagreb	4,105,267	55,960
	Cyprus	Nicosia	1,205,649	9,240
	Czech Republic	Prague	10,708,981	77,240
	Denmark	Copenhagen	5,792,202	42,430
	Estonia	Tallinn	1,326,535	42,390
	Finland	Helsinki	5,540,720	303,890
	France	Paris	65,273,511	547,557
	Georgia	Tbilisi	3,990,618	69,490
	Germany	Berlin	83,783,942	348,560
	Greece	Athens	10,423,054	128,900
	Greenland	Nuuk	56,751	410,450
	Hungary	Budapest	9,660,351	90,530
	Iceland	Reykjavik	341,243	100,250
	Ireland	Dublin	4,937,786	68,890
	Italy	Rome	60,461,826	294,140
	Kosovo	Prishtina	1,821,000	4,210
	Latvia	Riga	1,886,198	62,200
	Liechtenstein	Vaduz	38,128	160

FLAGS	COUNTRIES	CAPITAL CITIES	POPULATION	LAND MASS KM²
	Lithuania	Vilnius	2,722,289	62,674
	Luxembourg	Luxembourg City	625,978	2,590
	Macedonia	Skopje	2,083,390	25,220
	Malta	Valletta	441,543	320
	Moldova	Chisinau	4,033,963	32,850
	Monaco	Monaco	39,242	2
	Montenegro	Podgorica	628,066	13,450
	Netherlands	Amsterdam	17,134,872	33,720
	Norway	Oslo	5,421,241	365,268

FLAGS	COUNTRIES	CAPITAL CITIES	POPULATION	LAND MASS KM²
	Poland	Warsaw	37,846,611	306,230
	Portugal	Lisbon	10,196,709	91,590
	Romania	Bucharest	19,237,691	230,170
	Russia	Moscow	145,934,462	16,376,870
	San Marino	San Marino	33,931	60
	Serbia	Belgrade	8,737,371	87,460
	Slovakia	Bratislava	5,459,642	48,088
	Slovenia	Ljubljana	2,078,938	20,140
	Spain	Madrid	46,754,778	498,800
	Sweden	Stockholm	10,099,265	410,340
	Switzerland	Bern	8,654,622	39,516
	Turkey	Istanbul	84,160,685	769,630
	Ukraine	Kiev	43,733,762	579,320
	United Kingdom	London	67,886,011	241,930
	Vatican City	Vatican City	801	0.44

COUNTRY	CURRENCY	OFFICIAL LANGUAGE/S	DIALLING CODES
Albania	Albanian Lek (ALL)	Albanian	+355
Andorra	Euro (EUR)	Catalan	+376
Austria	Euro (EUR)	German	+43
Azerbaijan	Azerbaijani Manat (AZN)	Azerbaijani	+994
Belarus	Belarusian Ruble (BYR)	Belarusian, Russian	+375
Belgium	Euro (EUR)	Dutch, French, German	+32
Bosnia and Herzegovina	Bosnia and Herzegovina Convertible Mark (BAM)	Bosnian, Croatian, Serbian	+387
Bulgaria	Bulgarian Lev (BGN)	Bulgarian	+359
Croatia	Croatian Kuna (HRK)	Croatian	+385
Cyprus	Euro (EUR)	Greek, Turkish	+357
Czech Republic	Czech Koruna (CZK)	Czech	+420
Denmark	Danish Krone (DKK)	Danish	+45
Estonia	Euro (EUR)	Estonian	+372
Finland	Euro (EUR)	Finnish, Swedish	+358
France	Euro (EUR)	French	+33
Georgia	Georgian Lari (GEL)	Georgian	+995
Germany	Euro (EUR)	German	+49
Greece	Euro (EUR)	Greek	+30
Greenland	Danish Krone (DKK)	Greenlandic	+299
Hungary	Hungarian Forint (HUF)	Hungarian	+36
Iceland	Second Icelandic Króna (ISK)	Icelandic	+354
Ireland	Euro (EUR)	Irish, English	+353
Italy	Euro (EUR)	Italian	+39
Kosovo	Euro (EUR)	Albanian, Serbian	+383
Latvia	Euro (EUR)	Latvian	+371
Liechtenstein	Swiss Franc (CHF)	German	+423
Lithuania	Euro (EUR)	Lithuanian	+370
Luxembourg	Euro (EUR)	Luxembourgish, German, French	+352
Macedonia	Macedonian Denar (MKD)	Macedonian, Albanian	+389
Malta	Euro (EUR)	Maltese, English	+356

COUNTRY	CURRENCY	OFFICIAL LANGUAGE/S	DIALLING CODES
Moldova	Moldovan Leu (MDL)	Moldovan, Romanian	+373
Monaco	Euro (EUR)	French	+377
Montenegro	Euro (EUR)	Montenegrin	+382
Netherlands	Euro (EUR)	Dutch	+31
Norway	Norwegian Krone (NOK)	Norwegian	+47
Poland	Polish Złoty (PLN)	Polish	+48
Portugal	Euro (EUR)	Portuguese	+351
Romania	Romanian Leu (RON)	Romanian	+40
Russia	Russian Ruble (RUB)	Russian	+7
San Marino	Euro (EUR)	Italian	+378
Serbia	Serbia Dinar (RSD)	Serbian	+381
Slovakia	Euro (EUR)	Slovak	+421
Slovenia	Euro (EUR)	Slovenian	+386
Spain	Euro (EUR)	Spanish	+34
Sweden	Swedish Krona (SEK)	Swedish	+46
Switzerland	Swiss Franc (CHF)	German, French, Italian, Romansh	+41
Turkey	Turkish Lira (TRY)	Turkish	+90
Ukraine	Ukrainian Hryvnia (UAH)	Ukranian	+380
United Kingdom	Pound Sterling (GBP)	English	+44
Vatican City	Euro (EUR)	Latin, Italian	+379

Country info – Africa

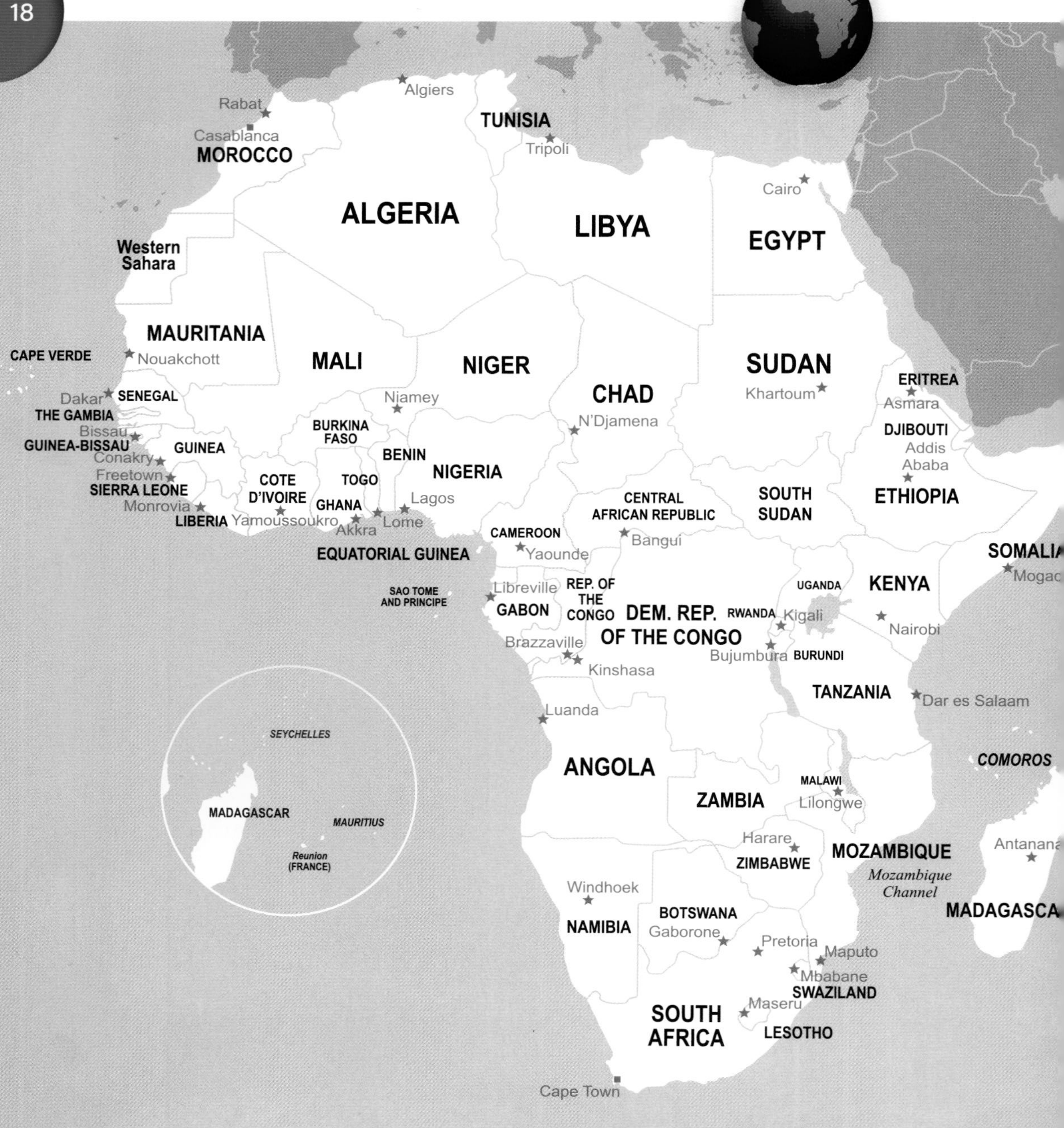

FLAGS	COUNTRIES	CAPITAL CITIES	POPULATION	LAND MASS KM²
	Algeria	Algiers	43,851,044	2,381,740
	Angola	Luanda	32,866,272	1,246,700
	Benin	Porto-Novo	12,123,200	112,760
	Botswana	Gaborone	2,351,627	566,730
	Burkina Faso	Ouagadougou	20,903,273	273,600
	Burundi	Gitega	11,890,784	25,680
	Cameroon	Yaoundé	25,680	4,030
	Cape Verde	Praia	26,545,863	472,710
	Central African Republic	Bangui	4,829,767	622,980
	Chad	N'Djamena	16,425,864	1,259,200
	Comoros Islands	Moroni	869,601	1,861
	Congo, the Democratic Republic of the	Kinshasa	5,518,087	341,500
	Congo, Republic of the	Brazzaville	89,561,403	2,267,050
	Djibouti	Djibouti	988,000	23,180
	Egypt	Cairo	102,334,404	995,450
	Equatorial Guinea	Malabo	1,402,985	28,050
	Eritrea	Asmara	3,546,421	101,000
	Eswatini	Mbabane	1,160,164	17,200
	Ethiopia	Addis Ababa	114,963,588	1,000,000
	Gabon	Libreville	2,225,734	257,670
	Gambia	Banjul	2,416,668	10,120
	Ghana	Accra	31,072,940	227,540
	Guinea	Conakry	13,132,795	245,720

FLAGS	COUNTRIES	CAPITAL CITIES	POPULATION	LAND MASS KM²
	Guinea Bissau	Bissau	1,968,001	28,120
	Ivory Coast	Yamoussoukro	26,378,274	318,000
	Kenya	Nairobi	53,771,296	569,140
	Lesotho	Maseru	2,142,249	30,360
	Liberia	Monrovia	5,057,681	96,320
	Libya	Tripoli	6,871,292	1,759,540
	Madagascar	Antananarivo	27,691,018	581,795
	Malawi	Lilongwe	19,129,952	94,280
	Mali	Bamako	20,250,833	1,220,190
	Mauritania	Nouakchott	4,649,658	1,030,700
	Mauritius	Port Louis	1,271,768	2,030
	Morocco	Rabat	36,910,560	446,300
	Mozambique	Maputo	31,255,435	786,380
	Namibia	Windhoek	2,540,905	823,290
	Niger	Niamey	24,206,644	1,266,700
	Nigeria	Abuja	206,139,589	910,770
	Réunion	Saint-Denis	895,312	2,500
	Rwanda	Kigali	12,952,218	24,670

FLAGS	COUNTRIES	CAPITAL CITIES	POPULATION	LAND MASS KM²
	São Tomé and Principe	São Tomé	219,159	960
	Senegal	Dakar	16,743,927	192,530
	Seychelles	Victoria	98,347	460
	Sierra Leone	Freetown	7,976,983	72,180
	Somalia	Mogadishu	15,893,222	627,340
	South Africa	Cape Town, Pretoria, Bloemfontein	59,308,690	1,213,090
	South Sudan	Juba	11,193,725	610,952
	Sudan	Khartoum	43,849,260	1,765,048
	Tanzania	Dodoma	59,734,218	885,800
	Togo	Lomé	8,278,724	54,390
	Tunisia	Tunis	11,818,619	155,360
	Uganda	Kampala	45,741,007	199,810
	Western Sahara* *Disputed territory claimed by Morocco and Saharawis seeking self-determination	Main town: Laayoune	597,339	266,000
	Zambia	Lusaka	18,383,955	743,390
	Zanzibar	Zanzibar City	1,303,569	2,461
	Zimbabwe	Harare	14,862,924	386,850

COUNTRY	CURRENCY	OFFICIAL LANGUAGE/S	DIALLING CODES
Algeria	Algerian Dinar (DZD)	Arabic	+213
Angola	Kwanza (AOA)	Portuguese	+244
Benin	West African CFA franc (XOF)	French	+229
Botswana	Pula (BWP)	English, Setswana	+267
Burkina Faso	West African CFA Franc (XOF)	French	+226
Burundi	Burundian Franc (BIF)	French, Kirundi	+257
Cameroon	Central African CFA Franc (XAF)	French, English	+237
Cape Verde	Cape Verdean Escudo (CVE)	Portuguese	+238
Central African Republic	Central African CFA Franc (XAF)	French, Sangho	+236
Chad	Central African CFA Franc (XAF)	French, Arabic	+235
Comoros Islands	Comorian Franc (KMF)	French, Arabic	+269
Congo, the Democratic Republic of the	Congolese Franc (CDF)	French	+243
Congo, Republic of the	Central African CFA Franc (XAF)	French	+242
Djibouti	Djiboutian Franc (DJF)	French, Arabic	+253
Egypt	Egyptian Pound (EGP)	Arabic	+20
Equatorial Guinea	Central African CFA Franc (XAF)	Spanish, French	+240
Eritrea	Eritrean Nakfa (ERN)	Tigrinya, English, Arabic	+291
Eswatini	Lilangeni (SZL)	English, Swazi	+268
Ethiopia	Ethiopian Birr (ETB)	Amharic	+251
Gabon	Central African CFA Franc (XAF)	French	+241
Gambia	Gambian Dalasi (GMD)	English	+220
Ghana	Ghanaian Cedi (GHS)	English	+233
Guinea	Guinean Franc	French	+224
Guinea Bissau	West African CFA Franc (XOF)	Portuguese	+245
Ivory Coast	West African Franc (XOF)	French	+225
Kenya	Kenyan Shilling (KES)	Swahili, English	+254
Lesotho	Lesotho Loti (LSL)	Southern Sotho, English	+266
Liberia	Liberian Dollar (LRD)	English	+231
Libya	Libyan Dinar (LYD)	Arabic	+218
Madagascar	Malagasy Ariary (MGA)	Malagasy, French	+261
Malawi	Malawian Kwacha (MWK)	English, Nyanja	+265

COUNTRY	CURRENCY	OFFICIAL LANGUAGE/S	DIALLING CODES
Mali	West African CFA Franc (XOF)	French	+223
Mauritania	Mauritanian Ouguiya (MRU)	Arabic	+222
Mauritius	Mauritian Rupee (MUR)	English, French	+230
Morocco	Moroccan Dirham (MAD)	Arabic	+212
Mozambique	Mozambican Metical (MZN)	Portuguese	+258
Namibia	Namibian Dollar (NAD)	English	+264
Niger	West African CFA Franc (XOF)	French	+227
Nigeria	Nigerian Naira (NGN)	English	+234
Réunion	Euro (EUR)	French	+262
Rwanda	Rwandan Franc (RWF)	Kinyarwanda, English, French	+250
São Tomé and Principe	São Tomé and Príncipe Dobra (STN)	Portuguese	+239
Senegal	West African CFA Franc (XOF)	French	+221
Seychelles	Seychellois Rupee (SCR)	French, English	+248
Sierra Leone	Sierra Leonean Leone (SLL)	English	+232
Somalia	Somali Shilling (SOS)	Somali	+252
South Africa	South African Rand (ZAR)	Afrikaans, English, Ndebele, Pedi, Sotho, Swati, Tshonga, Tswana, Venda, Xhosa, Zulu	+27
South Sudan	South Sudanese Pound (SDG)	English	+211
Sudan	Sudanese Pound (SDG)	Arabic, English	+249
Tanzania	Tanzanian Shilling (TZS)	Swahili, English	+255
Togo	West African CFA Franc (XOF)	French	+228
Tunisia	Tunisian Dinar (TND)	Arabic	+216
Uganda	Ugandan Shilling (UGX)	English	+256
Western Sahara	Algerian Dinar (DZD)	Arabic	+212
Zambia	Zambian Kwacha (ZMW)	English	+260
Zanzibar	Tanzanian Shilling (TZS)	Swahili, English, Arabic	+255
Zimbabwe	United States Dollar (USD)	Chewa, Chibarwe, English, Kalanga, Koisan, Nambya, Ndau, Ndebele, Shangani, Shona, sign language, Sotho, Tonga, Tswana, Venda & Xhosa	+263

Country info – Asia

FLAGS	COUNTRIES	CAPITAL CITIES	POPULATION	LAND MASS KM²
	Afghanistan	Kabul	38,928,346	652,860
	Armenia	Yerevan	2,963,243	28,470
	Azerbaijan	Baku	10,139,177	82,658
	Bahrain	Manama	1,701,575	760

FLAGS	COUNTRIES	CAPITAL CITIES	POPULATION	LAND MASS KM²
	Bangladesh	Dhaka	164,689,383	130,170
	Bhutan	Thimphu	771,608	38,117
	Brunei	Bandar Seri Begawan	437,479	5,270
	Cambodia	Phnom Penh	16,718,965	176,520
	China	Beijing	1,439,323,776	9,388,211
	Christmas Island	Flying Fish Cove	1,843	135
	Cocos Islands	West Island	596	14
	Georgia	Tbilisi	3,989,167	69,490
	Hong Kong	Hong Kong	7,496,981	1,050
	India	New Delhi	1,380,004,385	2,973,190
	Indonesia	Jakarta	273,523,615	1,811,570
	Iran	Tehran	83,992,949	1,628,550
	Iraq	Baghdad	40,222,493	434,320
	Israel	Jerusalem	8,655,535	21,640
	Japan	Tokyo	126,476,461	364,555
	Jordan	Amman	10,203,134	88,780
	Kazakhstan	Nur-Sultan	18,776,707	2,699,700
	Kuwait	Kuwait City	4,270,571	17,820
	Kyrgyzstan	Bishkek	6,524,195	191,800
	Laos	Vietiane	7,275,560	230,800
	Lebanon	Beirut	6,825,445	10,230
	Macau	Macau	649,335	30
	Malaysia	Kuala Lumpur	32,365,999	328,550

FLAGS	COUNTRIES	CAPITAL CITIES	POPULATION	LAND MASS KM²
	Maldives	Male	540,544	300
	Mongolia	Ulaanbaatar	3,278,290	1,553,560
	Myanmar	Naypyidaw	54,409,800	653,290
	Nepal	Kathmandu	29,136,808	143,350
	North Korea	Pyongyang	25,778,816	120,410
	Oman	Muscat	5,106,626	309,500
	Pakistan	Islamabad	220,892,340	770,880
	Palestine	Ramallah, East Jerusalem	5,101,414	6,020
	Philippines	Manila	109,581,078	298,170
	Qatar	Doha	2,881,053	11,610
	Russia	Moscow	145,922,521	16,376,870
	Saudi Arabia	Riyadh	34,813,871	2,149,690
	Singapore	Singapore	5,850,342	700

FLAGS	COUNTRIES	CAPITAL CITIES	POPULATION	LAND MASS KM²
	South Korea	Seoul	51,269,185	97,230
	Sri Lanka	Colombo	21,413,249	62,710
	Syria	Damascus	17,500,658	183,630
	Taiwan	Taipei	23,816,775	35,410
	Tajikistan	Dushanbe	9,537,645	139,960
	Thailand	Bangkok	69,799,978	510,890
	Tibet	Lhasa	3,180,000	1,228,400
	Timor-Leste	Dili	1,318,445	14,870
	Turkey	Ankara	84,339,067	769,630
	Turkmenistan	Ashgabat	6,031,200	469,930
	United Arab Emirates	Abu Dhabi	9,890,402	83,600
	Uzbekistan	Tashkent	33,469,203	425,400
	Vietnam	Hanoi	97,338,579	310,070
	Yemen	Sanaa	29,825,964	527,970

COUNTRY	CURRENCY	OFFICIAL LANGUAGE/S	DIALLING CODES
Afghanistan	Afghan Afghani (AFN)	Pashto, Dari	+93
Armenia	Armenian Dram (AMD)	Armenian	+374
Azerbaijan	Azerbaijani Manat (AZN)	Azerbaijani	+994
Bahrain	Bahraini Dinar (BHD)	Arabic	+973
Bangladesh	Bangladeshi Taka (BDT)	Bengali	+880
Bhutan	Bhutanese Ngultrum (BTN)	Dzongkha	+975
Brunei	Brunei Dollar (BND)	Mala	+673
Cambodia	Cambodian Riel (KHR)	Khmer	+855
China	Renminbi (CNY)	Mandarin	+86
Christmas Island	Australian Dollar (AUD)	Chinese, Malay, English	+61
Cocos Islands	Australian Dollar (AUD)	English, Malay	+891
Georgia	Georgian Lari (GEL)	Georgian	+995
Hong Kong	Hong Kong Dollar (HKD)	English, Chinese	+852
India	Indian Rupee (INR)	Hindi, English	+91
Indonesia	Indonesian Rupiah (IDR)	Indonesian	+62
Iran	Iranian Rial (IRR)	Persian	+98
Iraq	Iraqi Dinar (IQD)	Arabic, Kurdish	+964
Israel	Israeli New Shekel (ILS)	Hebrew	+972
Japan	Japanese Yen (JPY)	Japanese	+81
Jordan	Jordanian Dinar (JOD)	Arabic	+962
Kazakhstan	Kazakhstani Tenge (KZT)	Russian, Kazakh	+7
Kuwait	Kuwaiti Dinar (KWD)	Arabic	+965
Kyrgyzstan	Kyrgyzstani Som (KGS)	Kyrgyz, Russian	+996
Laos	Laotian Kip (LAK)	Lao	+856
Lebanon	Lebanese Pound (LBP)	Arabic	+961
Macau	Macanese Pataca (MOP)	Portuguese, Cantonese	+853
Malaysia	Malaysian Ringgit (MYR)	Malaysian	+60
Maldives	Maldivian Rufiyaa (MVR)	Dhivehi	+960
Mongolia	Mongolian tögrög (MNT)	Mongolian	+976
Myanmar	Myanmar Kyat (MMK)	Burmese	+95
Nepal	Nepalese Rupee (NPR)	Nepali	+977
North Korea	North Korean Won (KPW)	Korean	+850
Oman	Omani Rial (OMR)	Arabic	+968
Pakistan	Pakistani Rupee (PKR)	Urdu, English	+92

COUNTRY	CURRENCY	OFFICIAL LANGUAGE/S	DIALLING CODES
Palestine	Jordanian Dinar (JOD), Israeli New Shekel (ILS)	Arabic	+970
Philippines	Philippine Peso (PHP)	Filipino, English	+63
Qatar	Qatari Riyal (QAR)	Arabic	+974
Russia	Russian Ruble (RUB)	Russian	+7
Saudi Arabia	Saudi Arabian Riyal (SAR)	Arabic	+966
Singapore	Singapore Dollar (SGD)	English, Malay, Tamil, Mandarin	+65
South Korea	South Korean Won (KRW)	Korean	+82
Sri Lanka	Sri Lankan Rupee (LKR)	Sinhala, Tamil	+94
Syria	Syrian Pound (SYP)	Arabic	+963
Taiwan	New Taiwan Dollar (TWD)	Mandarin	+886
Tajikistan	Tajikistani Somoni (TJS)	Tajik	+992
Thailand	Thai Baht (THB)	Thai	+66
Tibet	Renminbi (RMB)	Tibetan	+895
Timor-Leste	United States Dollar (USD)	Portuguese, Tetum	+670
Turkey	Turkish Lira (TRY)	Turkish	+90
Turkmenistan	Turkmenistan Manat (TMT)	Turkmen	+993
United Arab Emirates	United Arab Emirates Dirham (AED)	Arabic	+971
Uzbekistan	Uzbekistani Som (UZS)	Uzbek, Russian	+998
Vietnam	Vietnamese Dong (VND)	Vietnamese	+84
Yemen	Yemeni Rial (YER)	Arabic	+967

Country info – North and Central America

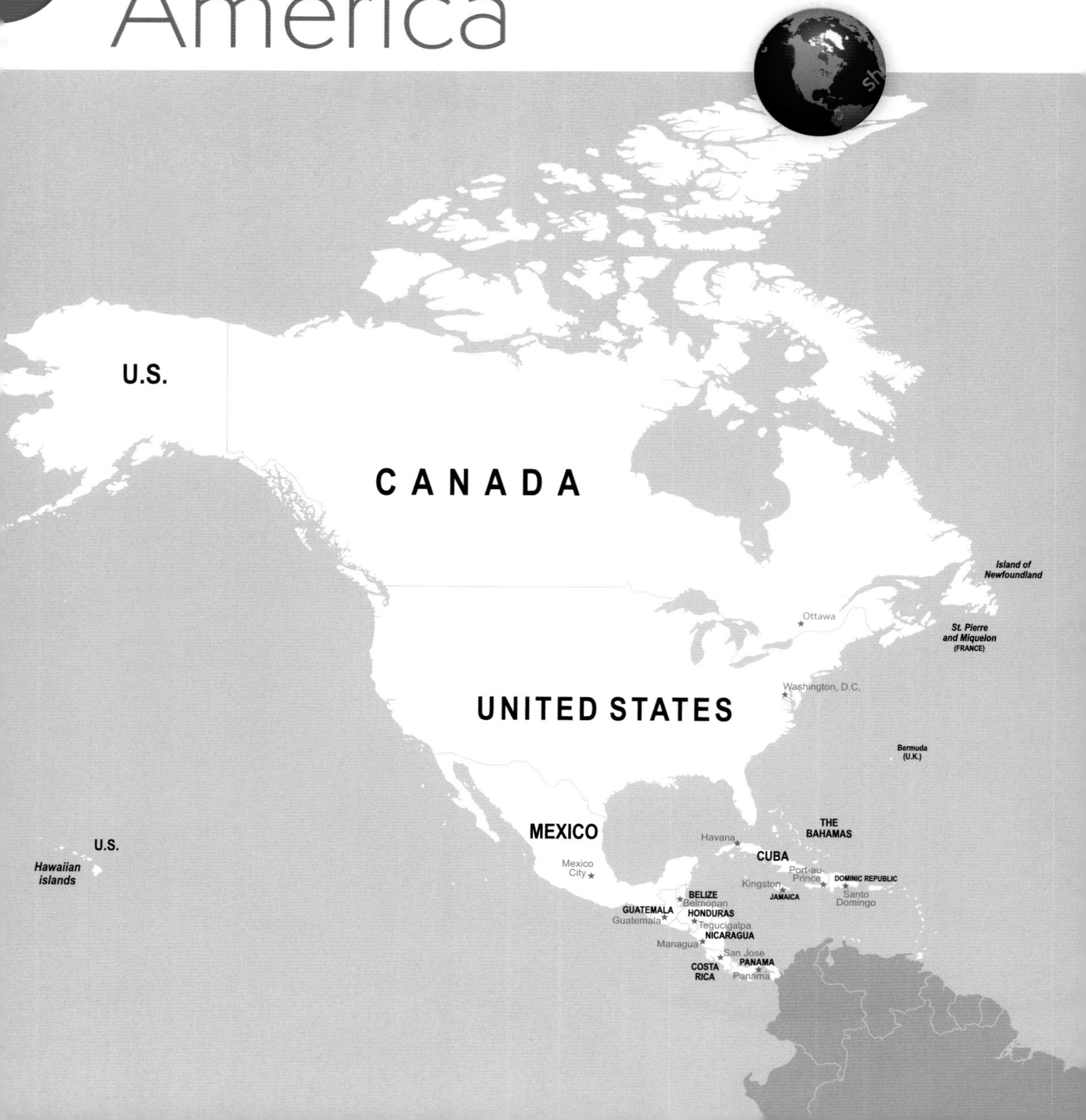

U.S.

CANADA

Island of Newfoundland

Ottawa

St. Pierre and Miquelon (FRANCE)

Washington, D.C.

UNITED STATES

Bermuda (U.K.)

MEXICO

Mexico City

U.S.

Hawaiian islands

THE BAHAMAS

Havana

CUBA

Port-au-Prince

DOMINIC REPUBLIC

Santo Domingo

Kingston

JAMAICA

BELIZE

Belmopan

GUATEMALA

Guatemala

HONDURAS

Tegucigalpa

NICARAGUA

Managua

San Jose

COSTA RICA

PANAMA

Panama

FLAGS	COUNTRIES	CAPITAL CITIES	POPULATION	LAND MASS KM²
	Anguilla	The Valley	15,003	90
	Antigua and Barbuda	Saint John's	97929	440
	Aruba	Oranjestad	106,766	180
	Bahamas	Nassau	393,244	10,010
	Barbados	Bridgetown	287,375	430
	Bermuda	Hamilton	50	62,321
	Belize	Belmopan	397,628	22,810
	British Virgin Islands	Road Town	30,231	150
	Canada	Ottawa	37,677,480	9,093,510

FLAGS	COUNTRIES	CAPITAL CITIES	POPULATION	LAND MASS KM²
	Cayman Islands	George Town	65,722	240
	Cuba	Havana	5,094,118	51,060
	Costa Rica	San José	11,326,616	106,440
	Dominica	Roseau	71,986	750
	Dominican Republic	Santo Domingo	10,847,910	48,320
	El Salvador	San Salvador	6,486,205	20,720
	Grenada	Saint George's	112,523	340
	Guadeloupe	Basse-Terre	400,124	1,690
	Guatemala	Guatemala City	17,915,568	107,160
	Haiti	Port-au-Prince	11,402,528	27,560
	Honduras	Tegucigalpa	9,904,607	111,890
	Jamaica	Kingston	2,961,167	10,830
	Martinique	Fort-de-France	375,265	1,060
	Mexico	Mexico City	128,932,753	1,943,950
	Montserrat	Brades	4,992	100
	Nicaragua	Managua	6,624,554	120,340
	Panama	Panama City	4,314,767	74,340

FLAGS	COUNTRIES	CAPITAL CITIES	POPULATION	LAND MASS KM²
	Puerto Rico	San Juan	2,860,853	8,870
	Saint Kitts and Nevis	Basseterre	53,199	260
	Saint Lucia	Castries	183,627	610
	Saint Vincent and the Grenadines	Kingstown	110,940	390
	Trinidad and Tobago	Port-of-Spain	1,399,488	5,130
	Turks and Caicos Islands	Cockburn Town	38,717	950
	US Virgin Islands	Charlotte Amalie	104,425	350
	United States	Washington D.C.	330,626,450	9,147,420

COUNTRY	CURRENCY	OFFICIAL LANGUAGE/S	DIALLING CODES
Anguilla	East Caribbean Dollar (XCD)	English	+1264
Antigua and Barbuda	East Caribbean Dollar (XCD)	English	+1268
Aruba	Aruban Florin (AWG)	Dutch, Papiamento	+297
Bahamas	Bahamian Dollar (BSD)	English	+1242
Barbados	Barbadian Dollar (BBD)	English	+1246
Bermuda	Bermudian Dollar (BMD)	English	+1441
Belize	Belize Dollar (BZD)	English	+501
British Virgin Islands	United States Dollar (USD)	English	+1284
Canada	Canadian Dollar (CAD)	English, French	+1
Cayman Islands	Cayman Islands Dollar (KYD)	English	+1345
Cuba	Cuban Peso (CUP)	Spanish	+53
Costa Rica	Costa Rican Colón (CRC)	Spanish	+506
Dominica	East Caribbean Dollar (XCD)	English	+1767
Dominican Republic	Dominican Peso (DOP)	Spanish	+1809
El Salvador	United States Dollar (USD)	Spanish	+503
Grenada	East Caribbean Dollar (XCD)	English	+1473
Guadeloupe	Euro (EUR)	French	+590
Guatemala	Guatemalan Quetzal (GTQ)	Spanish	+502
Haiti	Haitian Gourde (HTG)	Haitian Creole French, French	+509
Honduras	Honduran Lempira (HNL)	Spanish	+504
Jamaica	Jamaican Dollar (JMD)	Jamaican English	+1876
Martinique	Euro (EUR)	French	+596
Mexico	Mexican Peso (MXN)	Spanish	+52
Montserrat	East Caribbean Dollar (XCD)	English	+1664
Netherlands Antilles	Netherlands Antillean Guilder (ANG)	Dutch, English, Papiamentu	+599
Nicaragua	Nicaraguan Córdoba (NIO)	Spanish	+505

COUNTRY	CURRENCY	OFFICIAL LANGUAGE/S	DIALLING CODES
Panama	United States Dollar (USD), Balboa (PAB)	Spanish	+507
Puerto Rico	United States Dollar (USD)	Spanish, English	+1787
Saint Kitts and Nevis	East Caribbean Dollar (XCD)	English	+1869
Saint Lucia	East Caribbean Dollar (XCD)	English	+1758
Saint Vincent and the Grenadines	East Caribbean Dollar (XCD)	English	+1784
Trinidad and Tobago	Trinidad and Tobago Dollar (TTD)	English	+1868
Turks and Caicos Islands	United States Dollar (USD)	English	+1
US Virgin Islands	United States Dollar (USD)	English	+1340
United States	United States Dollar (USD)	English	+1

Country info – South America

FLAGS	COUNTRIES	CAPITAL CITIES	POPULATION	LAND MASS KM²
	Argentina	Buenos Aires	45,195,774	2,736,690
	Bolivia	La Paz, Sucre	11,673,021	1,083,300
	Brazil	Brasilia	212,559,417	8,358,140

FLAGS	COUNTRIES	CAPITAL CITIES	POPULATION	LAND MASS KM²
	Chile	Santiago	19,116,201	743,532
	Colombia	Bogotá	50,882,891	1,109,500
	Ecuador	Quito	17,643,054	248,360
	French Guiana	Cayenne	298,682	82,200
	Guyana	Georgetown	786,552	196,850
	Paraguay	Asunción	7,132,538	397,300
	Peru	Lima	32,971,854	1,280,000
	Suriname	Paramaribo	586,632	156,000
	Uruguay	Montevideo	3,473,730	175,020
	Venezuela	Caracas	28,435,940	882,050

COUNTRY	CURRENCY	OFFICIAL LANGUAGE/S	DIALLING CODES
Argentina	Argentine Peso (ARS)	Spanish	+54
Bolivia	Bolivian Boliviano (BOB)	Spanish, Aymara, Quechua	+591
Brazil	Brazilian Real (BRL)	Portuguese	+55
Chile	Chilean Peso (CLP)	Spanish	+56
Colombia	Columbian Peso (COP)	Spanish	+57
Ecuador	United States Dollar (USD)	Spanish	+593
French Guiana	Euro (EUR)	French	+594
Guyana	Guyanese Dollar (GYD)	English	+592
Paraguay	Paraguayan Guaraní (PYG)	Spanish, Paraguayan Guaraní	+595
Peru	Peruvian Nuevo Sol (PEN)	Spanish	+51
Suriname	Surinamese Dollar (SRD)	Dutch	+597
Uruguay	Uruguayan Peso (UYU)	Spanish	+598
Venezuela	Venezuelan Bolívar (VEF)	Spanish	+58

Country info – Australia and Oceania

FLAGS	COUNTRIES	CAPITAL CITIES	POPULATION	LAND MASS KM²
	American Samoa	Pago Pago	55,191	200
	Australia	Canberra	25,499,884	7,682,300
	Cook Islands	Avarua	17,564	240
	Fiji	Suva	896,445	18,270
	French Polynesia	Papeete	280,908	3,660
	Guam	Hagåtña	168,775	540
	Kiribati	Tarawa	119,449	810
	Marshall Islands	Majuro	59,190	180
	Micronesia	Palikir	115,023	700
	Nauru	Yaren District	10,824	20
	New Caledonia	Nouméa	285,498	18,280
	New Zealand	Wellington	4,822,233	263,310
	Niue	Alofi	1,626	260

FLAGS	COUNTRIES	CAPITAL CITIES	POPULATION	LAND MASS KM²
	Norfolk Island	Kingston	1,748	36
	Northern Mariana Islands	Saipan	57,559	460
	Palau	Ngerulmud	18,094	460
	Papua New Guinea	Port Moresby	8,947,024	452,860
	Pitcairn Islands	Adamstown	50	47
	Samoa	Apia	198,414	2,830
	Solomon Islands	Honiara	686,884	27,990
	Tokelau	Nukunonu	1,357	10
	Tonga	Nuku'alofa	105,695	720
	Tuvalu	Funafuti	11,792	30
	United States Minor Outlying Islands	Washington D.C.	300	34
	Vanuatu	Port Vila	307,145	12,190
	Wallis and Futuna	Mata-Utu	11,239	140

COUNTRY	CURRENCY	OFFICIAL LANGUAGE/S	DIALLING CODES
American Samoa	United States Dollar (USD)	Samoan, English	+684
Australia	Australian Dollar (AUD)	English	+61
Cook Islands	New Zealand Dollar (NZD)	Rarotongan, English	+682
Fiji	Fijian Dollar (FJD)	English, Fiji Hindi, Fiji	+679
French Polynesia	CFP Franc (CFP)	French	+689
Guam	United States Dollar (USD)	English	+1441
Kiribati	Australian Dollar (AUD)	English, Kiribati	+686
Marshall Islands	United States Dollar (USD)	Marshallese, English	+692
Micronesia	United States Dollar (USD)	English	+691
Nauru	Australian Dollar (AUD)	English, Nauruan	+674
New Caledonia	CFP Franc (CFP)	French	+687
New Zealand	New Zealand Dollar (NZD)	English, Māori	+64
Niue	New Zealand Dollar (NZD)	English, Niue	+683
Norfolk Island	Australian Dollar (AUD)	English, Norfuk	+672
Northern Mariana Islands	United States Dollar (USD)	English, Chamorro, Carolinian	+670
Palau	United States Dollar (USD)	English, Palauan	+680
Papua New Guinea	Papua New Guinean Kina (PGK)	Tok Pisin, English, Kiri Motu	+675
Pitcairn Islands	New Zealand Dollar (NZD)	English	+64
Samoa	Samoan Tālā (WST)	Samoan, English	+685
Solomon Islands	Solomon Islands Dollar (SBD)	English	+677
Tokelau	New Zealand Dollar (NZD)	Tokelauan	+690
Tonga	Tongan Pa'anga (TOP)	Tongan, English	+676
Tuvalu	Australian Dollar (AUD). Tuvaluan Dollar (TVD)	Tuvaluan, English	+688
United States Minor Outlying Islands	United States Dollar (USD)	English	+699
Vanuatu	Vanuatu Vatu (VUV)	French, English, Bislama	+678
Wallis and Futuna	CFP Franc (CFP)	French	+681

Country info – Antarctica

Antarctica does not have a native population and there are no countries, although seven nations claim different parts of it: New Zealand, Australia, France, Norway, the United Kingdom, Chile, and Argentina.

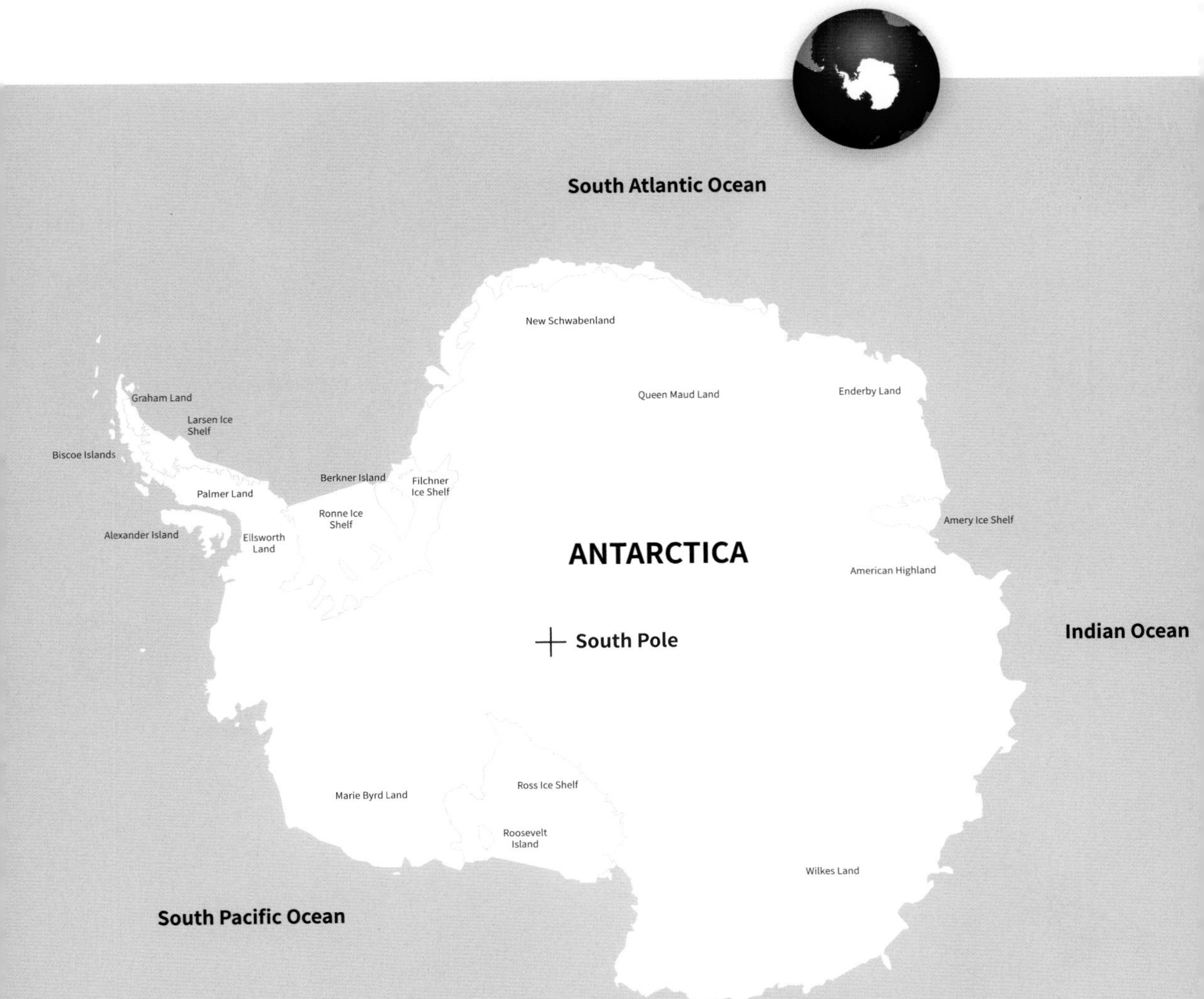

English counties

COUNTIES	TOWN
Bedfordshire	Bedford
Berkshire	Reading
Bristol	Bristol
Buckinghamshire	Aylesbury
Cambridgeshire	Cambridge
Cheshire	Chester
Cornwall	Truro
Cumbria	Carlisle
Derbyshire	Matlock
Devon	Exeter
Dorset	Dorchester
Durham	Durham
East Riding of Yorkshire	Kingston Upon Hull
East Sussex	Lewes
Essex	Chelmsford
Greater London	London
Greater Manchester	Manchester
Gloucestershire	Gloucester
Hampshire	Winchester
Herefordshire	Hereford
Hertfordshire	Hereford
Isle of Wight	Newton
Kent	Maidstone
Lancashire	Preston
Lincolnshire	Lincoln

COUNTIES	TOWN
Merseyside	Liverpool
Norfolk	Norwich
North Yorkshire	Northallerton
Northamptonshire	Northampton
Northumberland	Alnwick
Nottinghamshire	West Bridgford
Oxfordshire	Oxford
Rutland	Oakham
Shropshire	Shrewsbury
Somerset	Taunton
South Yorkshire	Sheffield
Staffordshire	Stafford
Suffolk	Ipswich
Surrey	Guildford
Sussex	Chichester
Tyne and Wear	Newcastle upon Tyne
Warwickshire	Warwick
West Midlands	Birmingham
West Sussex	Chichester
West Yorkshire	Bradford
Wiltshire	Trowbridge
Worcestershire	Worcester
Leicestershire	Leicester

West Yorkshire

Welsh counties

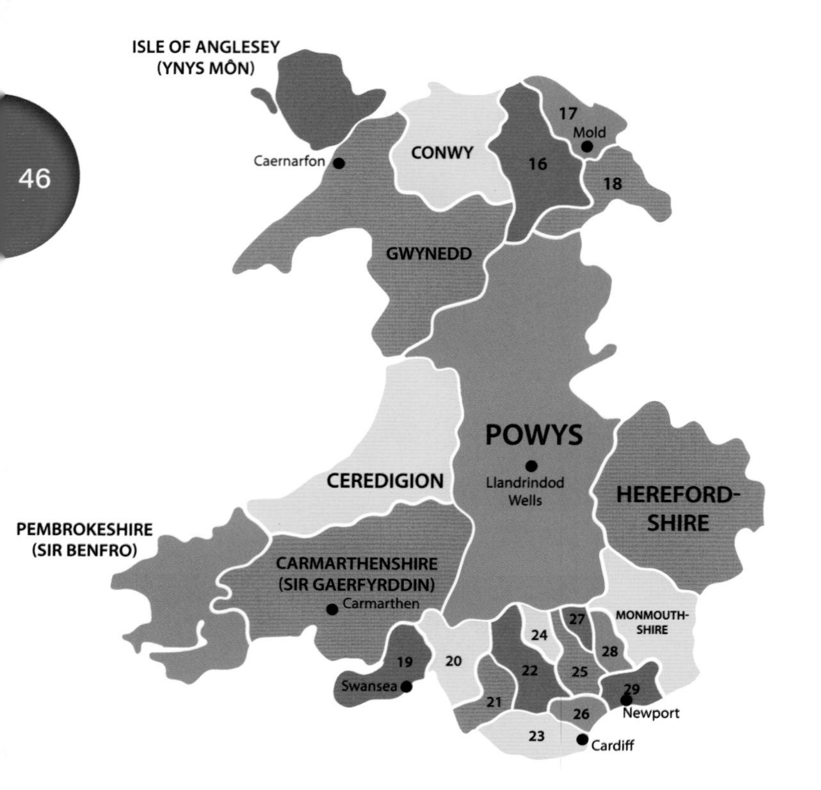

16. DENBIGHSHIRE (SIR DDINBYCH)
17. FLINTSHIRE (SIR Y FLINT)
18. WREXHAM (WRECSAM)
19. SWANSEA (ABERTAWE)
20. NEATH PORT TALBOT (CASTELL-NEDD PORT TALBOT)
21. BRIDGEND (PEN-Y-BONT AR OGWR)
22. RHONDDA CYON TAFF
23. VALE OF GLAMORGAN (BRO MORGANNWG)
24. MERTHYL TIDFIL (MERTHYL TIDFUL)
25. CAERPHILLY (CAERFFILI)
26. CARDIFF (CAERDYDD)
27. BLANEAU GWENT
28. TORFAEN (TOR-FAEN)
29. NEWPORT (CASNEWYDD)

COUNTIES	TOWN
Anglesey	Llangefni
Blaenau Gwent	Ebbw Vale
Bridgend	Bridgend
Caerphilly	Caerphilly
Carmarthenshire	Caernarfon
Conwy	Conwy
Denbighshire	Ruthin
Flintshire	Mold
Gwynedd	Caernarfon
Merthyr Tydfil	Merthyr Tydfil
Monmountshire	Newport

COUNTIES	TOWN
Neath Port Talbot	Neath
Newport	Newport
Pembrokeshire	Haverford-west
Powys	Newtown
Rhondda Cynon Taf	Aberdare
Torfaen	Pontypool
Swansea	Swansea
Vale of Glamorgan	Cardiff
Wrexham	Wrexham

Scottish counties

COUNTIES	TOWN
Aberdeenshire	Aberdeen
Angus	Forfar
Argyll and Bute	Lochgilphead
Ayrshire	Ayr
Clackmannanshire	Alloa
Dumfries and Galloway	Dumfries
Dunbartonshire	Dumbarton
East Lothian	Haddington
Falkirk	Falkirk
Fife	Cupar
Highland	Inverness
Inverclyde	Greenock
Lanarkshire	Hamilton
Midlothian	Edinburgh
Morayshire	Elgin
Perth and Kinross	Perth
Renfrewshire	Renfrew
Scottish Borders	Newtown St Boswells
Stirlingshire	Stirling
West Lothian	Linlithgow

1. CLACKMANNANSHIRE
2. WEST DUNBARTONSHIRE
3. EAST DUNBARTONSHIRE
4. FALKIRK
5. WEST LOTHIAN
6. CITY OF EDINBURGH
7. MIDLOTHIAN
8. EAST LOTHIAN
9. INVERCLYDE
10. RENFREWSHIRE
11. GLASGOW CITY
12. NORTH LANARKSHIRE

Scottish council areas and counties

Northern Irish disctricts

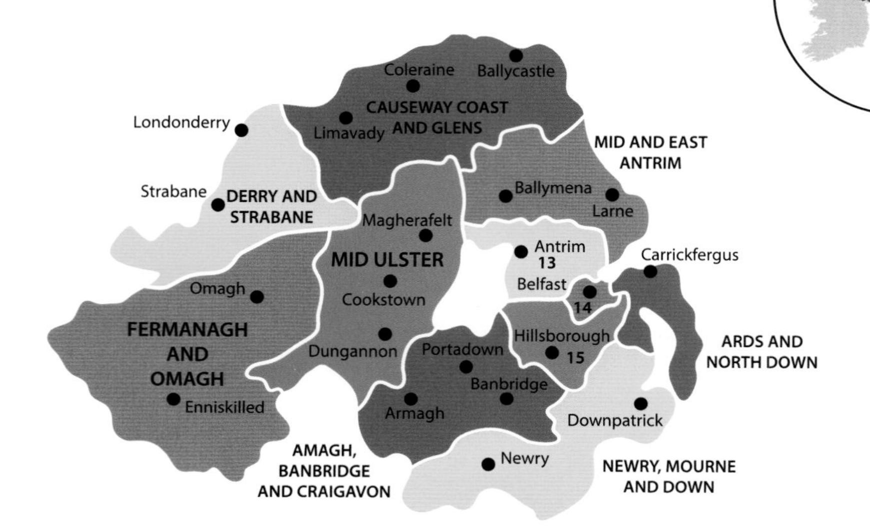

13. ANTRIM AND NEWTOWNABBEY
14. BELFAST
15. LISBURN AND CASTLEREAGH

COUNTIES	TOWN
Antrim and Newtownabbey	Belfast
Ards and North Down	Carrickfergus
Armagh, Banbridge and Craigavon	Armagh
Causeway Coast and Glens	Ballycastle
Derry and Strabane	Londonderry
Fermanagh and Omagh	Enniskillen
Lisburn and Castlereagh	Hillsborough
Mid and East Antrim	Ballymena
Mid Ulster	Dungannon
Newry, Mourne and Down	Downpatrick
Tyrone	Omagh

Irish counties

REPUBLIC OF IRELAND COUNTIES		
Carlow	Leitrim	Waterford
Cavan	Limerick	Westmeath
Clare	Longford	Wexford
Cork	Louth	Wicklow
Donegal	Mayo	
Dublin	Meath	
Galway	Monaghan	
Kerry	Offaly	
Kildare	Roscommon	
Kilkenny	Sligo	
Laois	Tipperary	

Indian states and territories

STATE	CAPITALS	POPULATION	AREA (KM²)
Andhra Pradesh	Hyderabad (de jure) Amaravati (de facto)	49,506,79	160,20
Arunachal Pradesh	Itanagar	1,383,727	83,743
Assam	Dispur	31,205,57	78,550
Bihar	Patna	104,099,452	94,163
Chhattisgarh	Naya Raipur	25,545,198	135,194
Goa	Panaji	1,458,545	3,702
Gujarat	Gandhinagar	60,439,692	196,024
Haryana	Chandigarh	25,351,462	44,212

STATE	CAPITALS	POPULATION	AREA (KM²)
Himachal Pradesh	Shimla (Summer) Dharamshala (Winter)	6,864,602	55,673
Jharkhand	Ranchi	32,988,134	74,677
Karnataka	Bangalore	61,095,297	191,791
Kerala	Thiruvananthapuram	33,406,061	38,863
Madhya Pradesh	Bhopal	72,626,809	308,252
Maharashtra	Mumbai (Summer) Nagpur (Winter)	112,374,333	307,713
Manipur	Imphal	2,855,794	22,347
Meghalaya	Shillong	2,966,889	22,720
Mizoram	Aizawl	1,097,206	21,081
Nagaland	Kohima	1,978,502	16,579
Orrisa	Bhubaneswar	41,974,218	155,820
Punjab	Chandigarh	27,743,338	50,362
Rajasthan	Jaipur	68,548,437	342,269
Sikkim	Gangtok	610,577	7,096
Tamil Nadu	Chennai	72,147,030	130,058
Telangana	Hyderabad[a]	35,193,978	114,840
Tripura	Agartala	3,673,917	10,492
Uttar Pradesh	Lucknow	199,812,341	243,286
Uttarakhand	Gairsain (Summer) Dehradun (Winter)	10,086,292	53,483
West Bengal	Kolkata	91,276,115	88,752

UNION TERRITORY	CAPITALS	POPULATION	AREA (KM²)
Andaman and Nicobar Islands	Port Blair	380,581	8,249
Punjab Chandigarh	Chandigarh	1,055,450	114
Dadra and Nagar Haveli and Daman and Diu	Daman	586,956	603
Delhi	New Delhi	16,787,941	1,490
Jammu and Kashmir	Srinagar (Summer) Jammu (Winter)	12,258,433	55,538
Ladakh	Leh (Summer) Kargil (Winter)	290,492	174,852
Lakshadweep	Kavaratti	64,473	32
Puducherry	Pondicherry	1,247,953	492

US states

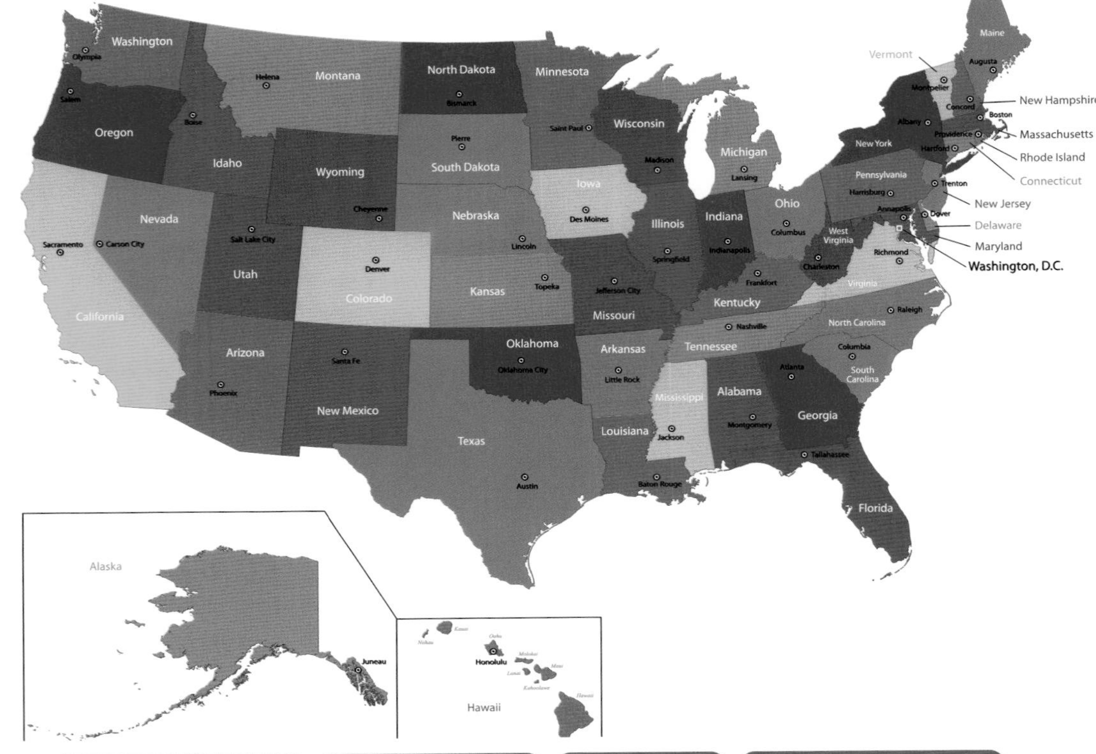

STATE NAMES	CAPITALS	POPULATION	AREA (KM²)
Alabama (AL)	Montgomery	4,849,00	131,426.36
Alaska (AK)	Juneau	737,000	1,481,346
Arizona (AZ)	Phoenix	6,731,000	294,313.30
Arkansas (AR)	Little Rock	2,966,000	134,856.00
California (CA)	Sacramento	38,803,000	403,931.96
Colorado (CO)	Denver	5,356,00	268,698.39
Connecticut (CT)	Hartford	3,597,000	268,628.39
Delaware (DE)	Dover	936,000	5,060.84
Florida (FL)	Tallahassee	19,893,000	139,760.29
Georgia (GA)	Atlanta	10,097,000	149,975.85
Hawaii (HI)	Honolulu	1,420,000	16,635.49
Idaho (ID)	Boise	1,634,000	214,313.75
Illinois (IL)	Springfield	12,881,000	143,961.90
Indiana (IN)	Indianapolis	6,597,000	92,895.10

STATE NAMES	CAPITALS	POPULATION	AREA (KM²)
Iowa (IA)	Des Moines	3,107,000	144,700.05
Kansas (KS)	Topeka	2,904,000	211,899.88
Kentucky (KY)	Frankfort	4,413,000	102,895.05
Louisiana (LA)	Baton Rouge	4,650,000	112,825.06
Maine (ME)	Augusta	1,330,000	79,932.21
Maryland (MD)	Annapolis	5,976,000	206,188.95
Massachusetts (MA)	Boston	6,745,000	20,305.51
Michigan (MI)	Lansing	9,910,000	147,121.68
Minnesota (MN)	Saint Paul	5,457,000	206,188.95
Mississippi (MS)	Jackson	2,994,000	121,488.72
Missouri (MO)	Jefferson City	6,064,000	178,413.92
Montana (MT)	Helena	1,024,000	376,977.95
Nebraska (NE)	Lincoln	1,882,000	199,097.57
Nevada (NV)	Carson City	2,839,000	284,448.03
New Hampshire (NH)	Concord	1,327,000	23,227.01
New Jersey (NJ)	Trenton	8,938,000	19,209.94
New Mexico (NM)	Santa Fe	2,086,000	314,310.60
New York (NY)	Albany	19,746,000	122,283.70
North Carolina (NC)	Raleigh	9,944,000	126,160.91
North Dakota (ND)	Bismarck	739,000	178,647.02
Ohio (OH)	Columbus	11,594,000	106,054.83
Oklahoma (OK)	Oklahoma City	3,878,000	177,846.71
Oregon (OR)	Salem	3,970,000	268,631.09
Pennsylvania (PA)	Harrisburg	12,787,000	116,075.50
Rhode Island (RI)	Providence	1,055,000	2,706.54
South Carolina (SC)	Columbia	4,832,000	77,981.95
South Dakota (SD)	Pierre	853,000	196,541.25
Tennessee (TN)	Nashville	6,549,000	106,751.54
Texas (TX)	Austin	26,957,000	678,051.12
Utah (UT)	Salt Lake City	2,943,000	212,751.98
Vermont (VT)	Montpelier	627,000	23,957.39
Virginia (VA)	Richmond	8,326,000	102,547.99
Washington (WA)	Olympia	7,062,000	172,348.17
West Virginia (WV)	Charleston	1,855,413	62,361.73
Wisconsin (WI)	Madison	5,758,000	140,662.25
Wyoming (WY)	Cheyenne	584,000	251,487.85

Canada

PROVINCES & TERRITORIES	CAPITALS	POPULATION	AREA (KM²)
Alberta (AB)	Edmonton	4,286,134	640,081.87
British Columbia (BC)	Victoria	4,817,160	922,509.29
Manitoba (MB)	Winnipeg	1,338,109	552,329.52
New Brunswick (NB)	Fredericton	759,655	552,239.52
Newfoundland & Labrador (NL)	St. John's	528,817	71,377.18
Nova Scotia (NS)	Halifax Regional Municipality	953,869	52,939.44
Northwest Territories (NT) - Territory	Yellowknife	44,520	270,510.76
Nunavut (NU) - Territory	Iqaluit	37,996	1,877,787.62
Ontario (ON)	Toronto	14,193,384	908,607.67
Prince Edward Island (PE)	Charlottetown	152,021	5,685.73
Quebec (QC)	Quebec City	8,394,034	1,356,547.02
Saskatchewan (SK)	Regina	1,163,925	588,239.21
Yukon (YT) - Territory	Whitehorse	38,459	474,712.64

Australia

STATES AND TERRITORIES	CAPITALS	POPULATION	AREA (KM²)
Ashmore and Cartier Islands (Territory)	N/A	Uninhabited	5
Australia and Australian Capital Territory (Inc. Jervis Bay Territory)	Canberra	401,737	2431
Australian Antarctic Territory	Davis Station	Under 1,000	5,896,500
Christmas Island (Territory)	Flying Fish Cove	2,072	135
Cocos (Keeling) Islands (Territory)	West Island	596	14
Coral Sea Islands (Territory)	N/A	Uninhabited	780,000
Heard and McDonald Islands (Territory)	N/A	Uninhabited	372
New South Wales	Sydney	7,700,000	800,642
Norfolk Island (Territory)	Kingston	2,169	35
Northern Territory	Darwin	244,500	1,349,129
Queensland	Brisbane	4,900,000	1,730,648
South Australia	Adelaide	1,710,000	983,482
Tasmania	Hobart	519,166	68,401
Victoria	Melbourne	6,150,000	227,416
Western Australia	Perth	2,640,000	2,529,875

New Zealand

REGIONS AND TERRITORIES	POPULATION	AREA (KM²)
Auckland	1,527,100	5,600
Bay of Plenty	282,300	12,447
Canterbury	574,300	45,346
Cook Islands (Territory)	14,974	240
Gisborne	47,100	8,351
Hawke's Bay	159,000	14,164
Manawatu - Wanganui	232,000	22,215
Marlborough	44,800	12,484
Nelson - Tasman	49,100	9,786
Niue (Territory)	1,190	260
Northland	166,100	13,941
Otago	211,700	31,990
Ross Dependency (Territory)	Seasonal Estimate: 0-1,000	450,000
Southland	96,500	34,347
Taranaki	114,800	7,273
Tokelau (Territory)	1,411	10
Waikato	430,800	25,598
Wellington	491,500	8,124
West Coast	32,800	23,336

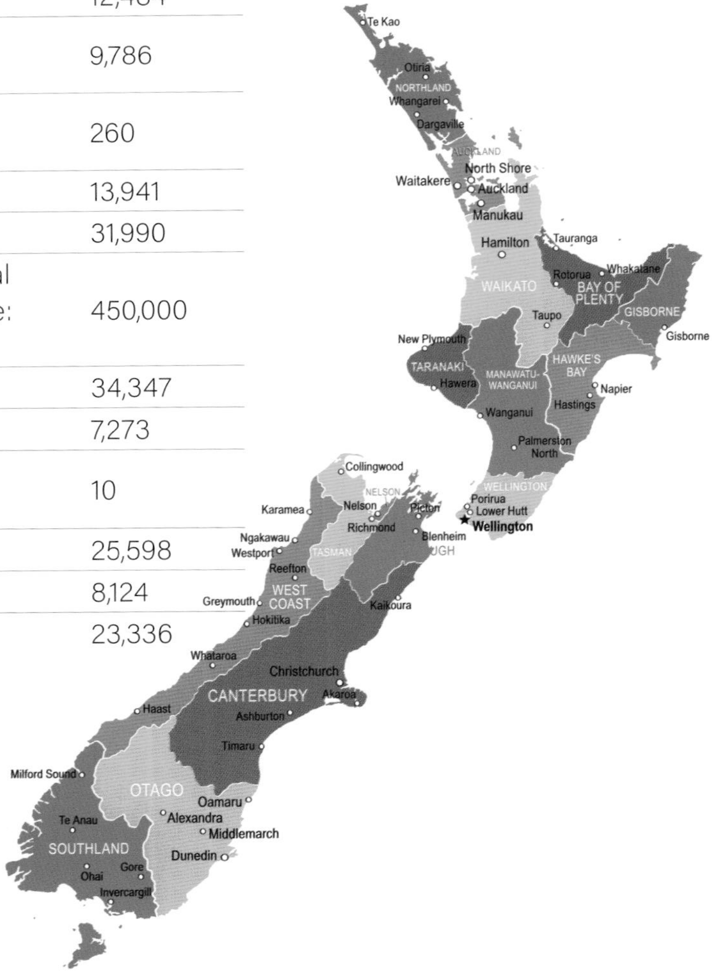

Bordering countries

Countries that share the most borders

COUNTRY	BORDER LENGTH (KM)	NO. COUNTRIES BORDERED
China	22,117	14
Russia	20,017	14
Brazil	14,681	10
Democratic Republic of the Congo	10,730	9
Germany	3,621	9
France	2,751	8
Zambia	5,667	8
Tanzania	3,861	8
Turkey	2,648	8
Austria	2,562	8
Serbia	2,027	8

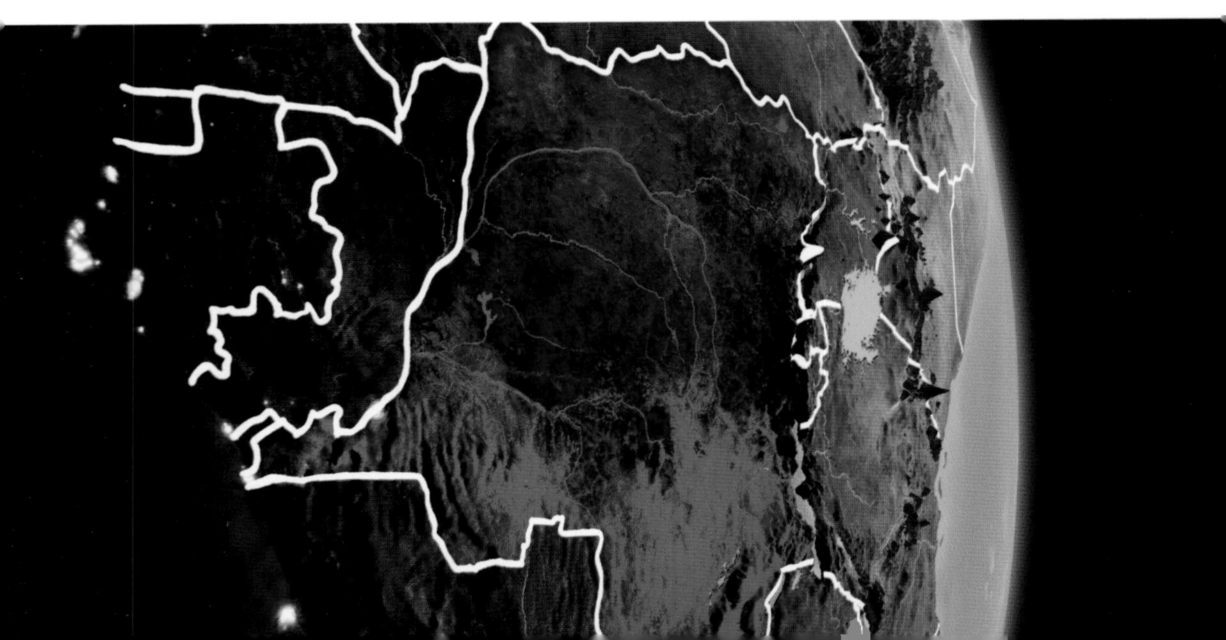

Largest landlocked countries

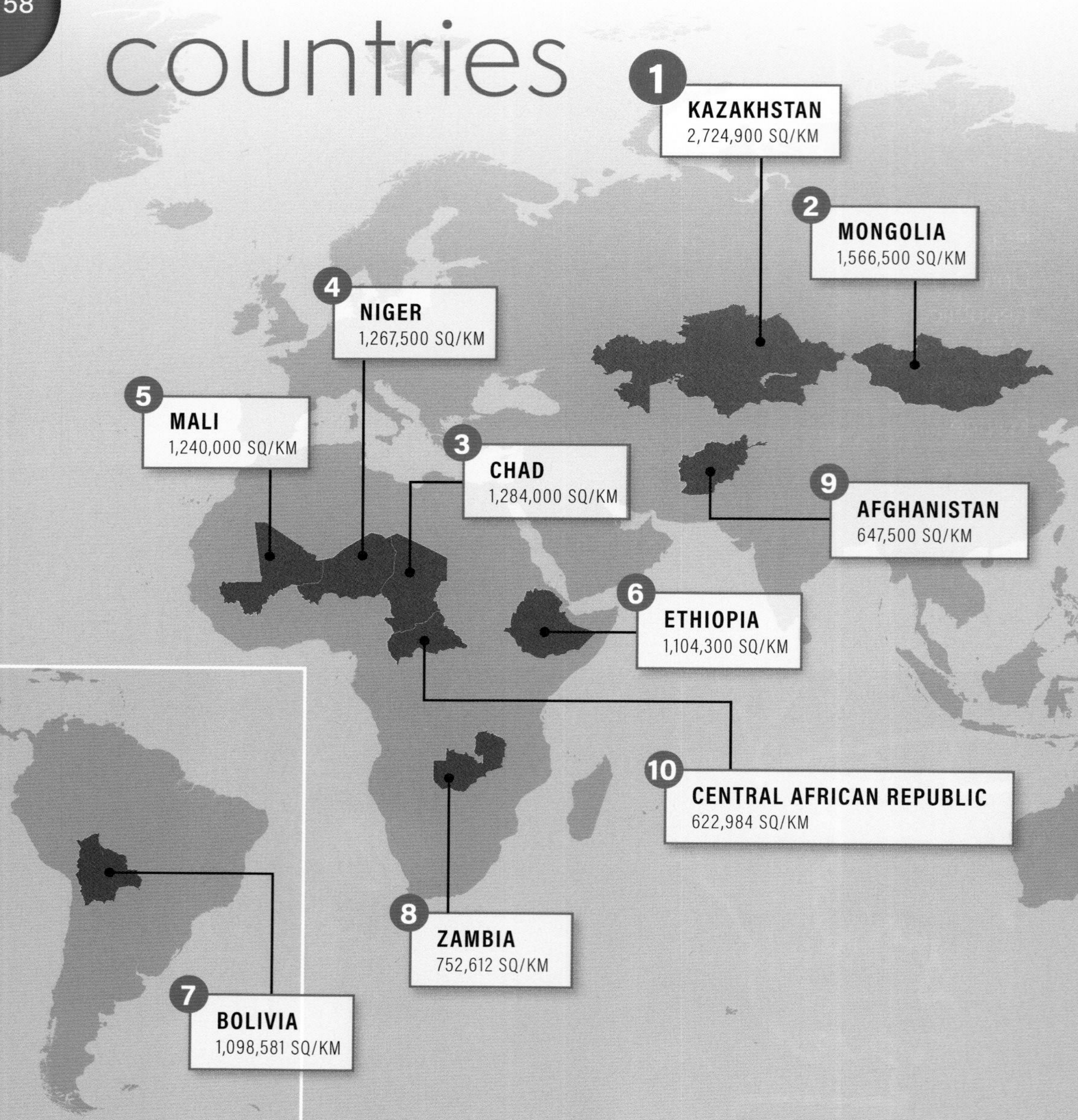

The only two doubly landlocked countries

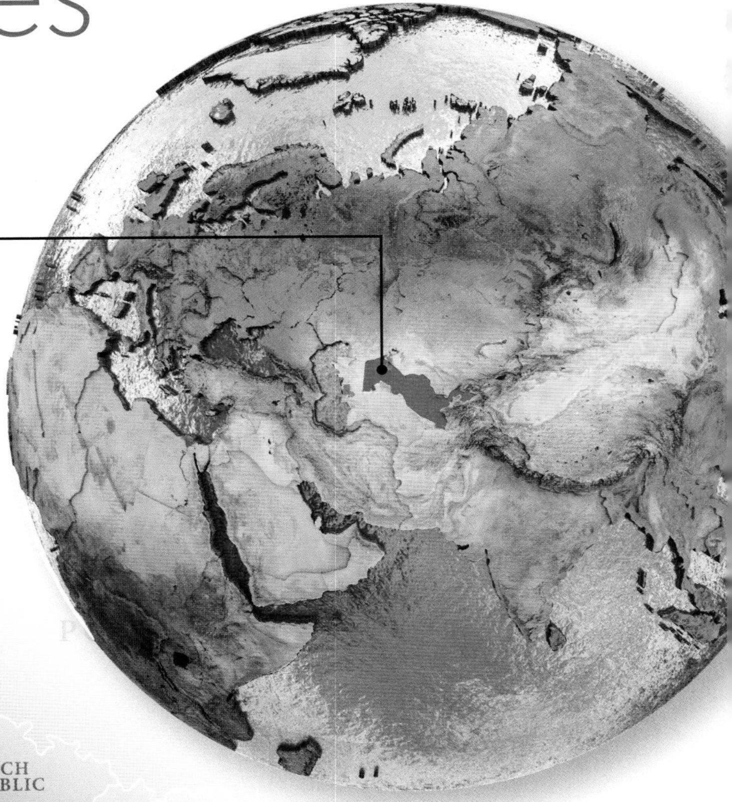

UZBEKISTAN
Surrounded by the landlocked countries of: Kazakhstan, Kyrgyzstan, Tajikistan, Afghanistan and Turkmenistan

LIECHTENSTEIN
Surrounded by the landlocked countries of Switzerland and Austria

Landlocked countries by continent

EUROPE	
San Marino	Liechtenstein
Moldova	Czech Republic
Belarus	Austria
Luxembourg	Serbia
Andorra	Slovakia
Hungary	Switzerland
Macedonia	Vatican City

AMERICA
Bolivia
Paraguay

10 highest mountains

ASIA

- Afghanistan
- Armenia
- Azerbaijan
- Bhutan
- Kazakhstan
- Kyrgyzstan
- Laos
- Mongolia
- Nepal
- Tajikistan
- Turkmenistan
- Uzbekistan

AFRICA

- Zimbabwe
- Zambia
- Central African Republic
- Uganda
- Botswana
- Mali
- South Sudan
- Niger
- Rwanda
- Chad
- Burundi
- Burkina Faso
- Eswatini
- Lesotho

10 largest oceans and seas

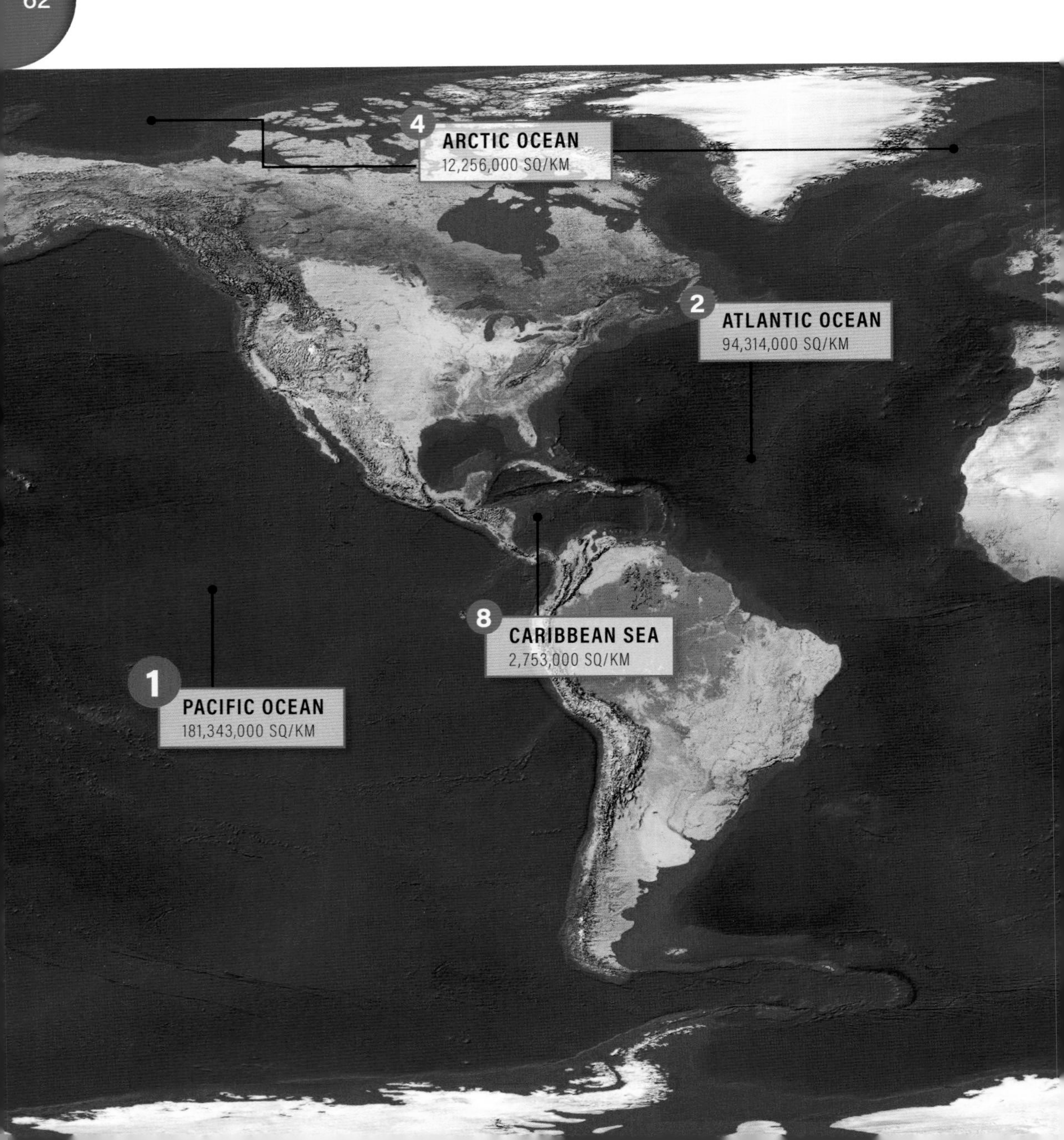

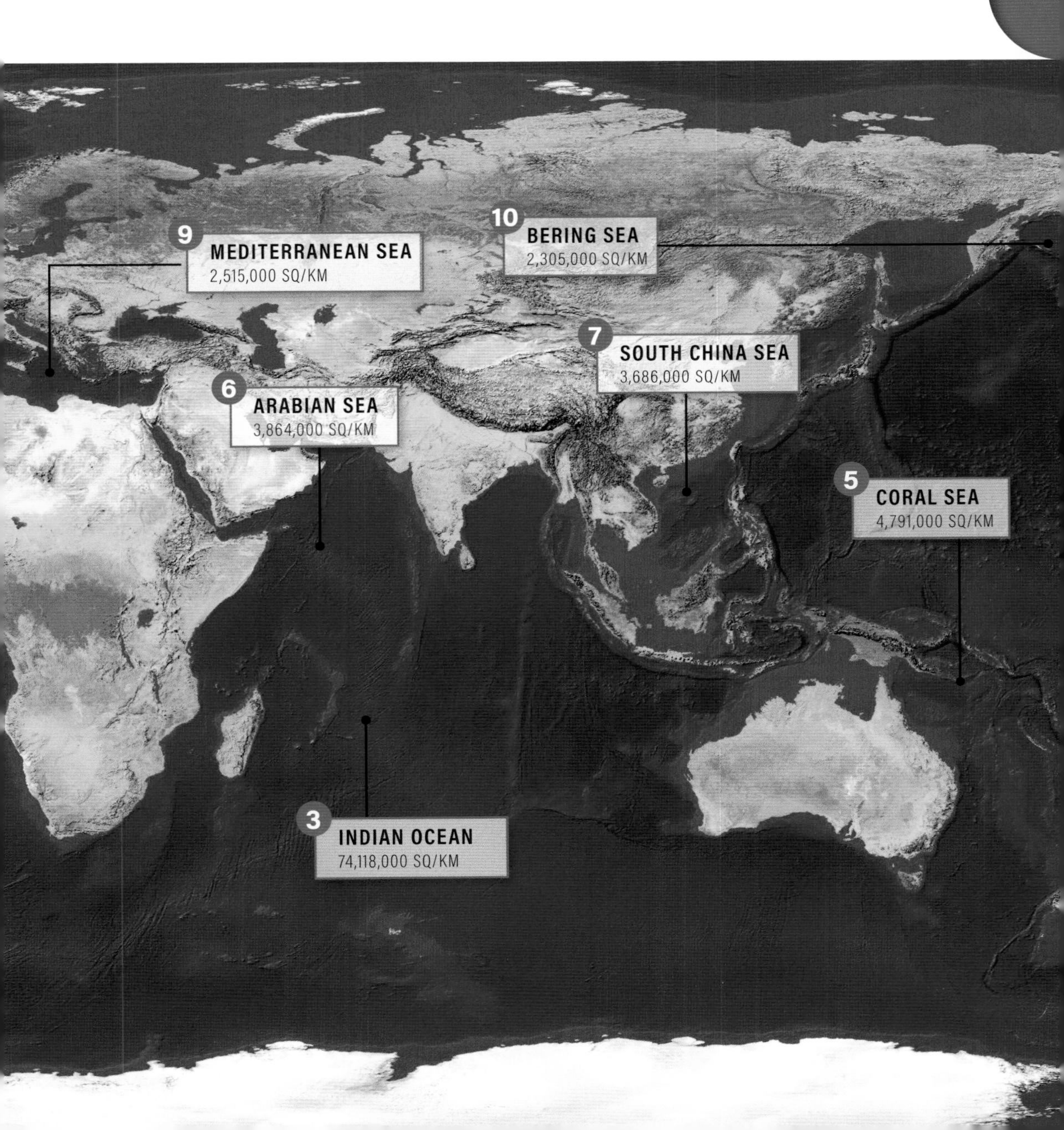
9
MEDITERRANEAN SEA
2,515,000 SQ/KM
10
BERING SEA
2,305,000 SQ/KM
7
SOUTH CHINA SEA
3,686,000 SQ/KM
6
ARABIAN SEA
3,864,000 SQ/KM
5
CORAL SEA
4,791,000 SQ/KM
3
INDIAN OCEAN
74,118,000 SQ/KM

10 longest rivers

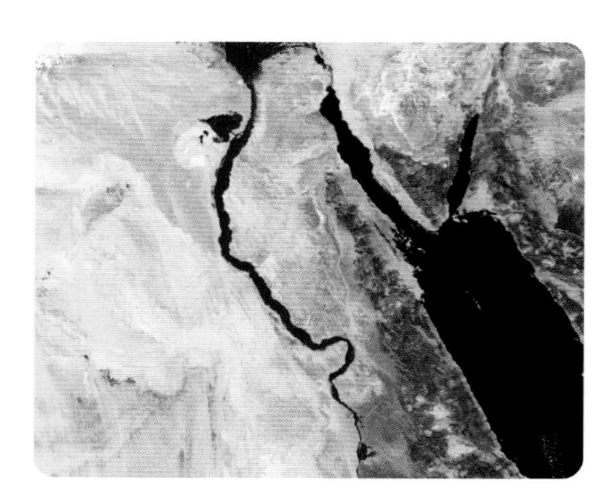

1

River: Nile
Length (km): 6,650
Source: White Nile, Blue Nile
Mouth: Mediterranean Sea
Location: Tanzania, Uganda, Rwanda, Burundi, the Democratic Republic of the Congo, Kenya, Ethiopia, Eritrea, South Sudan, Sudan and Egypt

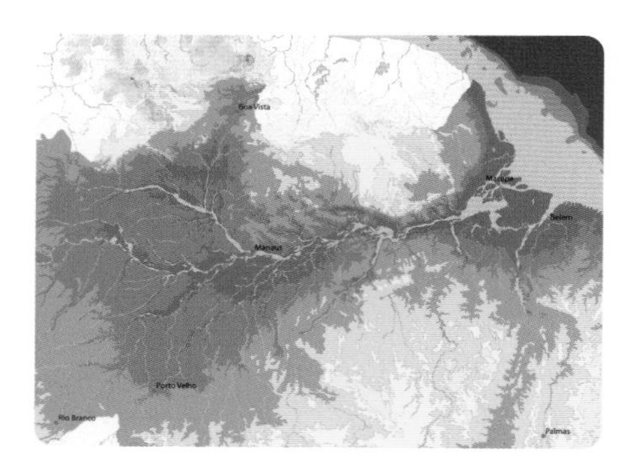

2

River: Amazon
Length (km): 6,400
Source: Mismi
Mouth: Atlantic Ocean
Location: Brazil, Bolivia, Peru, Ecuador, Colombia, Venezuela, Guyana and Suriname, French Guiana.

3

River: Yangtze
Length (km): 6,300
Source: Qinhai
Mouth: East China Sea
Location: China

	RIVER NAME	LENGTH (KM)	SOURCE	MOUTH	LOCATION
4	The Mississippi-Missouri	6,275	Lake Itasca	Gulf of Mexico	United States of America
5	Yenisei	5,539	Mongolia	Arctic Ocean, Yeniesi Gulf, Kara Sea	Russia, China, Mongolia
6	Yellow River	5,464	Bayan Har Mountains	Bohai Sea	China
7	Ob-Irtysh	5,410	Katun River, Belukha Mountain, Altai Republic	Gulf of Ob	Russia, Kazakhstan, China, Mongolia
8	Congo	4,700	East African Rift, Chambeshi River	Atlantic Ocean	Democratic Reublic of Congo, Gabon, Cameroon
9	Amur	4,444	Shilka River, Argun River	Sea of Okhotsk, Strait of Tartary, Pacific Ocean	Russia, China, Mongolia
10	Lena	4,400	Baikal Mountains	Arctic Ocean	Russia

Lena River, Russia

10 largest lakes

	LAKE NAME	AREA (SQ.KM)	LENGTH (KM)	DEPTH (M)	LOCATION
1	Caspian Sea*	370,992	1,225	1,025	Iran, Azerbaijan, Russia, Kazakhstan, Turkmenistan,
2	Superior	82,103	560	406	U.S, Canada
3	Victoria	68,800	360	85	Tanzania, Uganda
4	Huron	59,600	330	229	U.S, Canada
5	Michigan	58,000	516	281	U.S
6	Aral	33,669	450	68	Kazakhstan, Uzbekistan
7	Tanganyika	32,900	675	1,435	Tanzania, Congo
8	Baikal	31,722	635	1,741	Russia
9	Great Bear	31,153	373	82	Canada
10	Nyasa	29,600	579	109	Malawi, Mozambique, Tanzania

*Caspian Sea can be called either a lake or a sea

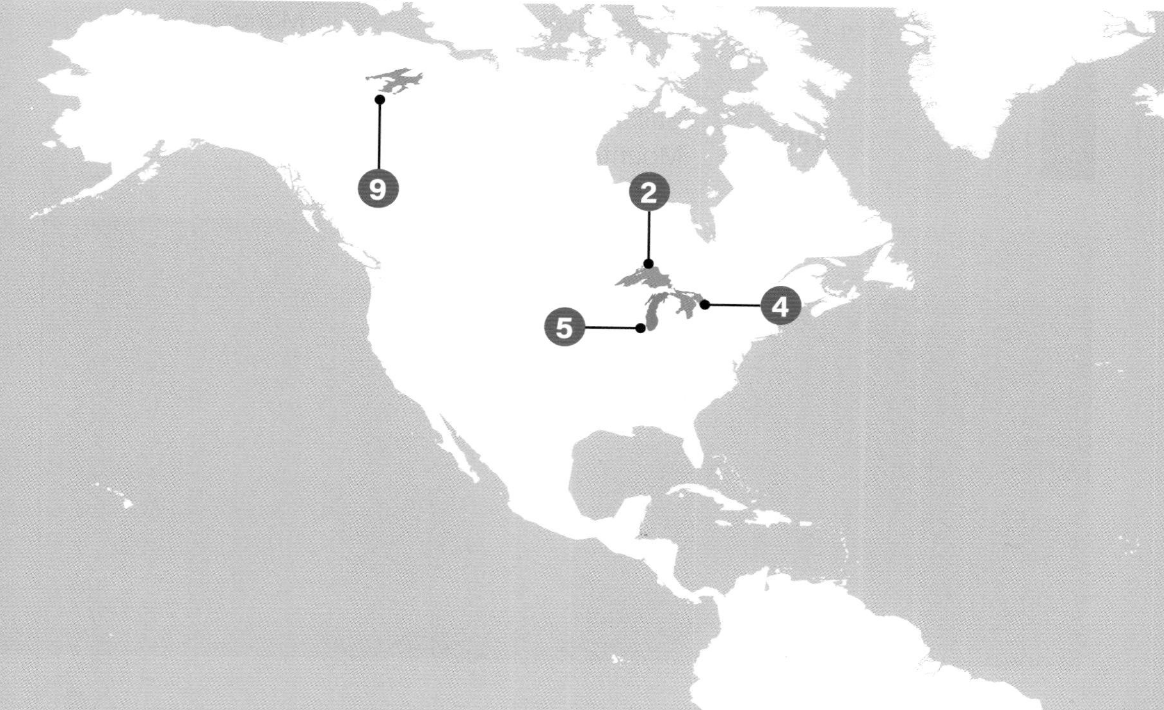

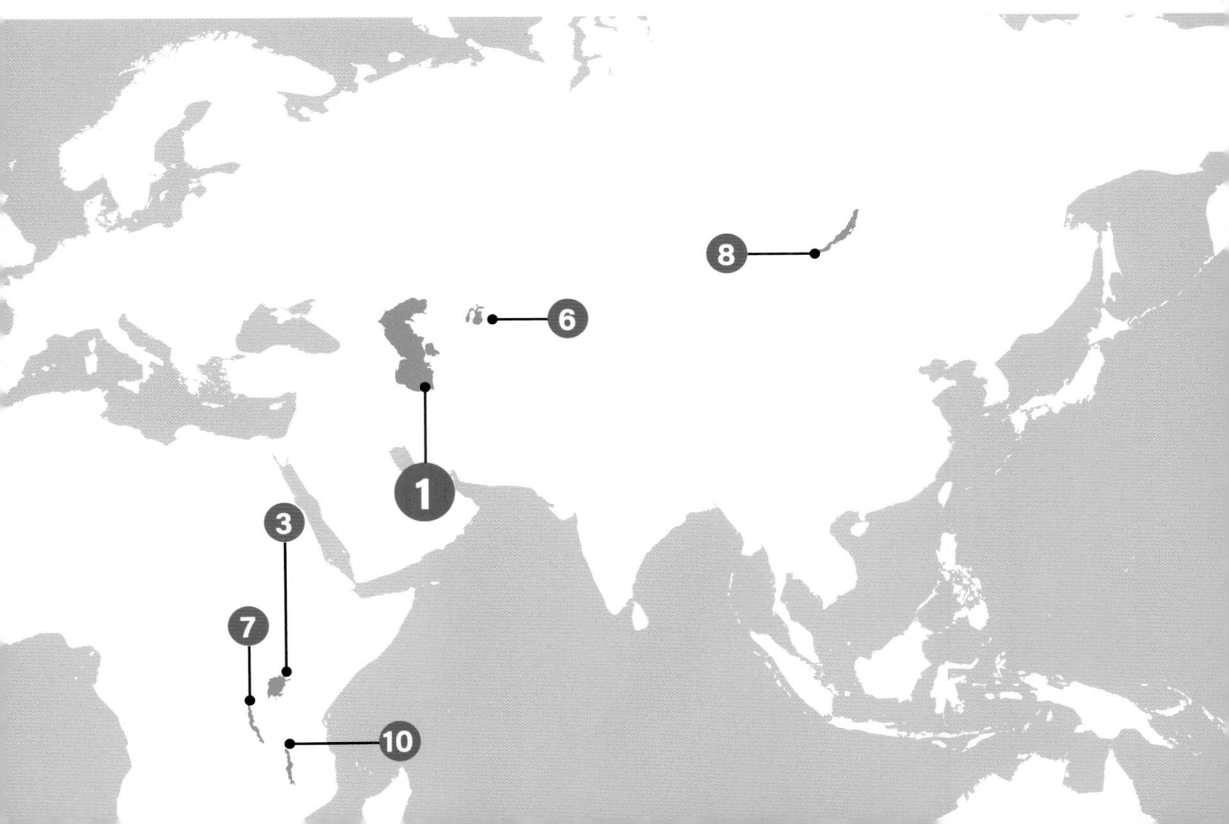
8
6
1
3
7
10

10 largest islands

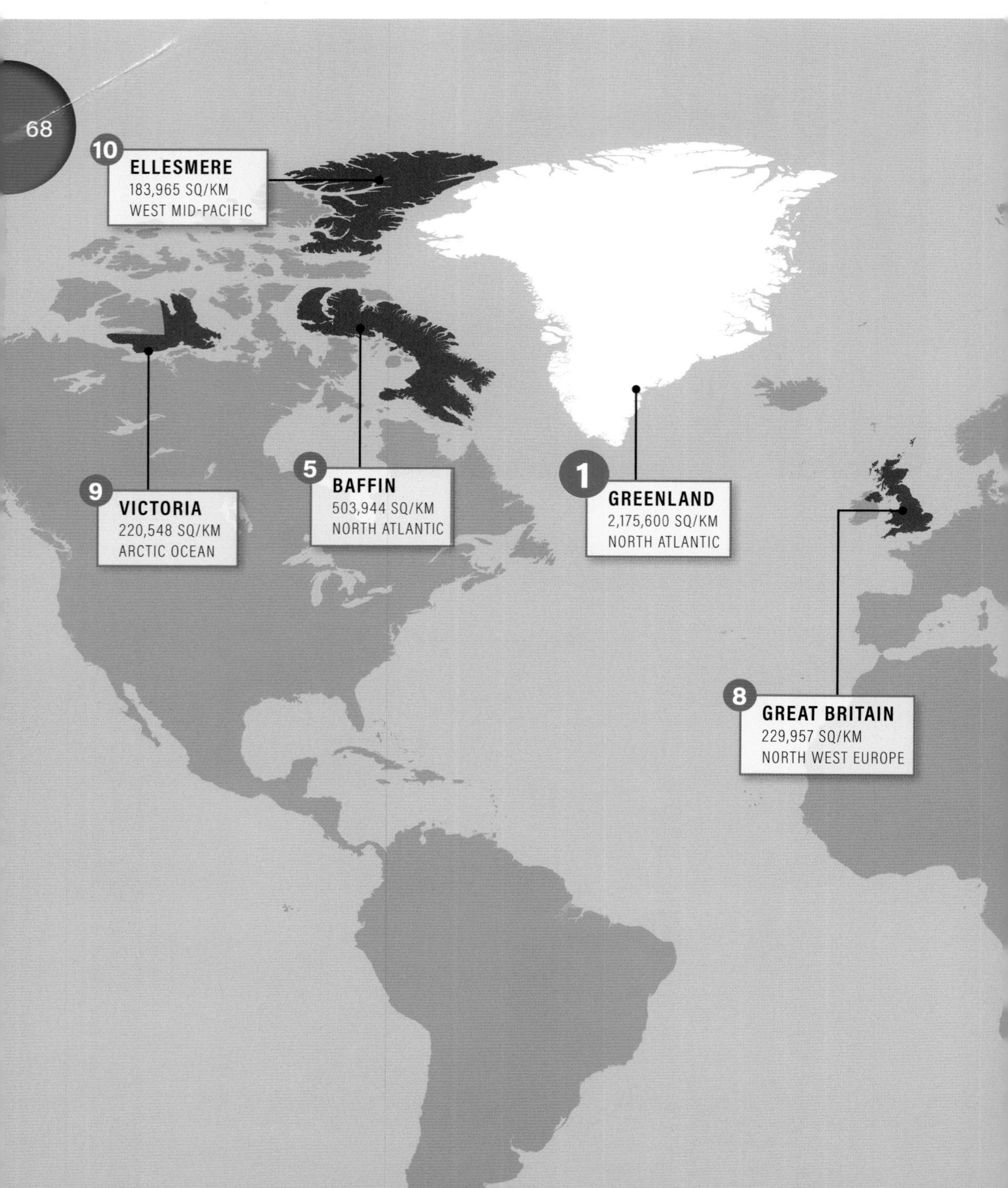

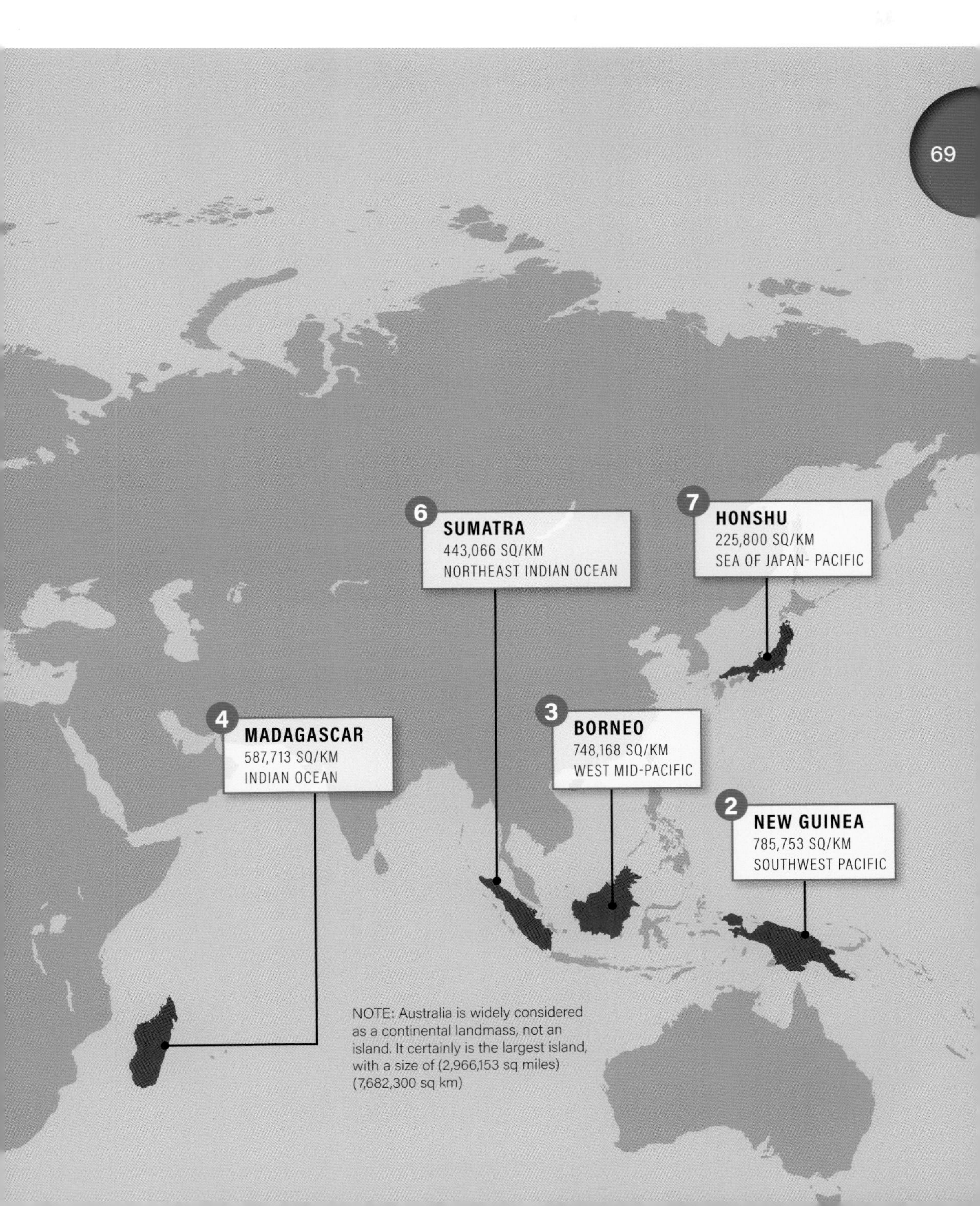
6
SUMATRA
443,066 SQ/KM
NORTHEAST INDIAN OCEAN
7
HONSHU
225,800 SQ/KM
SEA OF JAPAN- PACIFIC
4
MADAGASCAR
587,713 SQ/KM
INDIAN OCEAN
3
BORNEO
748,168 SQ/KM
WEST MID-PACIFIC
2
NEW GUINEA
785,753 SQ/KM
SOUTHWEST PACIFIC
NOTE: Australia is widely considered as a continental landmass, not an island. It certainly is the largest island, with a size of (2,966,153 sq miles) (7,682,300 sq km)

Major UK rivers

*and the towns/cities they pass through

ENGLAND	
RIVERS	TOWNS/CITIES THEY PASS THROUGH
Aire	Keighley, Bingley, Shipley, Leeds, Castleford, Knottingley
Avon	Malmesbury, Tetbury, Chippenham, Bradford on Avon, Bath
Avon (Wiltshire)	Devizes, Amesbury, Salisbury, Fordingbridge, Ringwood
Coquet	Rothbury, Alnwick, Morpeth, Ashington, Blindburn, Alwinton
Dart	Dartmoor, Buckfastleigh, Dartington, Totnes, Dartmouth,
Dee	Bala, Corwen, Llangollen, Chirk, Overton, Holt, Chester
Derwent	Derby
Don	Penistone, Sheffield, Rotherham, Mexborough, Conisbrough, Doncaster, Stainforth
Eden	Penrith, City of Carlisle, Kirkby Stephen, Wetheral, Mallerstang
Exe	Exeter, Exmouth, Exminster, Thorverton, Exford, Exebridge, Stoodleigh, Nether Exe, Rewe, Devon, Exton,
Fowey	Lostwithiel, Milltown, Cornwall
Great Ouse	Ely, Cambridgeshire, Bedford, St Ives, Huntingdon, St Neots
Humber	Hull, Grimsby, Immingham, Barton upon Humber, Cleethorpes
Kennet	Newbury, Marlborough, Wiltshire, Hungerford
Lune	Lancaster, Kirkby Lonsdale
Medway	Tonbridge, Maidstone, Medway
Mersey	Liverpool, Manchester
Nene	Northampton, Wellingborough, Wisbech, Thrapston, Irthlingborough
Parrett	Bridgwater, Langport, Cannington, Combwich
Ribble	Preston, Clitheroe, Settle, Ribchester, Southport, Wigan, Walton-le-Dale
Severn	Llanidloes, Shrewsbury, Worcester, Gloucester
Stour (Dorset)	Sturminster Newton, Gillingham
Stour (Essex)	Sudbury, Harwich, Haverhill, Cavendish
Stour (Kent)	Canterbury, Ashford, Sandwich
Stour (Warwickshire)	Shipston on Stour, Alderminster, Halford, Newbold on Stour, Atherstone on Stour, Clifford Chambers.
Stour (Worcestershire)	Romsley, Halesowen, Dudley, Stourbridge, Amblecote, Kinver, Stourton, Wolverley, Brierley Hill, Kidderminster, Stourport on Severn
Swale	Richmond, Skipton-on-Swale, Catton, Topcliffe, Asenby, Helperby, Myton-On-Swale
Taw	North Tawton, Barnstaple
Tamar	Plymouth, Saltash, Calstock, Bridgetown, Hele, Luffincott, Bridgerule
Tees	Hartlepool, Redcar, Middlesbrough
Test	Southampton

RIVERS	TOWNS/CITIES THEY PASS THROUGH
Thames	Cricklade, Lechlade, Oxford, Abingdon-on-Thames, Wallingford, Reading, Wargrave, Henley-on-Thames, Marlow, Maidenhead, Windsor and Eton, Staines-upon-Thames and Egham, Chertsey, Weybridge, Sunbury-on-Thames, Walton-on-Thames, Kingston upon Thames, Dagenham, Erith, Purfleet, Dartford, West Thurrock, Northfleet, Tilbury, Gravesend, London
Trent	Stoke-on-Trent, Nottingham, Derby, Burton upon Trent, Newark-on Trent, Lichfield, Rugeley, Stone, Scunthorpe, Beeston, Long Eaton, Gainsborough, Castle Donington,
Tyne	Newcastle upon Tyne
Ure	Ripon, Boroughbridge, Wensley, Mickley
Wear	Stanhope, Wolsingham, Bishop Auckland, Willington, Durham, Chester-le-Street, Sunderland
Welland	Market Harborough, Stamford, Crowland, Spalding
Wensum	Norwich, Fakenham, Trowse, Lyng, North Elmham, Sculthorpe, Great Ryburgh, Whissonsett
Wharfe	Ilkley, Otley, Grassington, Burnsall, Wetherby, Kettlewell, Buckden, Appletreewick, Collingham, Hubberholme, Ulleskelf
Witham	Grantham, Lincoln, Boston
Yare	Norwich, Great Yarmouth, Reedham, Surlingham

SCOTLAND	
RIVERS	CITIES AND TOWNS
Clyde	Glasgow, Greenock, Lanark, Bothwell
Dee	Bala, Corwen, Llangollen, Chirk, Overton, Holt, Chester
Ness	Inverness
Loch Lomomd	Argyll, Bute/Stirling,
Spey	Kingussie, Kincraig, Aviemore
Tay	Oban, Perth, Dundee
Tweed	Berwick upon Tweed

WALES	
RIVERS	**CITIES AND TOWNS**
Dovey	Machynlleth, Aberdyfi, Dinas Mawddwy
Severn	Shrewsbury, Worcester, Gloucester, Bristol
Taff	Cardiff, Merthyr Tydfil, Pontypridd, Treharris
Teifi	Cardigan, Newcastle Emlyn, Llandysul, Lampeter, Cenarth, Tregaron, Llanybydder
Towy	Llandeilo, Llandovery, Abergwili
Usk	Sennybridge, Crickhowell, Abergavenny, Newport
Wye	Ross-on-Wye, Hereford, Monmouth, Chepstow, Hay-on-Wye, Symonds Yat, Tintern, Builth Wells, Rhayader

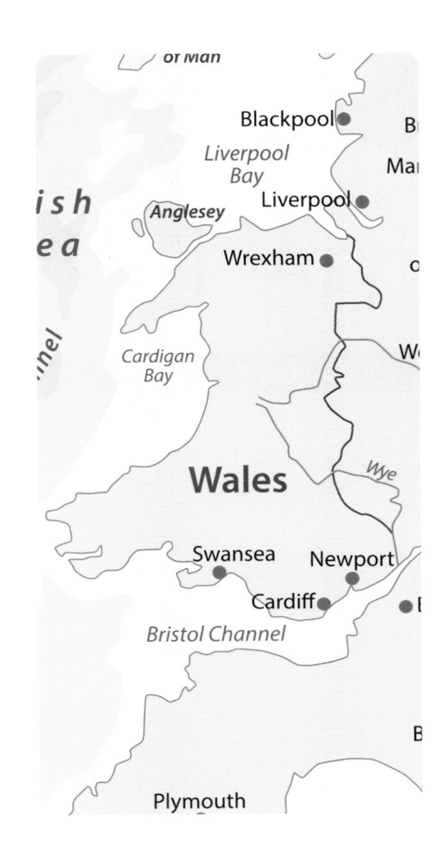

NORTHERN IRELAND	
RIVERS	**CITIES AND TOWNS**
Lagan	Belfast, Lambeg, Mazetown, Donaghcloney, Dromore
Bann	Coleraine, Agivey, Portglenone
Foyle	Londonderry
Six Mile Water	Ballyclare, Dunadry, Antrim
Bush	Bushmills, Stanocum, Armoy
River Erne	Belleek, Enniskillen

Sea areas around the UK

AREA NAMES	NAMED AFTER
Bailey	The sandbank in the North Atlantic Ocean
Biscay	The Bay of Biscay, west of France
Cromarty	The river estuary and place Cromarty in Scotland
Dogger	A sandbank in the North Sea
Dover	The town
Faeroes	The islands between Scotland and Iceland
Fair Isle	The isle between Orkney and Shetland
Fastnet	Fastnet Rock island in Southwest Ireland
Fisher	A sandbank off of the west coast of Denmark
Fitzroy	Vice Admiral Robert FitzRoy, the first head of the Met Office in 1854
Forth	The river estuary the Firth of Forth, Scotland
Forties	A sandbank in the North Sea
German Bight	A curve in the shoreline between the Netherlands and Denmark
Hebrides	The isle of Hebrides, northwest of Scotland's coast
Humber	The estuary of the River Humber in the east coast of North England
Irish Sea	The sea between England and Ireland
Lundy	The island Lunde in the Bristol Channel
Malin	Malin Head on the Inishowen Peninsula, Ireland
North Utsire	The island of Utsire off of Norway's west coast
Plymouth	The city Plymouth in Devon, Southwest England
Portland	The man made harbour, south of Weymouth
Rockall	The rock stack in the North Atlantic Ocean
Shannon	Named after the Shannon river estuary in Ireland
Sole	The Great and Little Sole Banks, west of the Isles of Scilly
South Utsire	The island Utsire off of Norway's west coast
Southeast Iceland	Southeast Iceland
Thames	The River Thames estuary
Trafalgar	The headland Cape Trafalgar in the south of Spain and after the Battle of Trafalgar in 1805
Tyne	The River Tyne, North East England
Viking	A sandbank in the North Sea
Wight	The Isle of Wight

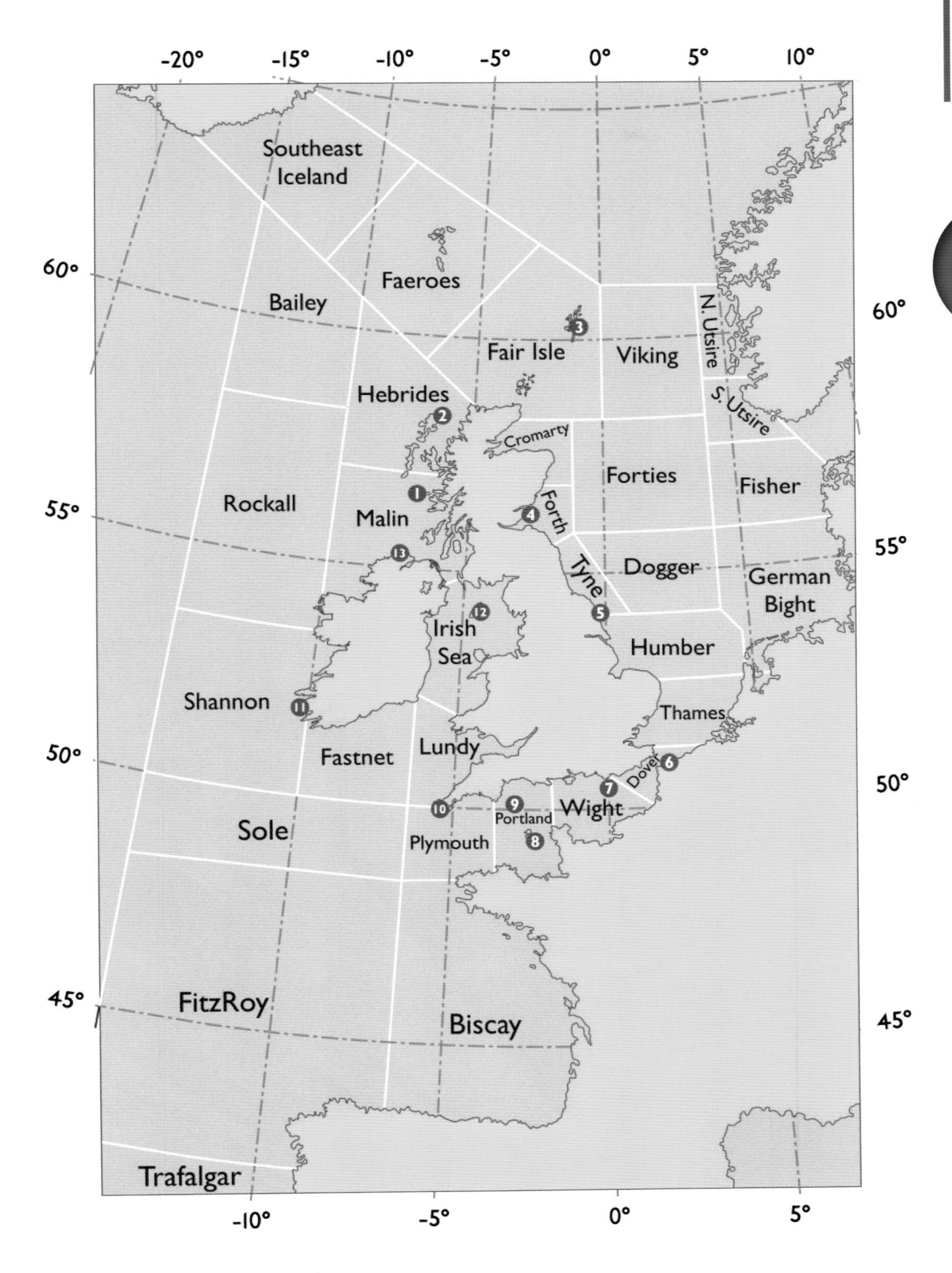
-20°
-15°
-10°
-5°
0°
5°
10°
60°
55°
50°
45°
Southeast Iceland
Faeroes
Bailey
Fair Isle
Viking
N. Utsire
S. Utsire
Hebrides
Cromarty
Forties
Fisher
Rockall
Malin
Forth
Tyne
Dogger
German Bight
Irish Sea
Humber
Shannon
Thames
Fastnet
Lundy
Dover
Wight
Portland
Plymouth
Sole
FitzRoy
Biscay
Trafalgar
-10°
-5°
0°
5°

The world's most expansive road networks

	COUNTRY	LENGTH (KM)
1	United States of America	6.58 million
2	China	4.24 million
3	India	4.1 million
4	Brazil	1.6 million
5	Russia	1.28 million
6	Japan	1.21 million
7	Canada	1.04 million
8	France	1.02 million
9	Australia	823,000
10	Spain	683,000

History

World wonders

SEVEN WONDERS OF THE ANCIENT WORLD
Great Pyramid of Giza, Egypt
Hanging Gardens of Babylon, Iraq
Statue of Zeus at Olympia, Greece
Temple of Artemis at Ephesus, Turkey
Mausoleum at Halicarnassus, Turkey
Colossus of Rhodes, Greece
Lighthouse of Alexandria, Egypt

SEVEN WONDERS OF NATURE
Amazon Rainforest and River, South America
Jeju Island, South Korea
Ha Long Bay, Vietnam
Iguazú Falls, Argentina and Brazil
Puerto Princesa Subterranean River National Park, Philippines
Komodo Island, Indonesia
Table Mountain, South Africa

SEVEN WONDERS OF THE MODERN WORLD
Christ the Redeemer, Brazil
Great Wall of China
Petra, Jordan
The Colosseum, Italy
Chichén Itzá, Mexico
Machu Picchu, Peru
Taj Mahal, India

Some of the greatest empires in history

British Empire

FOUNDED	1603
AREA (SQ. KM)	35,500,000
POPULATION	500 million
GOVERNMENT	Constitutional monarchy
CAPITALS	London

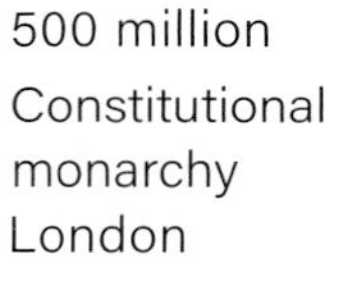

Mongol Empire

FOUNDED	1206
AREA (SQ. KM)	24,000,000
POPULATION	110 million
GOVERNMENT	Elective monarchy
CAPITALS	Khanbaliq, Avarga, Karakorum

Russian Empire

FOUNDED	1721
AREA (SQ. KM)	22,800,000
POPULATION	181.5 million
GOVERNMENT	Tsarist autocracy, Autocracy, Absolute monarchy
CAPITALS	St Petersburg, Moscow

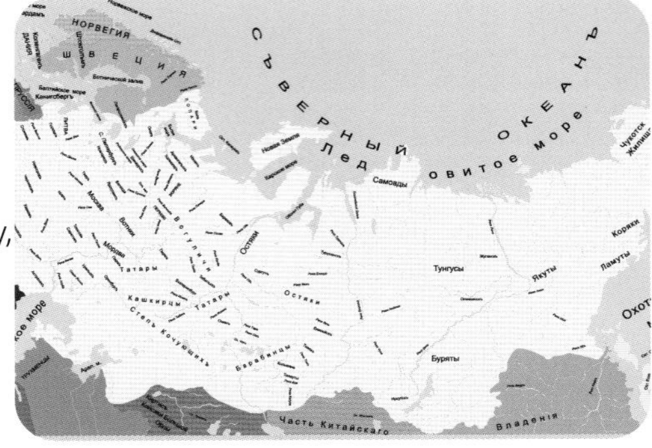

Qing Dynasty

FOUNDED	1644
AREA (SQ. KM)	13,150,000
POPULATION	140 million
GOVERNMENT	Absolute monarchy
CAPITALS	Beijing

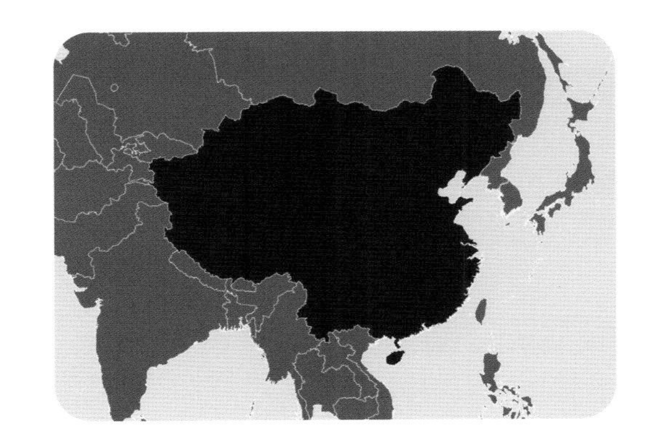

Umayyad Caliphate Empire

FOUNDED	661
AREA (SQ. KM)	11,000,000
POPULATION	34 million
GOVERNMENT	Caliphate
CAPITALS	Damascus, Harran, Córdoba (capital in exile)

Han Dynasty

FOUNDED	206BC
AREA (SQ. KM)	6,000,000
POPULATION	57.6 million
GOVERNMENT	Autocracy
CAPITALS	Chang'an, Luoyang, Xuchang

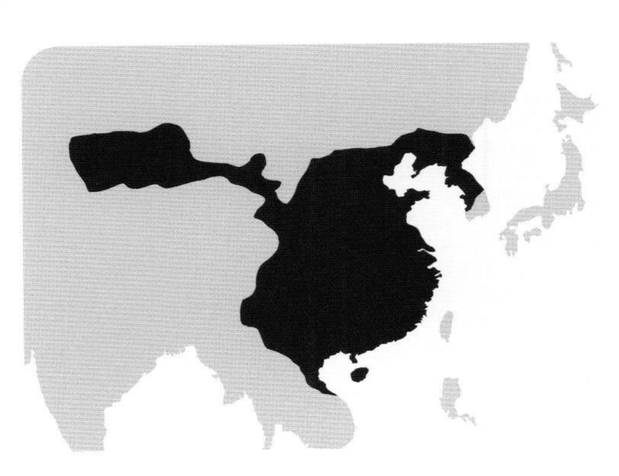

Persian Empire

FOUNDED	550BC
AREA (SQ. KM)	5,500,000
POPULATION	50 million
GOVERNMENT	Monarchy
CAPITALS	Babylon, Susa

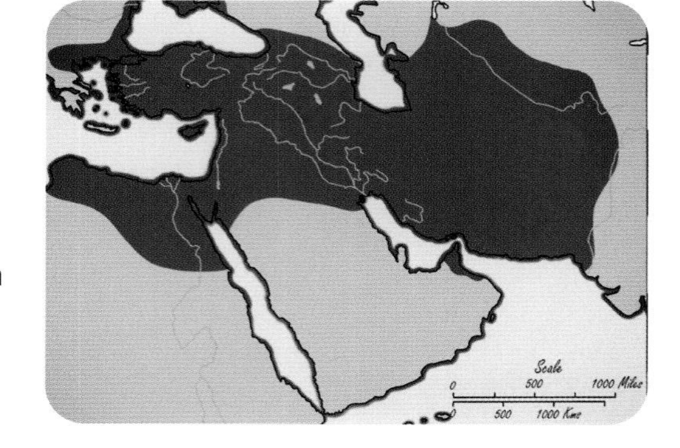

Ottoman Empire

FOUNDED	1299
AREA (SQ. KM)	5,200,000
POPULATION	14.63 million
GOVERNMENT	Absolute/ Constitutional monarchy
CAPITALS	Constantinople, Buursa, Söğüt, Edirne

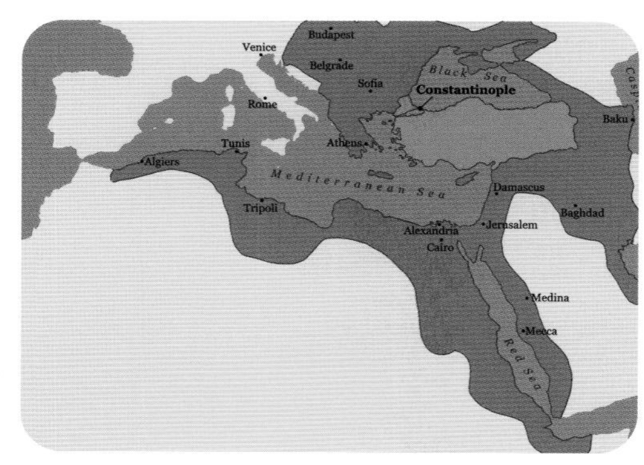

Roman Empire

FOUNDED	27BC
AREA (SQ. KM)	5,000,000
POPULATION	56.8 million
GOVERNMENT	Autocracy
CAPITALS	Ravenna, Rome, Constantinople, Mediolanum

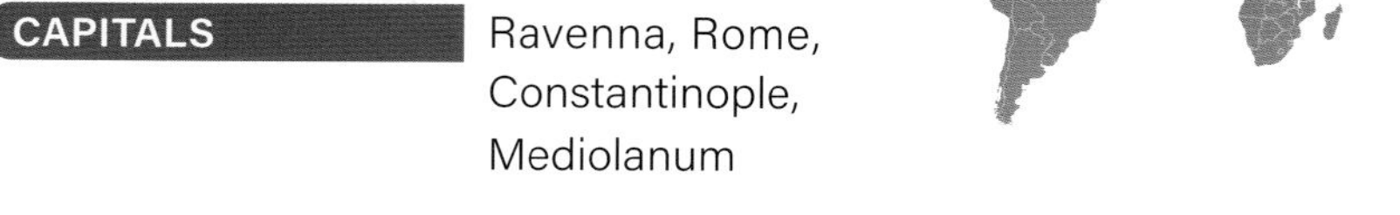

Byzantine Empire

FOUNDED	330
AREA (SQ. KM)	3,400,000
POPULATION	26 million
GOVERNMENT	Absolutism
CAPITALS	Constantinople, Luoyang, Xuchang

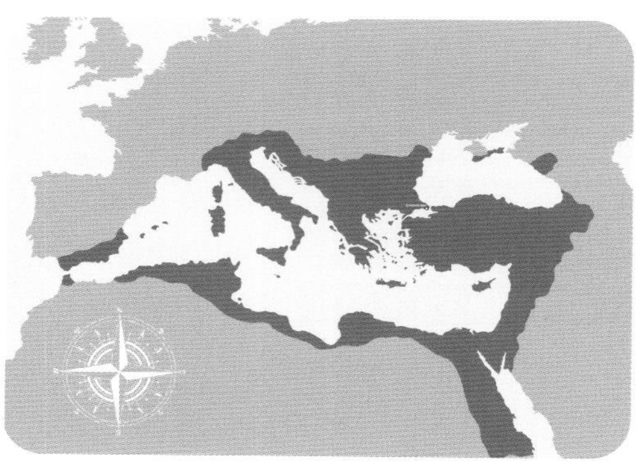

Popular Roman and Greek gods and goddesses

GREEK NAME	ROMAN NAME	DESCRIPTION
Aphrodite	Venus	Goddess of love and beauty. Wife of Hephaestus.
Apollo	Apollo	God of the Sun, arts and healing. Twin sister Artemis, son of Zeus.
Ares	Mars	God of war. Son of Zeus and Hera.
Artemis	Diana	Goddess of hunt, wild animals, childbirth and virginity. Twin sister of Apollo.
Athena	Minerva	Goddess of wisdom, courage, inspiration, strength and war strategy. Daughter of Zeus.
Cronus	Saturn	God of time. Ruler of the titans.
Demeter	Ceres	Goddess of agriculture. Sister of Zeus, mother of Persephone.

GREEK NAME	ROMAN NAME	DESCRIPTION
Dionysus	Bacchus	God of wine, vegetation and patron God of drama. Son of Zeus and Semele.
Gaia	Terra	Mother goddess of the Earth. Daughter of Chaos, mother of Uranus.
Hades	Pluto	God of the underworld, ruler of the dead. Brother of Zeus, husband of Persephone.
Hephaestus	Vulcan	God of fire and metalworking. Son of Zeus and Hera.
Hera	Juno	Goddess of marriage and childbirth. The queen of the Olympians. Mother of Hephaestus, Ares and Hebe.
Hermes	Mercury	Messenger of the Gods. Son of Zeus.
Hestia	Vesta	Goddess of the hearth, architecture, domesticity and the family. Daughter of Cronus and Rhea.
Persephone	Proserpine	Goddess of the Underworld. Wife of Hades, daughter of Zeus and Demeter.
Poseidon	Neptune	God of the Sea and Earthquakes. Brother of Zeus.
Rhea	Ops	Titaness daughter of Gaia and Uranus. Mother of Zeus.
Uranus	Uranus	Primal Greek god, symbolising the sky. Father of the Titans.
Zeus	Jupiter	King of the Gods.

Patron saints of the British Isles

St. George

COUNTRY	England
NATIONAL HOLIDAY	23rd April

St. Patrick

COUNTRY	Ireland
NATIONAL HOLIDAY	17th March

St. Andrew

COUNTRY	Scotland
NATIONAL HOLIDAY	30th November

St. David

COUNTRY	Wales
NATIONAL HOLIDAY	1st March

Popes from 1800

NAME	PONTIFICATE	PLACE OF BIRTH
Pius VII	1800-1823	Romagna, Italy
Leo XII	1823-1829	Marche, Italy
Pius VIII	1829-1830	Marche, Italy
Gregory XVI	1831-1846	Venice, Italy
Blessed Pius IX	1846-1878	Marche, Italy
Leo XIII	1878-1903	Lazio, Italy
St Pius X	1903-1914	Lombardy-Venetia, Austrian Empire
Benedict XV	1914-1922	Pegli, Italy
Pius XI	1922-1939	Lombardy-Venetia, Austrian Empire
Pius XII	1939-1958	Rome, Italy
St John XXIII	1958-1963	Bergamo, Italy
Paul VI	1963-1978	Brescia, Italy
John Paul I	Aug 1978-Sept 1978	Veneto, Italy
St John Paul II	1978-2005	Wadowice, Polish Republic
Benedict XVI	2005-2013	Bavaria, Germany
Francis	2013-present	Buenos Aires, Argentina

Pope Francis

Some historic battles

BATTLE OF ACTIUM		
WAR	DATE	LOCATION
Final War of the Roman Republic	Sept 31 BC	Ionian Sea, near the city of Actium in Greece

BATTLE OF SALAMIS		
WAR	DATE	LOCATION
Greco-Persian Wars	Sept 480 BC	Straits of Salamis

BATTLE OF TOURS		
WAR	DATE	LOCATION
Battle of Tours	Oct 732	Between Tours and Poitiers, France

BATTLE OF HASTINGS		
WAR	DATE	LOCATION
Norman Conquest of England	Oct 1066	Hastings, England

SIEGE OF ORLÉANS

WAR	DATE	LOCATION
Hundred Years of War	12 Oct 1428-8 May 1429	Orléans, France

BATTLE OF CAJAMARCA

WAR	DATE	LOCATION
Spanish Conquest of Peru	Nov 1532	Cajamarca, Inca Empire (present day Peru)

BATTLE OF YORKTOWN

WAR	DATE	LOCATION
Ameri-can Rev-olution	19 Oct 1781	Yorktown, Virginia

BATTLE OF WATERLOO

WAR	DATE	LOCATION
Napo-leonic Wars	18 June 1815	South of Brussels in modern Belgium

BATTLE OF STALINGRAD

WAR	DATE	LOCATION
World War II	Jul 1942-Feb 1943	Stalingrad, Russia

BATTLE OF HUAIHAI

WAR	DATE	LOCATION
Chinese Civil War	6 Nov 1948-10 Jan 1949	Shandong, Jiangsu, Anhi, Henan, China

Stained glass window representing Joan of Arc after the Siege of Orleans, Eglise Saint-Sulpice church

Famous ships and sailors

SAILOR	SHIP
Ronald Amundsen	Fram
Blackbeard	Queen Anne's Revenge
Captain William Bligh	Mary Celeste
Sir Francis Chichester	Gipsy Moth IV
Christopher Columbus	Santa Maria, Nina, Pinta

SAILOR	SHIP
Captain James Cook	HMS Endeavour
Charles Darwin	HMS Beagle
Francis Drake	Golden Hind (originally Pelican)
Vasco Da Gama	São Gabriel
Henry VIII	Mary Rose
Henry Hudson	Half Moon
Captain William Kidd	Adventure Galley
Ferdinand Magellan	Victoria
Henry Morgan	Oxford
Horatio Nelson	HMS Victory
Walter Raleigh	Ark Royal
Robert Falcon Scott	Discovery
Ernest Shackleton	Nimrod, Endurance
Myles Standish	Mayflower

A full sized replica of the Golden Hind in London

Henry VIII and the Mary Rose

Maritime disasters

SHIP	SOULS LOST (EST.)
SS The Arctic	400
RMS Empress of Ireland	1012
RMS Lusitania	1198
RMS Titanic	1500
The Sultana	1700
MV Le Joola	1800
SS Mont-Blanc	2000
MV Doña Paz	4,000
RMS Lancastria	4000
MV Goya	6000
MV The Wilhelm Gustloff	9000

Castles of England

CASTLE NAME	LOCATION
Acton Burnell Castle	Shropshire
Alnwick Castle	Northumberland
Appleby Castle	Cumbria
Arundel Castle	West Sussex
Ashby-de-la-zouch Castle	Leicestershire
Askerton Castle	Cumbria
Aydon Castle	Northumberland
Baconsthorpe Castle	Norfolk
Bamburgh Castle	Northumberland
Barnard Castle	County Durham
Bedford Castle	Bedfordshire
Beeston Castle	Cheshire
Bellister Castle	Northumberland
Belsay Castle	Northumberland
Berkeley Castle	Gloucestershire
Berkhamsted Castle	Hertfordshire
Berry Pomeroy Castle	Devon
Berwick Castle	Northumberland
Bewcastle Castle	Cumbria
Bewley Castle	Cumbria
Biggleswade Castle	Bedfordshire
Blenkinsop Castle	Northumberland
Boarstall Tower	Buckinghamshire
Bodiam Castle	East Sussex
Bolingbroke Castle	Lincolnshire
Bolsover Castle	Derbyshire
Bolton Castle	Yorkshire
Bowes Castle	County Durham

Ashby-de-la-zouch Castle

CASTLE NAME	LOCATION
Bramber Castle	West Sussex
Brinklow Castle	Warwickshire
Brough Castle	Cumbria
Buckden Palace	Cambridgeshire
Bungay Castle	Suffolk
Bywell Castle	Northumberland
Cainhoe Castle	Bedfordshire
Caister Castle	Norfolk
Calshot Castle	Hampshire
Camber Castle	East Sussex
Canterbury Castle	Kent
Carisbrooke Castle	Isle of Wight
Carlisle Castle	Cumbria
Cartington Castle	Northumberland
Castle Acre Castle	Norfolk
Castle Howe	Cumbria
Castle Rising Castle	Norfolk
Chalgrave Castle	Bedfordshire
Chester Castle: Agricola Tower	Cheshire
Chillingham Castle	Northumberland
Christchurch Castle	Dorset
Clare Castle	Suffolk
Clifford Castle	Herefordshire
Clitheroe Castle	Lancashire
Clun Castle	Shropshire
Cockermouth Castle	Cumbria
Colchester Castle	Essex
Conisbrough Castle	Yorkshire
Corfe Castle	Dorset
Dartmouth Castle	Devon
Dacre Castle	Cumbria
Dalton Castle	Cumbria
Dane John Mound	Kent
Deal Castle	Kent

Bodiam Castle

Camber Castle

Castle Rising Castle

Dartmouth Castle

Deal Castle

Edingham Castle

Goodrich Castle

Hastings Castle

CASTLE NAME	LOCATION
Donnington Castle	Berkshire
Deddington Castle	Oxfordshire
Devizes Castle	Wiltshire
Dover Castle	Kent
Dunstanburgh Castle	Northumberland
Durham Castle	County Durham
Edlingham Castle	Northumberland
Egremont Castle	Cumbria
Elsdon Castle	Northumberland
Elton Hall	Cambridgeshire
Etal Castle	Northumberland
Eye Castle	Suffolk
Eynsford Castle	Kent
Farleigh Hungerford Castle	Somerset
Farnham Castle Keep	Surrey
Flamborough Castle	Yorkshire
Fotheringhay Castle	Northamptonshire
Framlingham Castle	Suffolk
Goodrich Castle	Herefordshire
Greystoke Castle	Cumbria
Hadleigh Castle	Essex
Halton Castle	Runcorn
Hapton Castle	Lancashire
Hartshill Castle	Warwickshire
Hastings Castle	Sussex
Hedingham Castle	Essex
Helmsley Castle	Yorkshire
Herstmonceux Castle	East Sussex
Hever Castle	Kent
Hurst Castle	Hampshire
Hylton Castle	Northumberland
Kendal Castle	Cumbria
Kenilworth Castle	Warwickshire
Kilpeck Castle	Herefordshire

CASTLE NAME	LOCATION
Kimbolton Castle	Cambridgeshire
Kinnersley Castle	Herefordshire
Kirby Muxloe Castle	Leicestershire
Kirkoswald Castle	Cumbria
Kirtling Tower	Cambridgeshire
Knaresborough Castle	Yorkshire
Lancaster Castle	Lancashire
Launceston Castle	Cornwall
Leeds Castle	Kent
Lewes Castle	East Sussex
Lilbourne Castle	Northamptonshire
Lincoln Castle	Lincolnshire
Lindisfarne Castle	Northumberland
Longthorpe Tower	Cambridgeshire
Longtown Castle	Herefordshire
Ludgershall Castle	Wiltshire
Ludlow Castle	Shropshire
Lydford Castle	Devon
Meppershall Castle	Bedfordshire
Middleham Castle	Yorkshire
Mitford Castle	Northumberland
Morpeth Castle	Northumberland
Mount Bures Castle Motte	Essex
Muncaster Castle	Cumbria
Naworth Castle	Cumbria
Nether Stowey Castle	Somerset
Newark Castle	Nottinghamshire
Newcastle Castle Keep	Tyne and Wear
Norham Castle	Northumberland
Norwich Castle	Norfolk
Nunney Castle	Somerset
Oakham Castle	Rutland
Okehampton Castle	Devon
Old Sarum	Wiltshire

Launceston Castle

Ludgershall Castle

Muncaster Castle

Nunney Castle

Pendennis Castle

Raby Castle

St Michaels Mount

Shrewsbury Castle

CASTLE NAME	LOCATION
Old Wardour Castle	Wiltshire
Orford Castle	Suffolk
Oxford Castle	Oxfordshire
Pendennis Castle	Cornwall
Pendragon Castle	Cumbria
Penrith Castle	Cumbria
Pevensey Castle	East Sussex
Peveril Castle	Derbyshire
Pickering Castle	Yorkshire
Piel Castle	Cumbria
Pontefract Castle	Yorkshire
Portchester Castle	Hampshire
Powderham Castle	Exeter
Portland Castle	Dorset
Prudhoe Castle	Northumberland
Raby Castle	County Durham
Rayleigh Mount	Essex
Restormel Castle	Cornwall
Richmond Castle	Yorkshire
Rochester Castle	Kent
Rockingham Castle	Northamptonshire
Rose Castle	Cumbria
Rufus Castle	Dorset
Rye Castle	Sussex
St Briavels Castle	Gloucestershire
St Catherines Castle	Cornwall
St Mawes Castle	Cornwall
St Michaels Mount	Cornwall
Sandal Castle	Yorkshire
Scaleby Castle	Cumbria
Scarborough Castle	Yorkshire
Scotney Castle	Kent
Sherborne Old Castle	Dorset
Shrewsbury Castle	Shropshire
Skipsea Castle	Yorkshire

CASTLE NAME	LOCATION
Someries Castle	Yorkshire
Somerton Castle	Lincolnshire
Spofforth Castle	Yorkshire
Sutton Valence Castle	Lincolnshire
Tamworth Castle	Staffordshire
Thetford Castle	Norfolk
Thirlwall Castle	Northumberland
Thurleigh Castle	Bedfordshire
Tintagel Castle	Cornwall
Toddington Castle	Bedfordshire
Tonbridge Castle	Kent
Totnes Castle	Devon
Totternhoe Castle	Bedfordshire
Tower of London	Greater London
Triermain Castle	Cumbria
Tutbury Castle	Staffordshire
Tynemouth Castle and Priory	Tyne and Wear
Upnor Castle	Kent
Walmer Castle	Kent
Warkworth Castle	Northumberland
Warwick Castle	Warwickshire
Weeting Castle	Norfolk
Westenhanger Castle	Kent
Whittington Castle	Shropshire
Wigmore Castle	Herefordshire
Wilton Castle	Herefordshire
Winchester Castle	Hampshire
Windsor Castle	Berkshire
Wolvesey Castle	Hampshire
Yarmouth Castle	Isle of Wight
Yielden Castle	Bedfordshire

Windsor Castle

Kingdoms & monarchies of the world

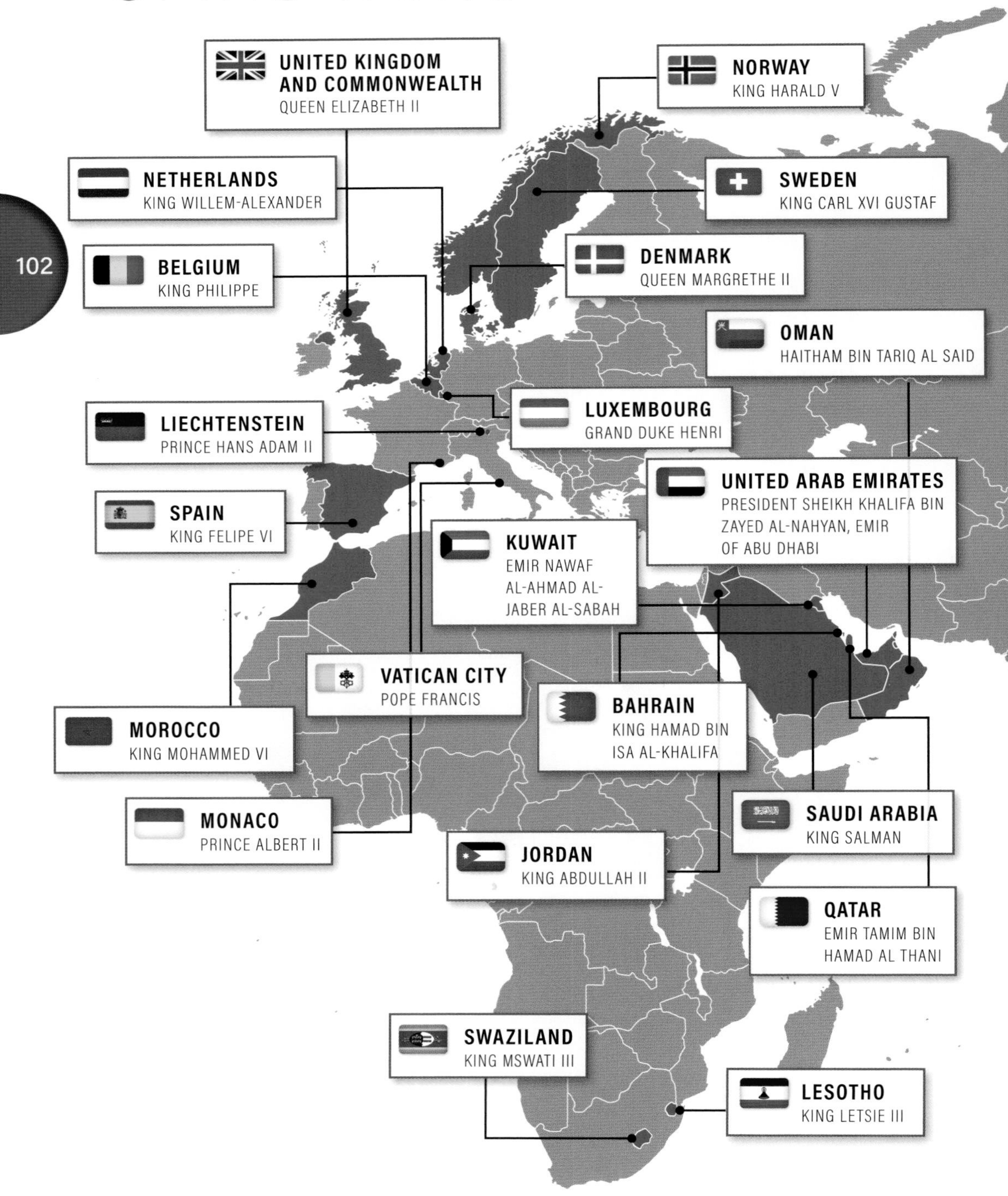

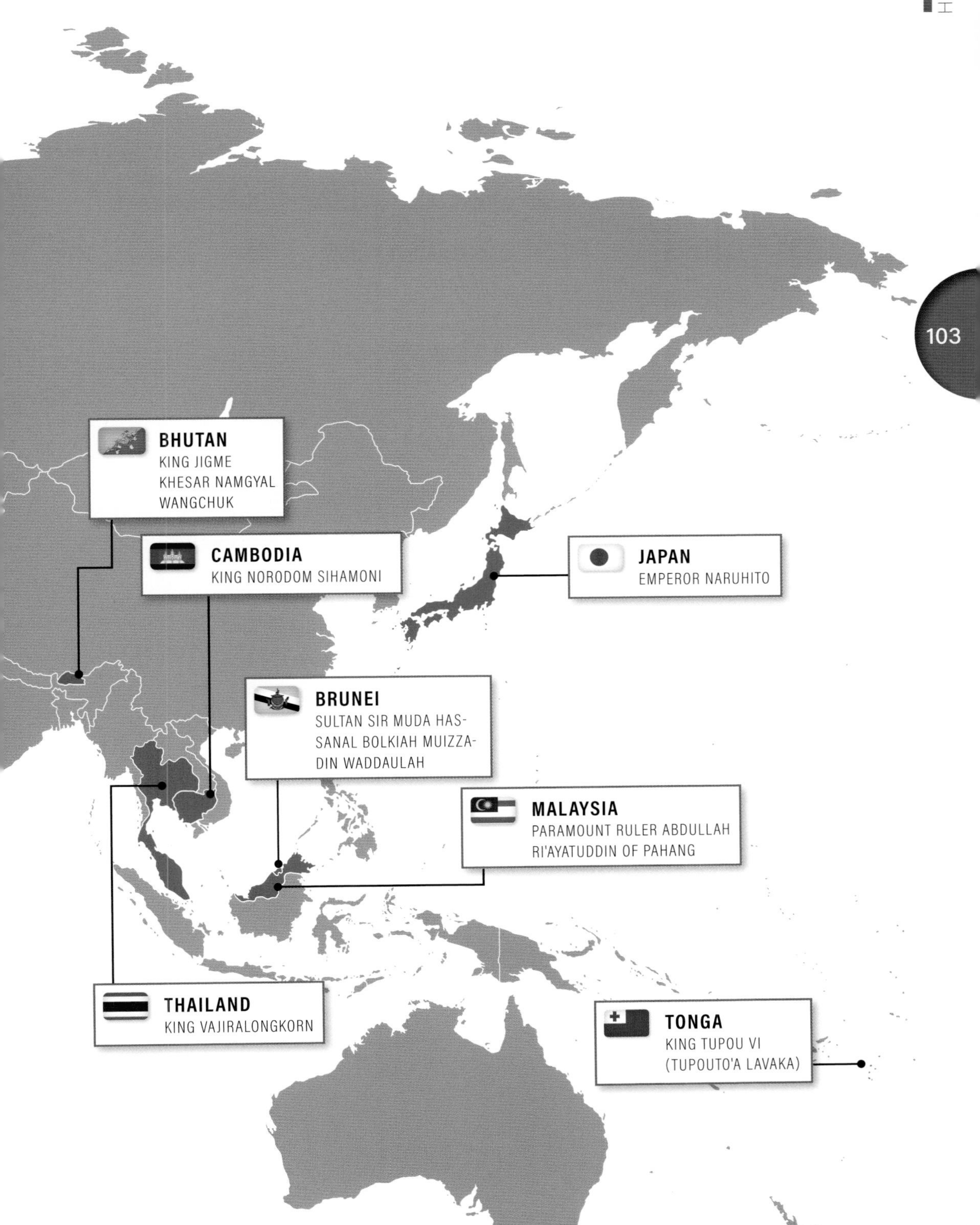
BHUTAN
KING JIGME
KHESAR NAMGYAL
WANGCHUK
CAMBODIA
KING NORODOM SIHAMONI
JAPAN
EMPEROR NARUHITO
BRUNEI
SULTAN SIR MUDA HAS-
SANAL BOLKIAH MUIZZA-
DIN WADDAULAH
MALAYSIA
PARAMOUNT RULER ABDULLAH
RI'AYATUDDIN OF PAHANG
THAILAND
KING VAJIRALONGKORN
TONGA
KING TUPOU VI
(TUPOUTO'A LAVAKA)

Kings and queens of England & Britain

SAXON KINGS		
DATES	NAME OF MONARCH	DESCRIPTION
978-1016	Aethelred II The Unready	Unready' because he was unable to organise a resistance against the Danes.
1016-1016	Edmund II of Ironside	Son of Aethelred II
1016-1035	Canute (Cnut The Great) The Dane	The Danish King who divided England into four earldoms of East Anglia, Mercia, Northumbria and Wessex
1035-1040	Harold I	Illegitimate son of Canute the Great
1040-1042	Harthacanute	Son of Canute the Great
1042-1066	Edward the Confessor	Son of Aethelred the Unready
1066-1066	Harold II	No royal bloodline, was elected by the Witan council
1066-1087	William I (The Conqueror)	Illegitimate son of Robert the Devil, whom he succeeded as Duke of Normandy in 1035
1087-1100	William II (Ruffus)	Son of William the Conqueror
1100-1135	Henry I	Fourth youngest son of William I
1135-1154	Stephen	Grandson of William I

Bayeux Tapestry depicting the Norman invasion of England in the 11th Century

THE PLANTAGENET KINGS		
DATES	NAME OF MONARCH	DESCRIPTION
1154-1189	Henry II	Ruled Count of Anjou, extended his French land in England
1189-1199	Richard I (The Lionheart)	Third son of Henry II
1199-1216	John	Fourth child of Henry II
1216-1272	Henry III	Son of King John, was nine years old when he became King

MONARCHS OF ENGLAND AND WALES		
DATES	NAME OF MONARCH	DESCRIPTION
1272-1307	Edward I	Son of Henry III
1307-1327	Edward II	Son of Edward I
1327-1377	Edward III	Son of Edward II
1377-1399	Richard II	Son of the Black Prince

HOUSE OF LANCASTER		
DATES	NAME OF MONARCH	DESCRIPTION
1399-1413	Henry IV	Son of John of Gaunt (Third son of Edward III)
1413-1422	Henry V	Son of Henry IV
1422-deposed in 1461	Henry VI	Son of Henry V. His reign marked the beginning of the War of the Roses

HOUSE OF YORK		
DATES	NAME OF MONARCH	DESCRIPTION
1461-1483	Edward IV	Son of Richard Duke of York (great grandson of Edward III)
1483-1483	Edward V	Son of Edward IV. After having reigned for only two months he and his brother Richard were murdered in the Tower of London
1483-1485	Richard III	Brother of Edward IV. His reign marks the end of the War of the Roses. Alleged for murdering his nephews

THE TUDORS		
DATES	NAME OF MONARCH	DESCRIPTION
1485-1509	Henry VII	Married Elizabeth of York, uniting the House of York and Lancaster
1509-1547	Henry VIII	Son of Henry VII
1547-1553	Edward VI	Son of Henry VIII, succeeded his father aged nine
1553-1553	Lady Jane Grey	Great granddaughter of Henry VII, known as 'the nine day queen', making her the shortest reigning monarch in British History.
1553-1558	Mary I (Bloody Mary)	Daughter of Henry VIII
1558-1603	Elizabeth I	Daughter of Henry VIII and Anne Boleyn

Queen Elizabeth I

THE STUARTS		
DATES	**NAME OF MONARCH**	**DESCRIPTION**
1603-1625	James I and VI of Scotland	Son of Mary Queen of Scots. First King to rule over Scotland and England
1625-1649	Charles I	Son of James I. His reign marks the outbreak of the English Civil War. With his Royalist forces defeated, the Commonwealth of England was declared and led by the Oliver Cromwell

Glamis Castle childhood home of Queen Mother with lead statue of King James I of England and King James VI of Scotland

THE COMMONWEALTH		
DATES	**NAME OF MONARCH**	**DESCRIPTION**
1649 – 1653	The Commonwealth	
1653-1658	Oliver Cromwell	An English military and political leader, later Lord Protector of the Commonwealth of England
1658-1659	Richard Cromwell	Son of Oliver Cromwell, took over as Lord Protector after the death of his father

THE RESTORATION OF THE STUARTS		
DATES	NAME OF MONARCH	DESCRIPTION
1660-1685	Charles II	Son of Charles I. The Great Plague of 1665 and the 1666 Fire of London took place in his reign
1685-1688	James II and VII of Scotland	Second surviving son of Charles I
1689-1702/1689-1694	William III and Mary II	Was sovereign Prince of Orange, the Dutch stadtholder and became King of England after the Glorious Revolution
1702-1714	Anne	Daughter of James II. During her reign the United Kingdom of Great Britain was created

THE HANOVARIANS		
DATES	NAME OF MONARCH	DESCRIPTION
1714-1727	George I	Great-grandson of James I
1727-1760	George II	Only son of George I
1760-1820	George III	Grandson of George II
1820-1830	George IV	Son of George III, known as the 'First Gentleman of Europe'
1830-1837	William IV	Brother of George IV, known as the 'Sailor King'
1837-1901	Victoria	Granddaughter of George III

Queen Victoria

HOUSE OF SAXE-COBURG AND GOTHA		
DATES	NAME OF MONARCH	DESCRIPTION
1901-1910	Edward VII	Son of Queen Victoria

Statue of King Edward

HOUSE OF WINDSOR		
DATES	NAME OF MONARCH	DESCRIPTION
1910-1936	George V	Son of Edward VII
June 1936-abdicated 1936	Edward VIII	Son of George V, abdicated due to the constitutional crisis caused by his proposal to marry American socialite Wallis Simpson
1936-1952	George VI	Son of George V
1952-present	Elizabeth II*	Daughter of George VI. Her coronation in 1953 was the first to be televised. In 2012 she celebrated her 60th year as Queen. Queen Elizabeth II became the longest-reigning British monarch on 9 September 2015.

* Queen Elizabeth II is also the Sovereign of 15 countries in the Commonwealth of Nations: Antigua and Barbuda, Australia, the Bahamas, Barbados, Belize, Canada, Grenada, Jamaica, New Zealand, Papua New Guinea, St. Kitts and Nevis, St. Lucia, St. Vincent and the Grenadines, the Solomon Islands, and Tuvalu.

Rulers of France

Dagobert I,

MEROVINGIAN	
DATE	RULER
481-511	Clovis I
511-558	Childebert I
558-562	Chlothar I
562-566	Caribert
566-584	Chilperic I
584-628	Chlothar II
628-637	Dagobert I
637-655	Clovis II
655-668	Chlothar III
668-674	Childeric II
674-691	Theuderic III
691-695	Clovis III
695-711	Childebert II
711-716	Dagobert III
716-721	Chilperic II
721-737	Theyderic IV
743-751	Childeric III, deposed by Pepin

CAROLINGIAN	
DATE	RULER
752-768	Pepin the Younger
768-771	Carloman I
768-814	Charlemagne (Charles I)
814-840	Louis I The Pious
840-877	Charles II The Bald
877-879	Louis II The Stammerer
879-882	Louis III
882-884	Carloman II
884-888	Charles III The Fat

ROBERTIAN	
DATE	RULER
888-898	Odo of Paris

CAROLINGIAN	
DATE	RULER
898-922	Charles III The Simple

LATER ROBERTIAN	
DATE	RULER
922-923	Robert I

BOSNOID	
DATE	RULER
923-936	Rudolph

LATER CAROLINGIAN	
DATE	RULER
936-954	Louis IV of Outremer
954-986	Lothair
986-987	Louis V The Lazy

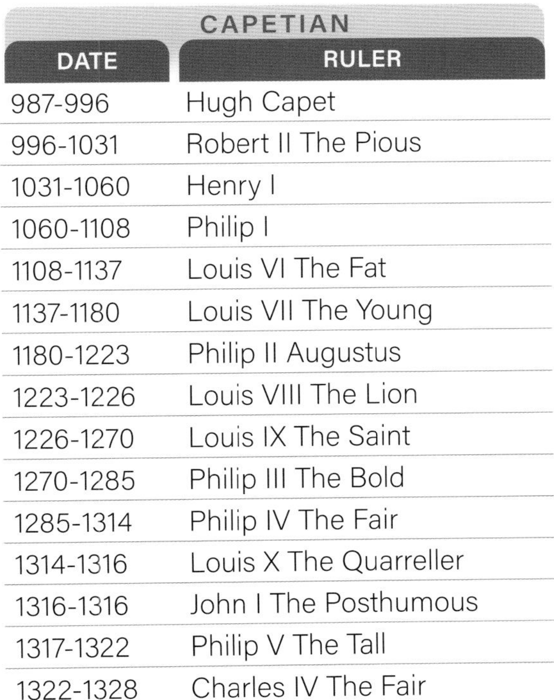

CAPETIAN	
DATE	RULER
987-996	Hugh Capet
996-1031	Robert II The Pious
1031-1060	Henry I
1060-1108	Philip I
1108-1137	Louis VI The Fat
1137-1180	Louis VII The Young
1180-1223	Philip II Augustus
1223-1226	Louis VIII The Lion
1226-1270	Louis IX The Saint
1270-1285	Philip III The Bold
1285-1314	Philip IV The Fair
1314-1316	Louis X The Quarreller
1316-1316	John I The Posthumous
1317-1322	Philip V The Tall
1322-1328	Charles IV The Fair

Odo of Paris

HOUSE OF VALOIS	
DATE	RULER
1328-1350	Philip VI
1350-1364	John II
1364-1380	Charles V
1380-1422	Charles VI

LATER HOUSE OF VALOIS	
DATE	RULER
1422-1461	Charles VII
1461-1483	Louis XI
1483-1498	Charles VIII

ORLÉANS BRANCH OF THE HOUSE OF VALOIS	
DATE	RULER
1498-1515	Louis XII

ORLÉANS- ANGOULÊME BRANCH OF THE HOUSE OF VALOIS	
DATE	RULER
1515-1547	Francis I
1547-1559	Henry II
1559-1560	Francis II
1560-1574	Charles IX
1574-1589	Henry III

HOUSE OF BOURBON	
DATE	RULER
1589-1610	Henry IV
1610-1643	Louis XIII
1643-1715	Louis XIV
1715-1774	Louis XV
1774-1792	Louis XVI

Charles X

Louis XIV

1ST REPUBLIC (CONT'D)	
DATE	RULER
1792–1795	National Convention
1795–1799	Directory (Directors)
1799–1804	Consulate

1ST EMPIRE (EMPORERS)	
DATE	RULER
1804–1814	Napoleon I
1814–1815	Louis XVIII (king)
1815	Napoleon I (2nd time)

HOUSE OF BOURBON (RESTORED)	
DATE	RULER
1814–1824	Louis XVIII
1824–1830	Charles X

ORLEANS	
DATE	RULER
1830–1848	Louis Philippe

2ND REPUBLIC (PRESIDENTS)	
DATE	RULER
1848	Louis Eugéne Cavaignac
1848–1852	Louis Napoleon (later Napoleon III)

2ND EMPIRE (EMPERORS)	
DATE	RULER
1852–1870	(Louis) Napoleon III

Louis Napoleon Bonaparte

3RD REPUBLIC (PRESIDENCY)	
DATE	RULER
1870-1871	Louis Jules Trochu
1871-1873	Adolphe Thiers
1873-1879	Patrice de MacMahon
1879-1887	Jules Grévy
1887-1894	Sadi Carnot
1894-1895	Sadi Carnot
1894-1895	Casimir Perier
1895-1899	Felix Faure
1899-1906	Emile Loubet
1906-1913	Armand Fallières
1913-1920	Raymond Poincaré
1920-1920	Paul Deschanel
1920-1924	Alexandre Millerand
1924-1931	Gaston Doumergue
1931-1932	Paul Doumer
1932-1940	Albert Lebrun

General Henri-Philippe Petain

FRENCH STATE	
DATE	RULER
1940-1944	Henri Philippe Petain

PROVISIONAL GOVERMENT (PRESIDENCY)	
DATE	RULER
1944-1946	Charles de Gaulle
1946-1946	Félix Gouin
1946-1946	Georges Bidault
1946-1947	Leon Blum

4TH REPUBLIC (PRESIDENCY)	
DATE	RULER
1947-1954	Vincent Auriol
1954-1958	René Coty

5TH REPUBLIC (PRESIDENCY)	
DATE	RULER
1958-1969	Charles de Gaulle
1969-1969	Alain Poher
1969-1974	Georges Pompidou
1974-1974	Alain Poher
1974-1981	Valéry Giscard d'Estaing
1981-1995	François Mitterrand
1995-2007	Jacques Chirac
2007-2012	Nicolas Sarkozy
2012-2017	François Holland
2017-present	Emmanuel Macron

Emmanuel Macron

Prime Ministers of the United Kingdom

William Pitt 'The Younger'

DATE	NAME	PARTY
1721-1742	Sir Robert Walpole	Whig
1742-1743	Earl of Wilmington	Whig
1743-1754	Henry Pelham	Whig
1754-1756	Duke of Newcastle	Whig
1756-1757	Duke of Devonshire	Whig
1757-1762	Duke of Newcastle	Whig
1762-1763	Earl of Bute	Tory
1763-1765	George Grenville	Whig
1765-1766	Marquess of Rockingham	Whig
1766-1768	Earl of Chatham, Pitt 'The Elder'	Whig
1768-1770	Duke of Grafton	Whig
1770-1782	Lord Frederick North	Tory
1782-1782	Marquess of Rockingham	Whig
1782-1783	Earl of Shelburne	Whig
1783-1783	Duke of Portland	Tory

DATE	NAME	PARTY
1783-1801	William Pitt, 'The Younger'	Tory
1801-1804	Henry Addington	Tory
1804-1806	William Pitt, 'The Younger'	Tory
1806-1807	Baron Grenville	Whig
1807-1809	Duke of Portland	Tory
1809-1812	Spencer Perceval	Tory
1812-1827	Earl of Liverpool	Tory
1827-1827	George Canning	Tory
1827-1828	Viscount Goderich	Tory
1828-1830	Duke of Wellington	Tory
1830-1834	Earl Grey	Whig
1834-1834	Viscount Melbourne	Whig
1834-1835	Sir Robert Peel	Tory
1835-1841	Viscount Melbroune	Tory
1841-1846	Sir Robert Peel	Tory
1846-1852	Earl Russell	Whig
1852-1852	Earl of Derby	Whig
1852-1855	Earl of Aberdeen	Tory
1855-1858	Viscount Palmerston	Liberal
1858-1859	Earl of Derby	Conservative
1859-1865	Viscount Palmerston	Liberal

Duke of Wellington

Marquess of Salisbury

DATE	NAME	PARTY
1859-1866	Earl Russell	Whig
1866-1868	Earl of Derby	Conservative
1868-1868	Earl of Beaconsfield	Conservative
1868-1874	William Gladstone	Liberal
1874-1880	Benjamin Disraeli	Conservative
1880-1885	William Gladstone	Liberal
1885-1886	Marquess of Salisbury	Conservative
1886-1886	William Gladstone	Liberal
1886-1892	Marquess of Salisbury	Conservative
1892-1894	William Gladstone	Liberal
1895-1902	Earl of Rosebery	Liberal
1895-1902	Marquess of Salisbury	Conservative
1902-1905	Arthur James Balfour	Conservative
1905-1908	Sir Henry Campbell-Bannerman	Liberal
1908-1916	Herbert Henry Asquith	Liberal
1916-1922	David Lloyd George	Liberal
1922-1923	Andrew Bonar Law	Conservative
1923-1924	Stanley Baldwin	Conservative
1924-1924	Ramsay MacDonald	Labour

Herbert Henry Asquith

Sir Winston Churchill

DATE	NAME	PARTY
1924-1929	Stanley Baldwin	Conservative
1929-1935	Ramsay MacDonald	Labour
1935-1937	Stanley Baldwin	Conservative
1937-1940	Neville Chamberlain	Conservative
1940-1945	Winston Churchill	Conservative
1945-1951	Clement Attlee	Labour
1951-1955	Sir Winston Churchill	Conservative
1955-1957	Sir Anthony Eden	Conservative
1957-1963	Harold Macmillan	Conservative
1963-1964	Sir Alec Douglas-Home	Conservative
1964-1970	Harold Wilson	Labour
1970-1974	Edward Heath	Conservative
1974-1976	Harold Wilson	Labour
1976-1979	James Callaghan	Labour
1979-1990	Margaret Thatcher	Conservative
1990-1997	John Major	Conservative
1997-2007	Tony Blair	Labour
2007-2010	Gordon Brown	Labour
2010-2016	David Cameron	Conservative
2016-2019	Theresa May	Conservative
2019-Present	Boris Johnson	Conservative

Margaret Thatcher

Boris Johnson

UK Parliaments and Assemblies

NORTHERN IRELAND ASSEMBLY – BELFAST

Established: 1973, 1999
Description/Powers: Initially established in 1973 but was abolished by 1974. It was then reintroduced in 1998 under the Good Friday Agreement and given full powers in 1999. The Northern Ireland Assembly has the power of primary legislation and domestic issues.

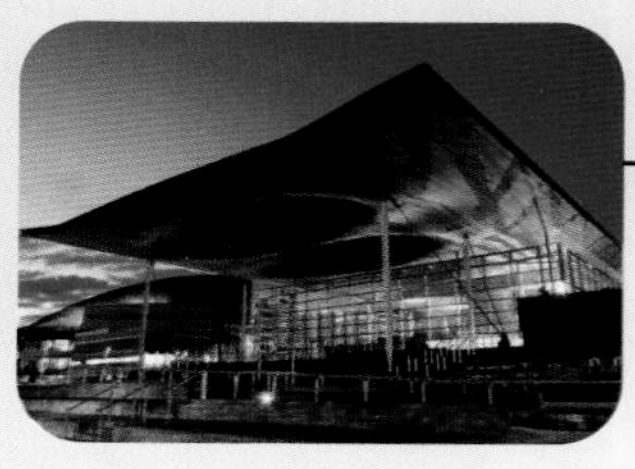

NATIONAL ASSEMBLY FOR WALES – CARDIFF

Established: 1st July 1999
Description/Powers: As an assembly, the Welsh have considerably fewer powers devolved to them than the Scottish Parliament. Similarly, to Scotland, the main policy areas dissolved to Wales are domestic issues such as Welsh education and health.

THE SCOTTISH PARLIAMENT – EDINBURGH

Established: 1st July 1999
Description/Powers: The Scottish Parliament was granted the power to make primary legislation for domestic issues such as Scottish education, health and local government.

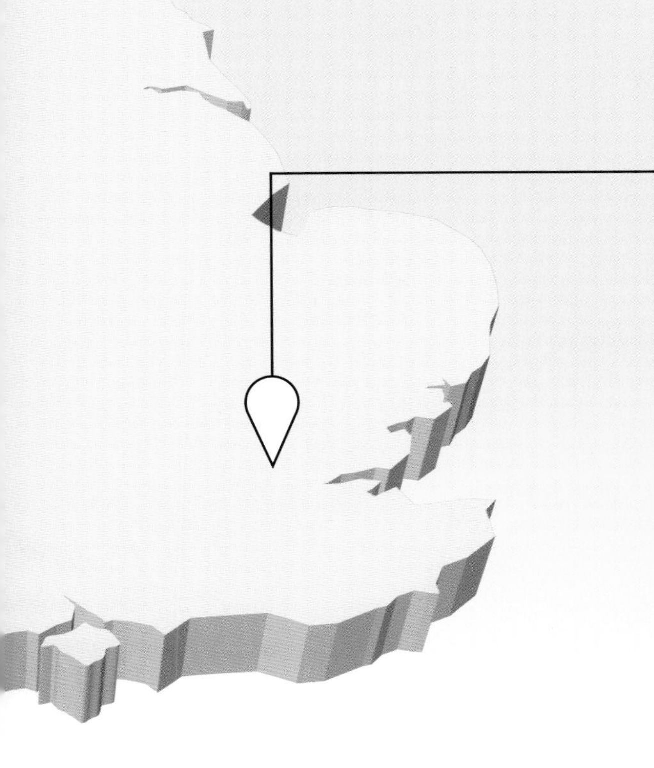

UK PARLIAMENT – WESTMINSTER

Established: 1688 (when Parliament began to assume its current role)
Description/Powers: The UK Parliament is a bicameral system as it has a House of Lords (Upper Chamber) and a House of Commons (Lower Chamber). It is the highest legislative authority as it includes the Queen of England.

U.S. presidents

DATE	PRESIDENT	PARTY
1789-1797	1. George Washington	None
1797-1801	2. John Adams	Federalist
1801-1809	3. Thomas Jefferson	Democratic-Republican
1809-1817	4. James Madison	Democratic-Republican
1817-1825	5. James Monroe	Democratic-Republican
1825-1829	6. John Quincy Adams	Democratic-Republican
1829-1837	7. Andrew Jackson	Democrat
1837-1841	8. Martin van Buren	Democrat
1841-1841	9. William H. Harrison	Whig
1841-1845	10. John Tyler	Whig
1845-1849	11. James K. Polk	Democrat
1849-1850	12. Zachary Taylor	Whig
1850-1853	13. Millard Fillmore	Whig
1853-1857	14. Franklin Pierce	Democrat
1857-1861	15. James Buchanan	Democrat
1861-1865	16. Abraham Lincoln	Republican
1865-1869	17. Andrew Johnson	National Union
1869-1877	18. Ulysses S. Grant	Republican
1877-1881	19. Rutherford Hayes	Republican
1881-1881	20. James Garfield	Republican
1881-1885	21. Chester Arthur	Republican
1885-1889	22. Grover Cleveland	Democrat
1889-1893	23. Benjamin Harrison	Republican

DATE	PRESIDENT	PARTY
1889-1893	23. Benjamin Harrison	Republican
1893-1897	24. Grover Cleveland	Democrat
1897-1901	25. William McKinley	Republican
1901-1909	26. Theodore Roosevelt	Republican
1909-1913	27. William Taft	Republican
1913-1921	28. Woodrow Wilson	Democrat
1921-1923	29. Warren Harding	Republican
1923-1929	30. Calvin Coolidge	Republican
1929-1933	31. Herbert C. Hoover	Republican
1933-1945	32. Franklin Delano Roosevelt	Democrat
1945-1953	33. Harry S Truman	Democrat
1953-1961	34. Dwight David Eisenhower	Republican
1961-1963	35. John Fitzgerald Kennedy	Democrat
1963-1969	36. Lyndon Baines Johnson	Democrat
1969-1974	37. Richard Milhous Nixon	Republican
1974-1977	38. Gerald R. Ford	Republican
1977-1981	39. James (Jimmy) Earl Carter, Jr.	Democrat
1981-1989	40. Ronald Wilson Reagan	Republican
1989-1993	41. George H. W. Bush	Republican
1993-2001	42. William (Bill) Jefferson Clinton	Democrat
2001-2009	43. George W. Bush	Republican
2009-2017	44. Barack Obama	Democrat
2017-present	45. Donald John Trump	Republican

Chinese dynasties

DATE	DYNASTY
2100-1600 BC	Xia Dynasty
1600-1050 BC	Shang Dynasty
	Zhou Dynasty
	Western Zhou (1050-771 BC)
	Eastern Zhou (771-256 BC)
221-206 BC	Qin Dynasty
206 BC-220	Han Dynasty
	Western Han (206 BC-9)
	Eastern Han (25-220)
220-589	Six Dynasties Period
	Three Kingdoms: Cao Wei, Shu Han, Dong Wu (220-265)
	Jin Dynasty (265-420)
	Period of the Northern and Southern Dynasties (386-589)
581-618	Sui Dynasty
618-906	Tang Dynasty
907-960	Five Dynasties Period
960-1279	Song Dynasty
	Northern Song Dynasty (960-1127)
	Southern Song Dynasty (1127-1279)
1279-1368	Yuan Dynasty
1368-1644	Ming Dynasty
1644-1911	Qing Dynasty
1912-1949	Republic Period
1949-present	People's Republic of China

Famous architects and their creations

ARCHITECT NAME	EXAMPLES OF THEIR WORK
Robert Adam	Harewood House; Kenwood House
Thomas Archer	Birmingham Cathedral; Chatsworth House, Derbyshire
Charles Barry	Manchester City Art Gallery; Parliament Square, Westminster
Norman Robert Foster	Millau Viaduct; Trafalgar Square Redevelopment, London; Millennium Bridge, London; Sackler Galleries, Royal Academy of Arts, London
Inigo Jones	Banqueting House, Whitehall, London; Queen's House, Greenwich, London; Hampton Court, London
A.W. Pugin	The Palace of Westminster, London
Sir George Gilbert Scott	St Pancras railway station and hotel, London; Kelham Hall, Nottinghamshire
G.E Street	All Saints, Clifton, Bristol; St Philip and St James Cathedrals, Oxford
Sir Christopher Wren	St Paul's Cathedral, London
James Wyatt	Ragley Hall, Warwickshire; Dodington Park, Gloucestershire
Sir John Vanburgh	Castle Howard, Yorkshire; Blenheim Palace, Oxfordshire

British architectural movements

English Baroque 17th and 18th century

Georgian 1714-1830

Victorian 1837-1901

Edwardian 1901-1914

Art Nouveau 1890-1915

Art Deco 1920s-1940s

Brutalist 1950s-1970s

Timeline of art movements

PERIOD	DATE	MOVEMENT	ARTISTS
Prehistory	2.5 million BC - 800 BC	Lower Paleolithic Era (2,500,000 BC); Middle Paleolithic Era (200,000 BC); Upper Maleolithic Era (40,000BC); Mesolithic Era (10,000 BC); Neolithic Era (8,000BC); Bronze Age (3,100 BC); Iron Age (1,250 BC)	
Art of Classical Antiquity	800 BC - 400	Ancient Greek Art (800 BC- 23 BC); Roman Period (27 BC - 330 AD); Christian Period (330-472)	
The Period of the Dark Ages	450-1050	Byzantine Art (500-1200); Medieval Christian Artworks (780-900)	
The European Revival	800-1387	Carolingian Art (750-900); Ottonian Art (900-1000); Romanesque Architecture (1050-1150); Gothic Art and Architecture (1100-1250); Proto-Renaissance Art and Architecture (1333-1400)	
The Renaissance	1400-1530	Italian Early Renaissance (1400-90); Italian High Renaissance (1490-1530)	Michaelangelo; Raphael; Titian; Sandro Botticelli; Giorgio Vasari; Leonardo Da Vinci
Flanders and Holland	1430-1580	Flemish painting (1430-1500); Netherlandish Renaissance Art (1430-1580)	Jan Van Eyck; Roger Van der Weyden; Hieronymus Bosch
Germany	1400-1550	German Gothic Art (1490-1520); German Renaissance Art (1430-1580)	Albrecht Durer; Tilman Riemenschneider

PERIOD	DATE	MOVEMENT	ARTISTS
Mannerism	1520-1600	Venetian Painting (1530-1600);	Caravaggio; Rubens; Velasquez; Anthony Van Dyck
Baroque	1600-1700		
Romanticism	1800-50		Eugene Delacroix; William Blake; Caspar David Friedrich; JMW Turner; Thomas Cole; John Constable
Pre-Raphaelite	1848-55		Dante Gabriel Rossetti
Realism	1850-present		Gustave Coubert; Edgar Degas; Ilya Repin; Honore Daumier; Jean-Francois Millet
Modern Art	1860-1979	French Naturalism (1880s-90s); Symbolism (1886-1900); Impressionism (1869-90); Post-Impressionism (1885-1990); Expressionist Art (1900-present); Cubist Art (1908-1914); Precisionism (1920s); Futurism (1909-1914); Rayonism (1912-1914); Art Nouveau (1890s-1910) Arts and Crafts (1910s-1920s); Art Deco (1920s-1940s); Surrealism (1920s-1930s)	Emil Zola; Claude Monet; Vincent Van Gough; William Morris; Henri Matisse; Gustav Klimt; Edvard Munch; Andre Breton; Salvador Dali; Pablo Picasso

A detail from *Guernica*, Pablo Picasso (1937)

Science & Nature

Space exploration

YEAR	EVENT	DETAILS	COUNTRY
4 Oct 1957	First artificial Earth satellite	Sputnik 1	U.S.S.R.
3 Nov 1957	First animal launched into space	Dog Laika aboard Sputnik 2	U.S.S.R.
14 Sep 1959	First spacecraft to hard-land on another celestial object (the Moon)	Luna 2	U.S.S.R.
1 Apr 1960	First applications satellite launched	TIROS 1 (weather observation)	U.S.
12 Apr 1961	First human to orbit Earth	Yury Gagarin on Vostok 1	U.S.S.R.
16 Jun 1963	First woman in space	Valentina Tereshkova on Vostok 6	U.S.S.R.
18 Mar 1965	First space walk	Aleksey Leonov on Voskhod 2	U.S.S.R.
3 Feb 1966	First spacecraft to soft-land on the Moon	Luna 9	U.S.S.R.
24 Dec 1968	First humans to orbit the Moon	Frank Borman, James Lovell, and William Anders on Apollo 8	U.S.
20 Jul 1969	First human to walk on the Moon	Neil Armstrong on Apollo 11	U.S.

Solar system planets

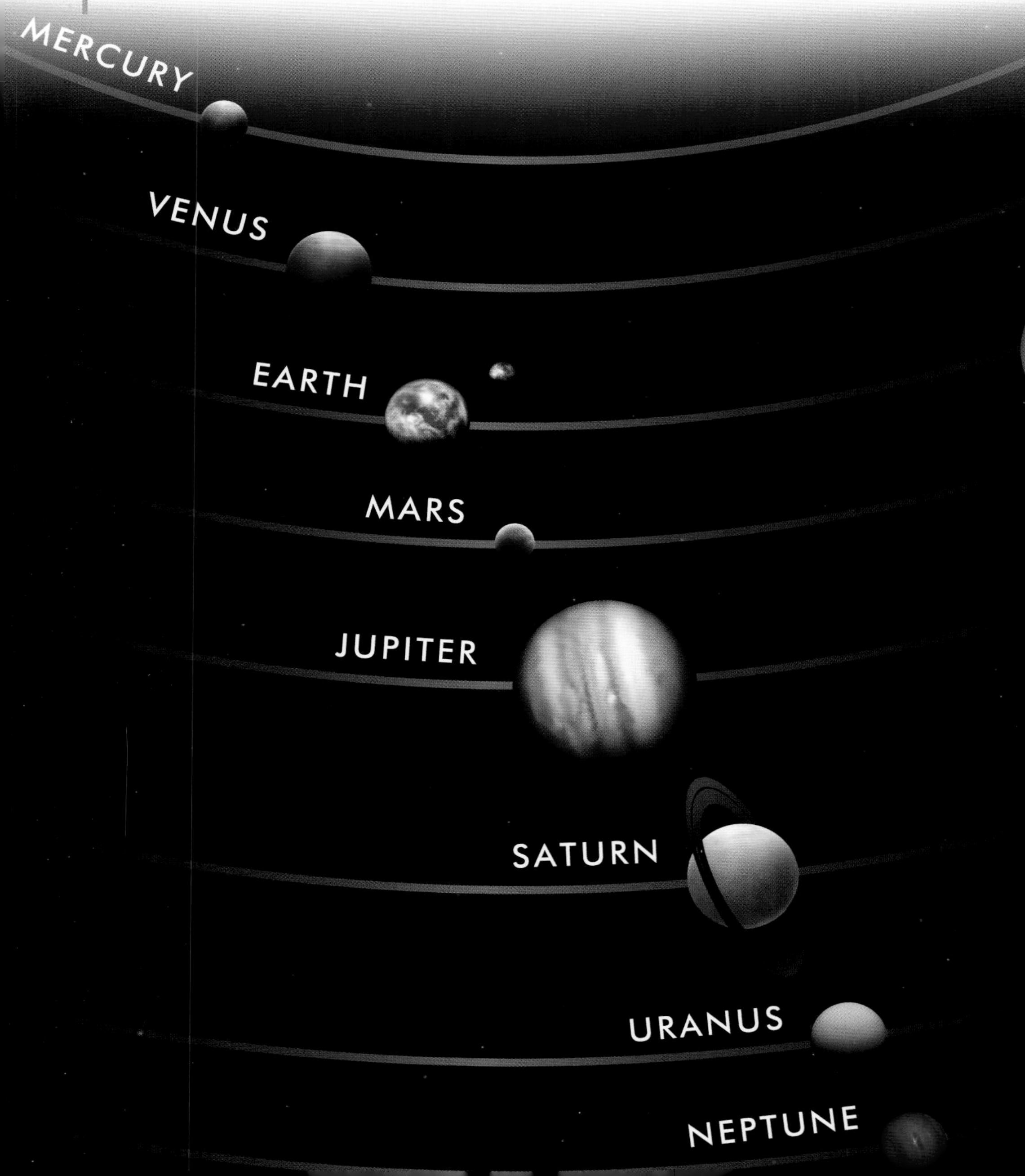

MERCURY

VENUS

EARTH

MARS

JUPITER

SATURN

URANUS

NEPTUNE

MERCURY			
DIAMETER	DISTANCE FROM SUN	LENGTH OF YEAR	NO. OF MOONS
4,879 km	57,909,227 km	88 Earth days	0

VENUS			
DIAMETER	DISTANCE FROM SUN	LENGTH OF YEAR	NO. OF MOONS
12,104 km	108,209,475 km	225 Earth days	0

EARTH			
DIAMETER	DISTANCE FROM SUN	LENGTH OF YEAR	NO. OF MOONS
12,742 km	149,598,262 km	365.24 days	1

MARS			
DIAMETER	DISTANCE FROM SUN	LENGTH OF YEAR	NO. OF MOONS
6,779 km	227,943,824 km	1.9 Earth years	2

JUPITER			
DIAMETER	DISTANCE FROM SUN	LENGTH OF YEAR	NO. OF MOONS
139,822 km	778,340,821 km	11.9 Earth years	79

SATURN			
DIAMETER	DISTANCE FROM SUN	LENGTH OF YEAR	NO. OF MOONS
116,464 km	1,426,666,422 km	29.5 Earth years	82

URANUS			
DIAMETER	DISTANCE FROM SUN	LENGTH OF YEAR	NO. OF MOONS
50,724 km	2,870,658,186 km	84.0 Earth years	27

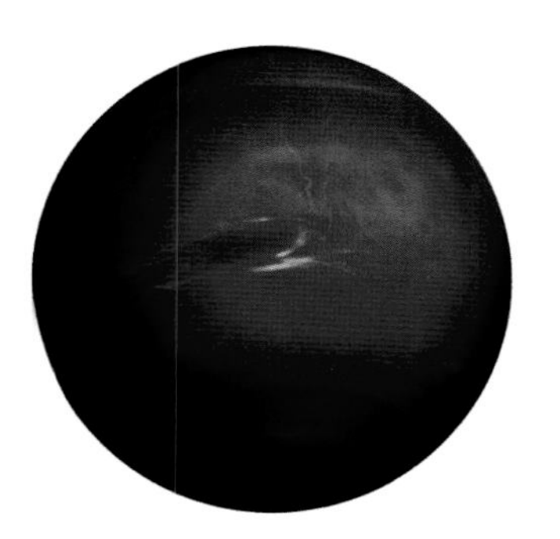

NEPTUNE			
DIAMETER	DISTANCE FROM SUN	LENGTH OF YEAR	NO. OF MOONS
49,244 km	4,498,396,441 km	164.8 Earth years	14

International Astronomical Union (IAU) downgraded the status of Pluto to that of "dwarf planet."

Revolutionary scientific theories

YEAR	THEORY	SCIENTIST	DESCRIPTION
1543	Heliocentrism	Nicolaus Copernicus	Theorises how the Earth revolves around the sun.
1778	Oxygen Theory of Combustion	Antoine-Laurent Lavoisier	Combustion is the chemical union of a substance with oxygen.
1859	Evolution by Natural Selection	Charles Darwin	Theorises how populations can evolve in such a way that they become better suited to their environments over time.
late 19th century	Statistical Mechanics	James Clerk Maxwell, Ludwig Boltzmann, J. Willard Gibbs	Made sense of thermodynamics and provided strong evidence for the reality of atoms.
1905	Special Relativity	Albert Einstein	Theorises how space and time are linked for objects that are moving at a consistent speed in a straight line.
1900-1926	Quantum Theory	Max Planck, Albert Einstein, Niels Bohr, Werner Heisenberg, Erwin Schrödinger, Max Born, Paul Dirac	Theorises the nature and behaviour of matter and energy on an atomic and subatomic level.
1915	General Relativity	Albert Einstein	The general theory of relativity describes the force of gravity.
1912 and 1960	Plate Tectonics	Alfred Wegener, Tuzo Wilson	Theorises that Earth's outer shell is divided into several plates that glide over the mantle, the rocky inner layer above the core.
1944	Game Theory	John von Neumann and Oskar Morgenstern	Branch of applied mathematics that provides tools for analysing situations in which players make decisions that are interdependent.
1948	Information Theory	Claude Shannon	A mathematical representation of the conditions and parameters affecting the transmission and processing of information.

The Periodic Table of Elements

Atomic Number — 8 15.999 — Atomic Mass
Symbol — O
OXYGEN — Name

PERIOD ↓ / GROUP →	1	2	3	4	5	6	7	8	9	10	11	12	13	14	15	16	17	18
1	1 1.008 H HYDROGEN																	2 4.003 He HELIUM
2	3 6.941 Li LITHIUM	4 9.012 Be BERYLLIUM											5 10.811 B BORON	6 12.011 C CARBON	7 14.007 N NITROGEN	8 15.999 O OXYGEN	9 18.998 F FLUORINE	10 20.180 Ne NEON
3	11 22.990 Na SODIUM	12 24.305 Mg MAGNESIUM											13 26.982 Al ALUMINIUM	14 28.086 Si SILICON	15 30.974 P PHOSPHORUS	16 32.066 S SULPHUR	17 35.453 Cl CHLORINE	18 39.948 Ar ARGON
4	19 39.098 K POTASSIUM	20 40.078 Ca CALCIUM	21 44.956 Sc SCANDIUM	22 47.867 Ti TITANIUM	23 50.942 V VANADIUM	24 51.996 Cr CHROMIUM	25 54.938 Mn MANGANESE	26 55.845 Fe IRON	27 58.933 Co COBALT	28 58.693 Ni NICKEL	29 63.546 Cu COPPER	30 65.38 Zn ZINC	31 69.723 Ga GALLIUM	32 72.64 Ge GERMANIUM	33 74.922 As ARSENIC	34 78.971 Se SELENIUM	35 79.904 Br BROMINE	36 83.798 Kr KRYPTON
5	37 85.468 Rb RUBIDIUM	38 87.62 Sr STRONTIUM	39 88.906 Y YTTRIUM	40 91.224 Zr ZIRCONIUM	41 92.906 Nb NIOBIUM	42 95.95 Mo MOLYBDENUM	43 98.907 Tc TECHNETIUM	44 101.07 Ru RUTHENIUM	45 102.91 Rh RHODIUM	46 106.42 Pd PALLADIUM	47 107.87 Ag SILVER	48 112.41 Cd CADMIUM	49 114.82 In INDIUM	50 118.71 Sn TIN	51 121.76 Sb ANTIMONY	52 127.60 Te TELLURIUM	53 126.90 I IODINE	54 131.29 Xe XENON
6	55 132.91 Cs CAESIUM	56 137.33 Ba BARIUM	57-71 La-Lu Lanthanide	72 178.49 Hf HAFNIUM	73 180.95 Ta TANTALUM	74 183.84 W TUNGSTEN	75 186.21 Re RHENIUM	76 190.23 Os OSMIUM	77 192.22 Ir IRIDIUM	78 195.08 Pt PLATINUM	79 196.97 Au GOLD	80 200.59 Hg MERCURY	81 204.38 Tl THALLIUM	82 207.2 Pb LEAD	83 208.98 Bi BISMUTH	84 (209) Po POLONIUM	85 (210) At ASTATINE	86 (222) Rn RADON
7	87 (223) Fr FRANCIUM	88 (226) Ra RADIUM	89-103 Ac-Lr Actinide	104 (261) Rf RUTHERFORDIUM	105 (262) Db DUBNIUM	106 (266) Sg SEABORGIUM	107 (264) Bh BOHRIUM	108 (269) Hs HASSIUM	109 (268) Mt MEITNERIUM	110 (281) Ds DARMSTADTIUM	111 (280) Rg ROENTGENIUM	112 (285) Cn COPERNICIUM	113 (286) Nh NIHONIUM	114 (289) Fl FLEROVIUM	115 (288) Mc MOSCOVIUM	116 (292) Lv LIVERMORIUM	117 (294) Ts TENNESSINE	118 (294) Og OGANESSON

Series															
Lanthanide Series	57 138.91 La LANTHANUM	58 140.12 Ce CERIUM	59 140.91 Pr PRASEODYMIUM	60 144.24 Nd NEODYMIUM	61 (145) Pm PROMETHIUM	62 150.36 Sm SAMARIUM	63 151.96 Eu EUROPIUM	64 157.25 Gd GADOLINIUM	65 158.93 Tb TERBIUM	66 162.50 Dy DYSPROSIUM	67 164.93 Ho HOLMIUM	68 167.26 Er ERBIUM	69 168.93 Tm THULIUM	70 173.05 Yb YTTERBIUM	71 174.97 Lu LUTETIUM
Actinide Series	89 (227) Ac ACTINIUM	90 232.04 Th THORIUM	91 231.04 Pa PROTACTINIUM	92 238.03 U URANIUM	93 (237) Np NEPTUNIUM	94 (244) Pu PLUTONIUM	95 (243) Am AMERICIUM	96 (247) Cm CURIUM	97 (247) Bk BERKELIUM	98 (251) Cf CALIFORNIUM	99 (252) Es EINSTEINIUM	100 (257) Fm FERMIUM	101 (258) Md MENDELEVIUM	102 (259) No NOBELIUM	103 (262) Lr LAWRENCIUM

ALKALI METAL · ALKALINE EARTH · TRANSITION METAL · BASIC METAL · SEMIMETAL · NONMETAL · HALOGEN · NOBLE GAS · LANTHANIDE · ACTINIDE

Famous inventions

The Wheel: Ancient Greeks

YEAR 3500 BC

First sailing ships: Ancient Egyptians

YEAR 3000 BC

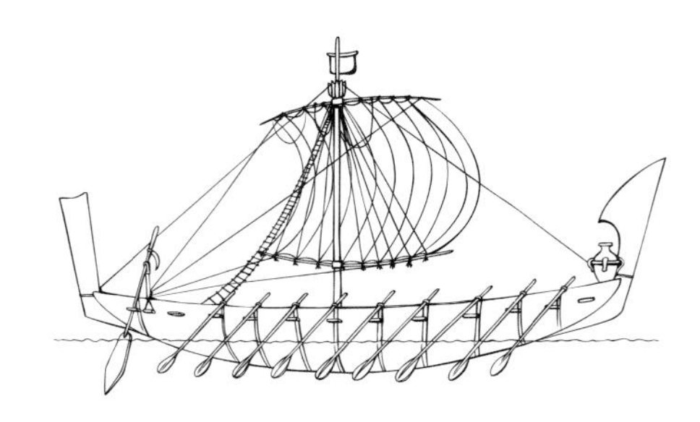

Earliest compass: Chinese

YEAR 2nd C BC - 1st C

Printing Press: Johannes Gutenburg

YEAR 1440

Seed drill: Jethro Tull

YEAR 1701

Carbon microphone: David Hughes

YEAR 1877

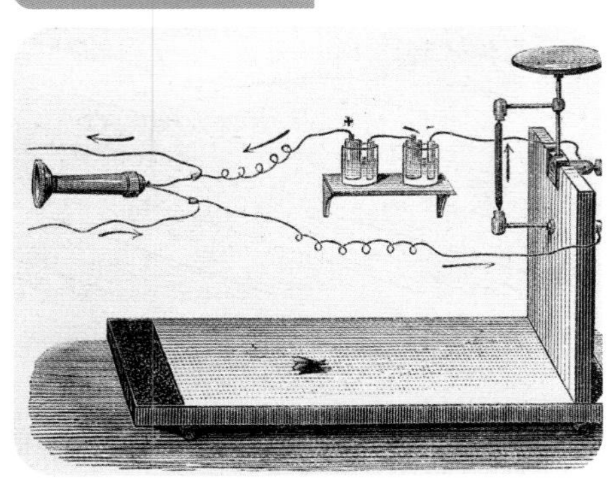

Electric lightbulb: Thomas Edison

YEAR 1878

First car: Karl Friedrich Benz & Gottleib Daimler

YEAR 1886

Television system: Philo Taylor Farnsworth

YEAR 1926

Penicillin: Alexander Fleming

YEAR 1928

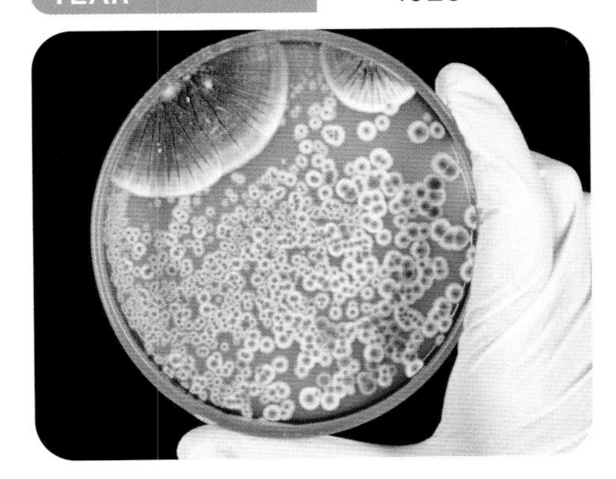

The internet: Vinton Cerf & Bob Kahn

YEAR 1960s

Important alloys and their uses

METAL	ALLOY AND USES	COMPOSITION OF ALLOY
Aluminium Alloys	Al-Li - military and commercial aerospace applications	Aluminium, lithium, sometimes mercury
	Alnico - small servomotors in aircraft, permanent magnets	Aluminium, nickel, copper
	Duralumin - aircrafts, boats, railroad cars, and machinery	Copper, aluminium
	Magnalium - aircraft and car parts; fireworks	Aluminium, 5% magnesium
	Magnox - used for cladding of the fuel elements	Magnesium oxide, aluminium
	Nambe - vase, candlestick or other serveware	Aluminium plus seven other unspecified metals
	Silumin - machine construction	Aluminium, silicon
	Zamak - used in die casting applications	Zinc, aluminium, magnesium, copper
Bismuth Alloys	Wood's metal - custom-shaped apertures and blocks	Bismuth, lead, tin, cadmium
	Rose metal – used as a solder and in the optical industry	Bismuth, lead, tin

Duralumin sheets with rivets

METAL	ALLOY AND USES	COMPOSITION OF ALLOY
Cobalt Alloys	Stellite - saw teeth, hardfacing, and acid-resistant machine parts	Cobalt, chromium, tungsten or molybdenum, carbon
	Talonite - aerospace use, knife blades	Cobalt, chromium
	Ultimet - valves, mixers, nozzles, and slurry pumps	Cobalt, chromium, nickel, molybdenum, iron, tungsten
Copper Alloys	Beryllium copper - electronics, automotive, aerospace industries	Copper, beryllium
	Billon - coins, medals, and token coins	Copper, silver
	Brass - decoration, plumbing, instruments	Copper, zinc
	Bronze - coins and medals, heavy gears, tools, electrical hardware	Copper, tin, aluminium or any other element
	Bell metal - casting of bells	Copper, tin
	Cupronickel - coinage, marine engineering	Copper, nickel
	Phosphor bronze - springs, electrical springs, boat propellers	Copper, tin, and phosphorus
	Nordic gold - 10,20 and 50 Euro coins	Copper, aluminium, zinc, tin
Gold Alloys	Electrum - first known coins in the Western world	Gold, silver, copper
	Tumbaga - used in pre-Columbian times to decorate the surfaces of objects made from low-gold alloys	Gold, copper
	Rose gold - jewellery	Gold, copper
	White gold - jewellery	Gold, nickel, palladium, or platinum

METAL	ALLOY AND USES	COMPOSITION OF ALLOY
Iron or Ferrous Alloys	Steel - structures, cutlery, car bodies, rails	Carbon
	Stainless steel - cutlery, surgical instruments	Chromium, nickel
	Elinvar - balance springs for watches and other physical instruments	Nickel, chromium
	Invar - surveying tapes, watches and various other temperature-sensitive devices	Nickel
	Kovar - plates, round bars, sheets, coils, wires and tubes	Cobalt
	Spiegeleisen - production of iron and steel	Manganese, carbon, silicon
Lead Alloys	Antimonial lead - used as a grid metal alloy in the lead acid storage battery	Lead, antimony
	Solder - used to connect metal workpieces	Lead, tin
	Terne - roofing, gutters, downspouts	Lead, tin
	Type metal - used to make type characters for printing, candlesticks	Lead, tin, antimony

White and rose gold rings

METAL	ALLOY AND USES	COMPOSITION OF ALLOY
Tin Alloys	Britannia - utensils, cookware, tableware, tankards	Tin, copper, antimony
	Pewter - decorative plates and vases	Tin, lead, copper
Silver Alloys	Argentium sterling silver - jewellery	Silver, copper, germanium
	Platinum sterling - fabrication of jewellery and flatware	Silver, platinum
	Sterling silver - jewellery, art objects, music instruments	Silver, copper

Pewter jugs

Popular gemstones

Popular herbs and spices

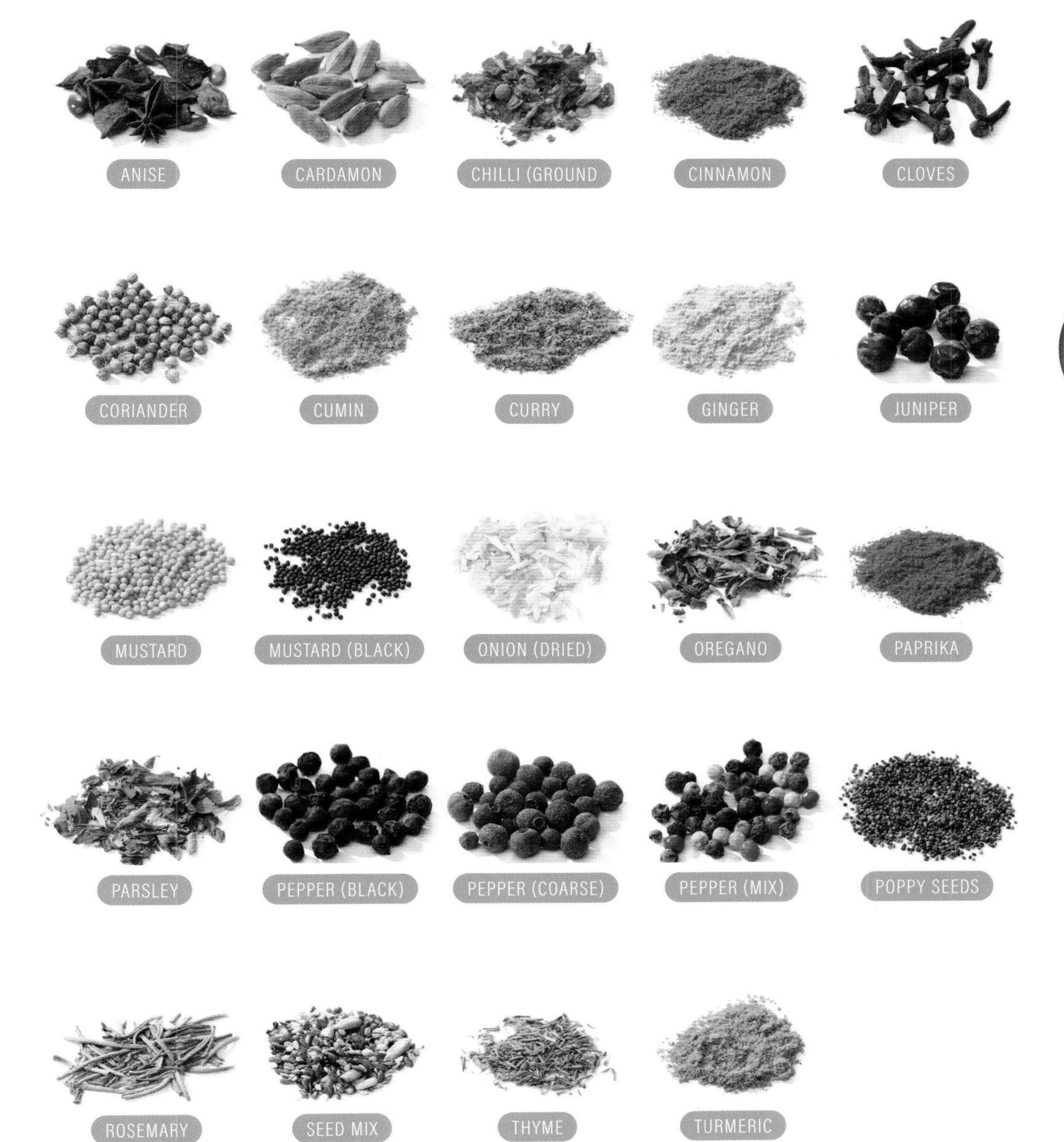

History's deadliest health epidemics

Epidemic Typhus/Camp Fever

YEAR STARTED 1846

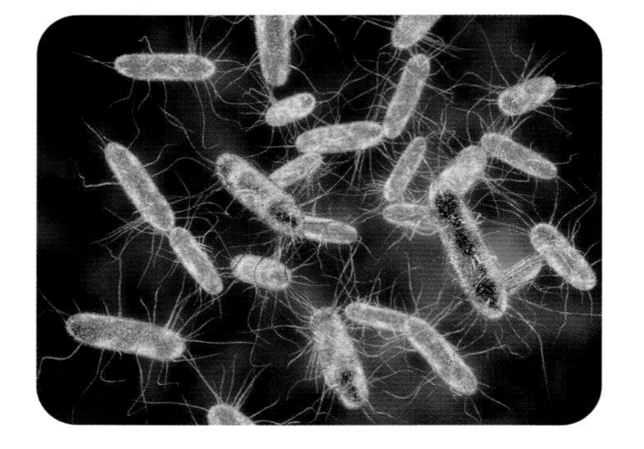

Spanish Influenza

YEAR STARTED 1918

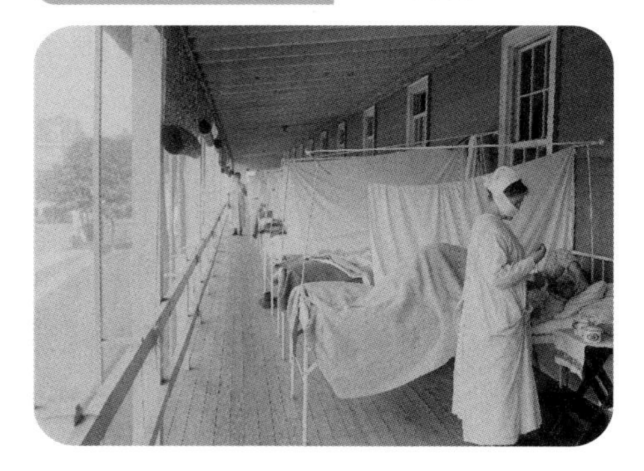

Bubonic Plague

YEAR STARTED 1347

Yellow Fever

YEAR STARTED 1648

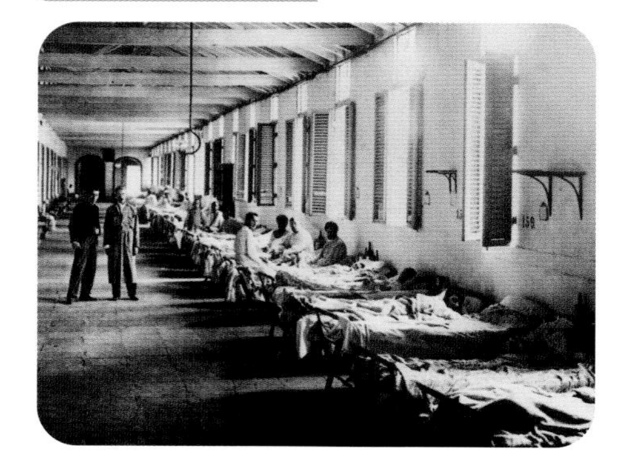

Cholera

YEAR STARTED 1817

Smallpox

YEAR STARTED 1500

Tuberculosis

YEAR STARTED 3000BC

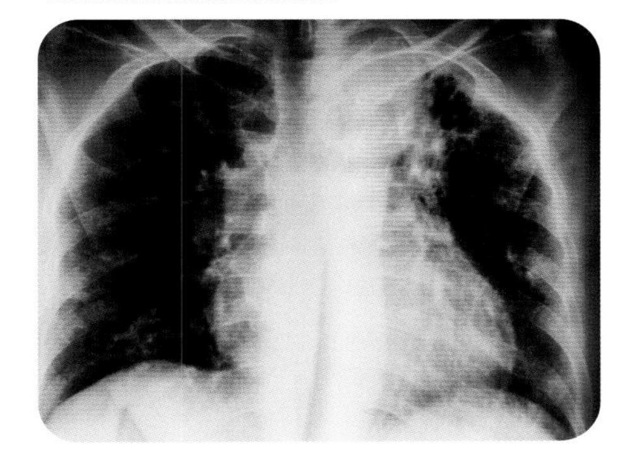

AIDS

YEAR STARTED 1981

Malaria

YEAR STARTED 2000BC

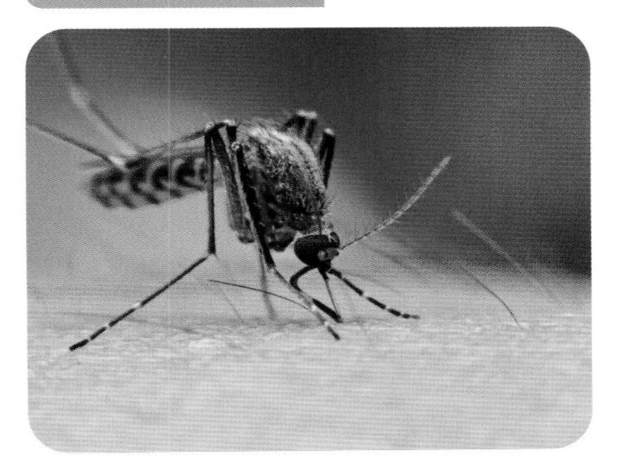

Coronavirus (COVID-19)

YEAR STARTED 2019

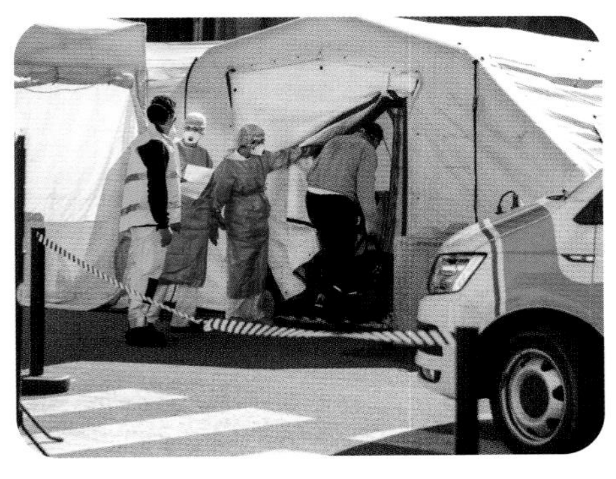

The human body

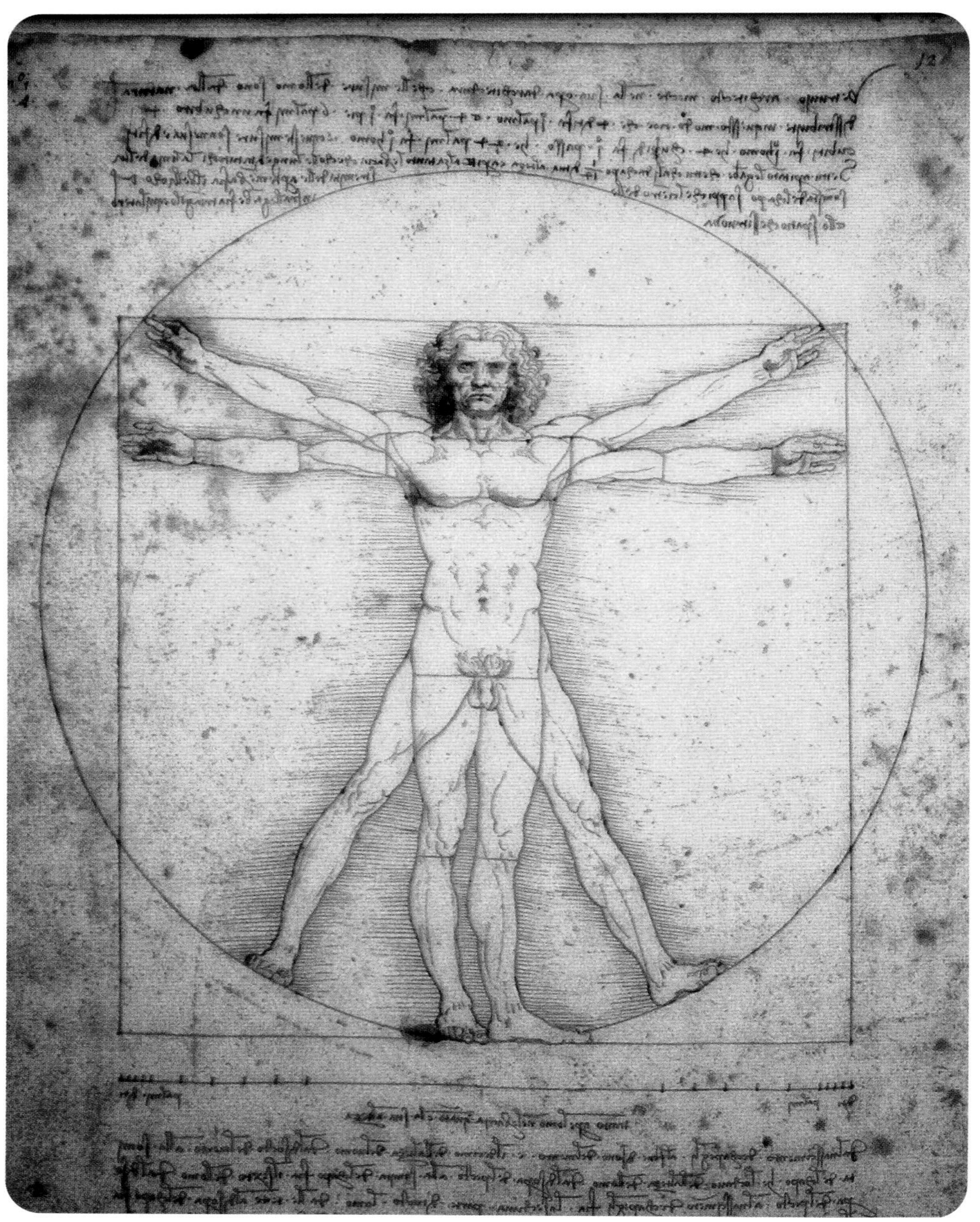

L'uomo vitruviano, Leonardo da Vinci est. 1490

The human arteries and veins

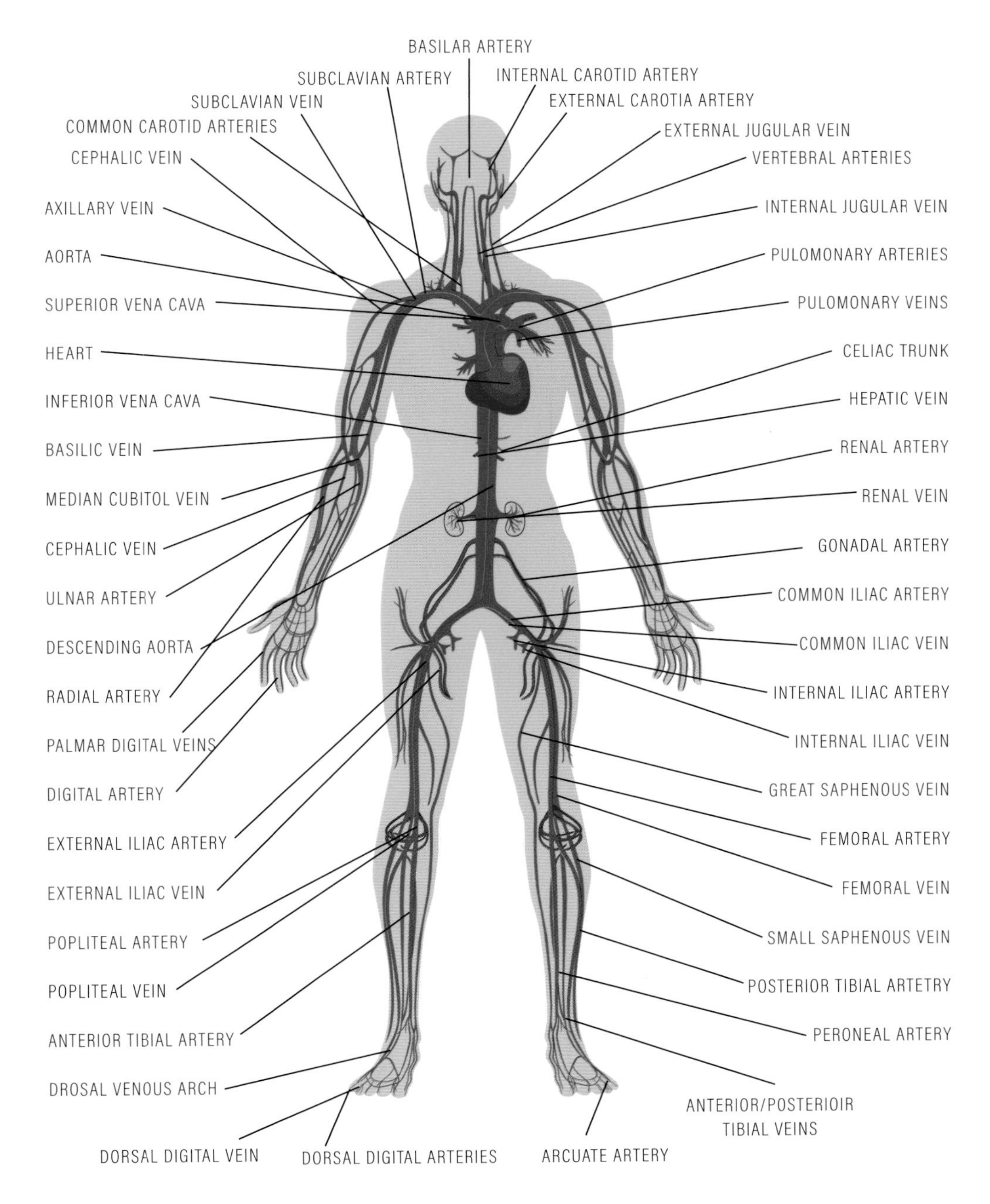

The human muscles system

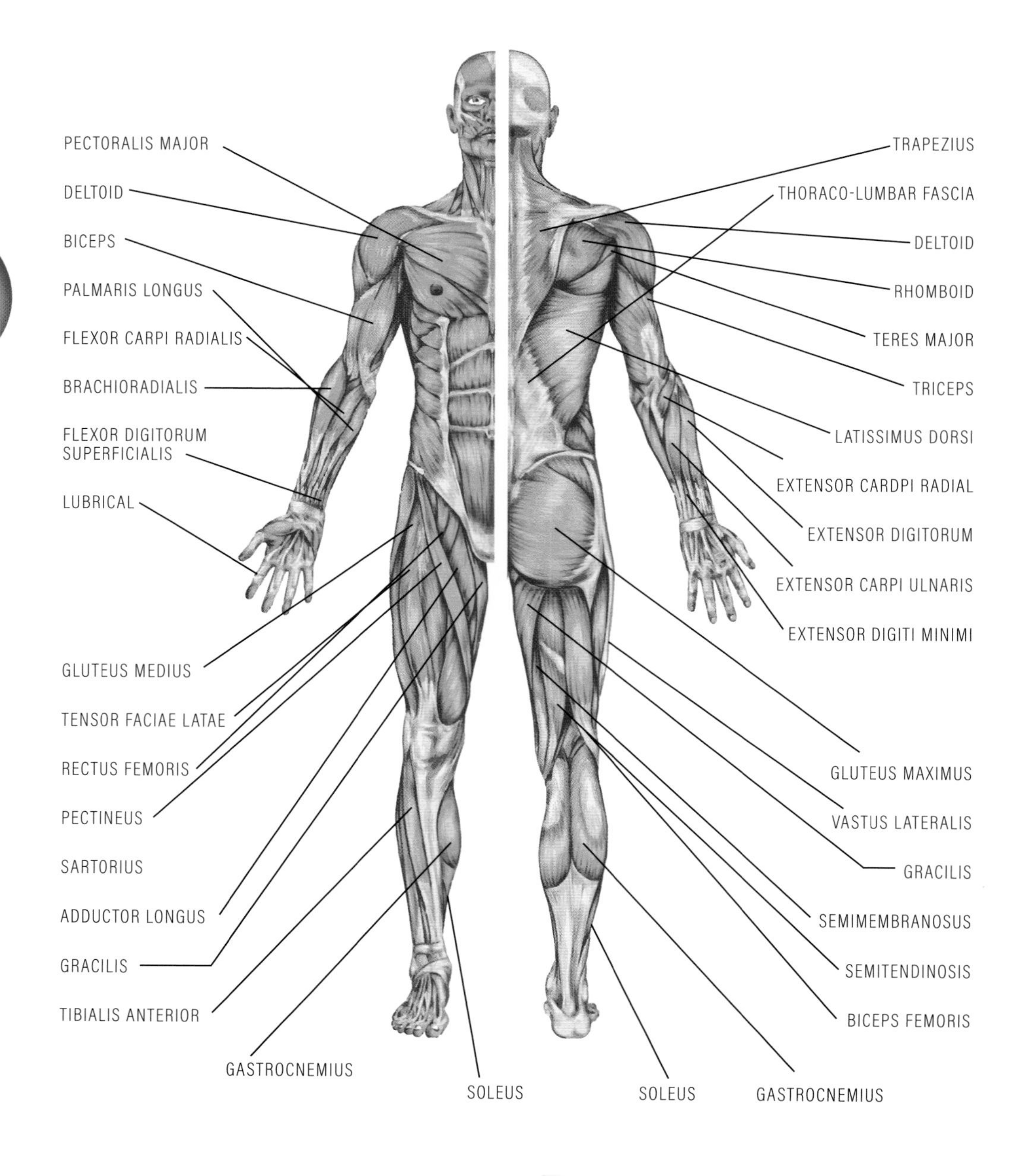

Muscles of the human head

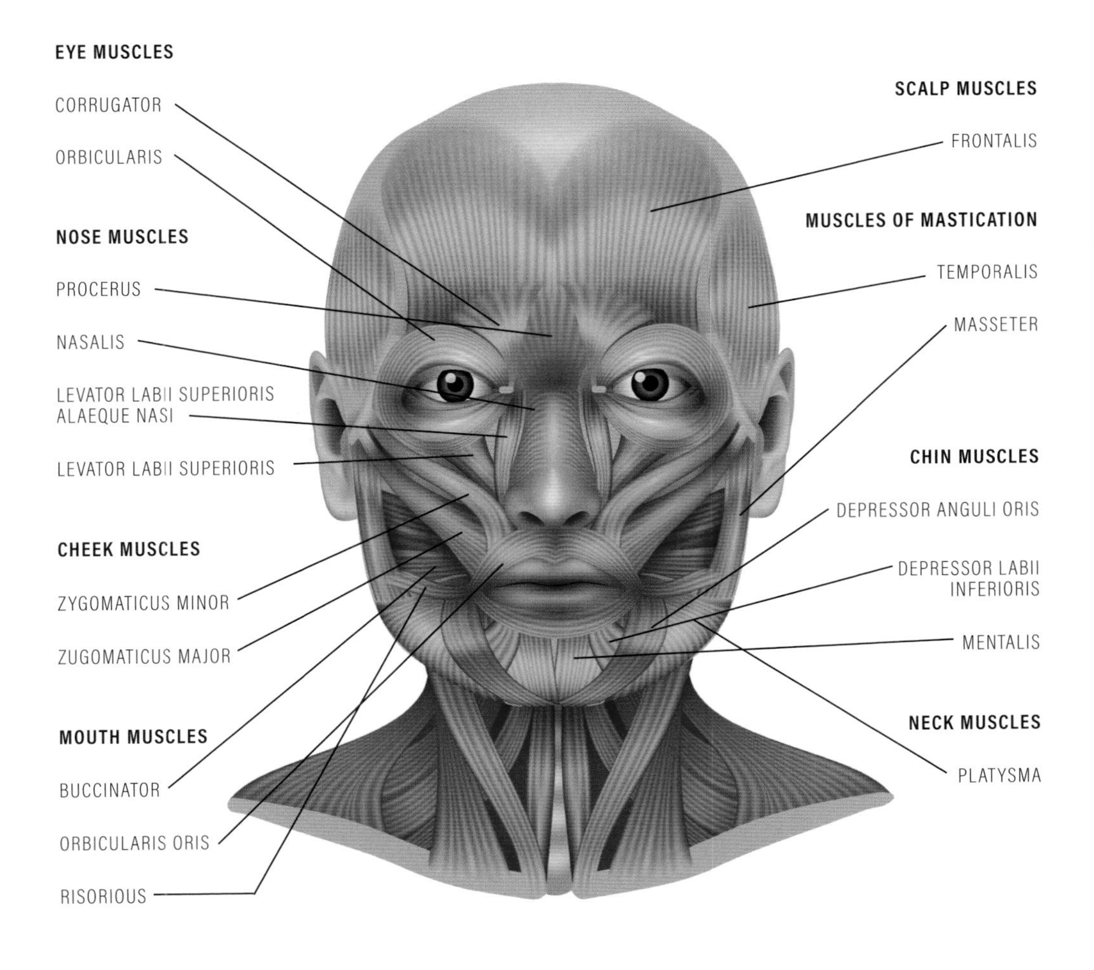

The human bones system

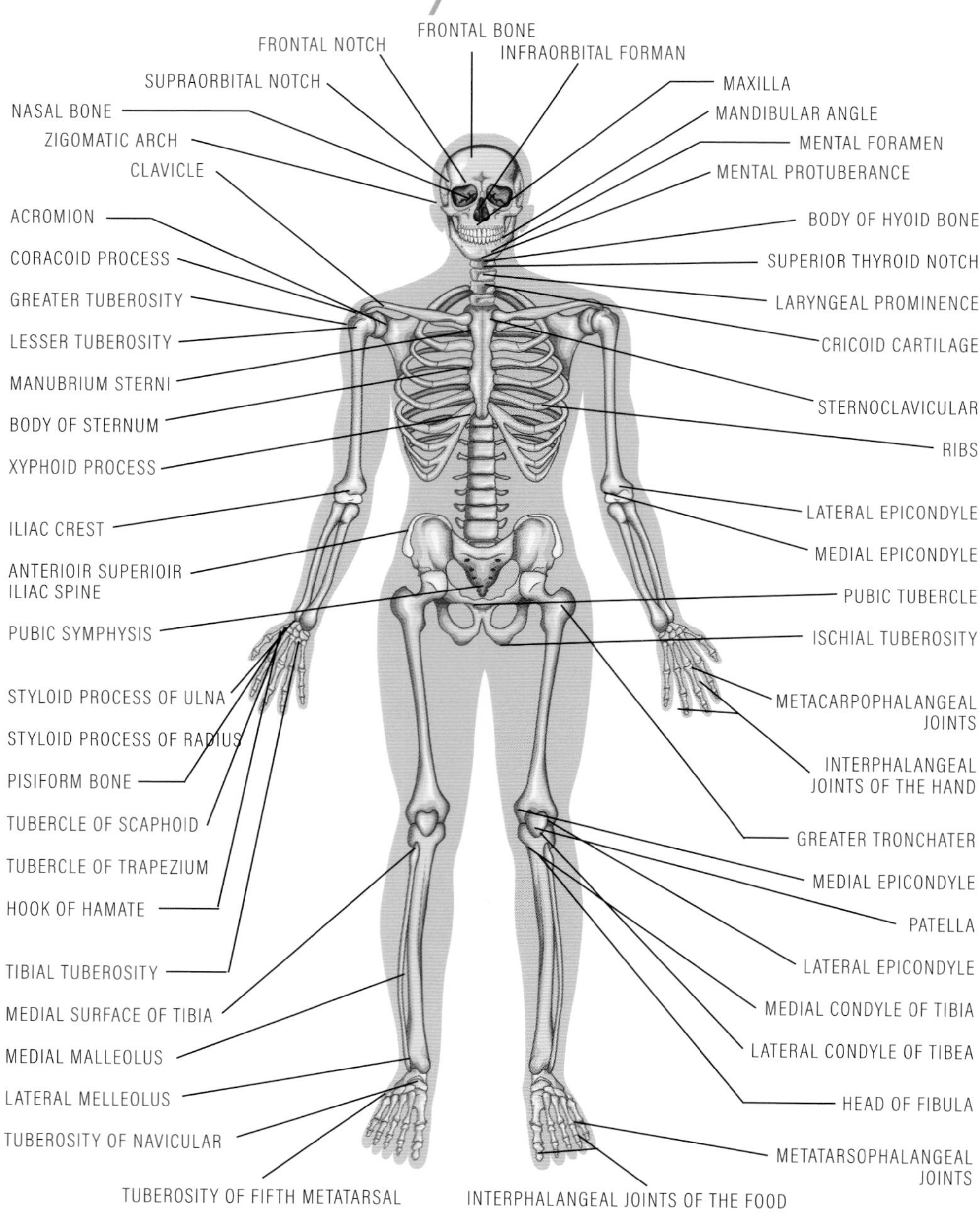

Taxonomic rank

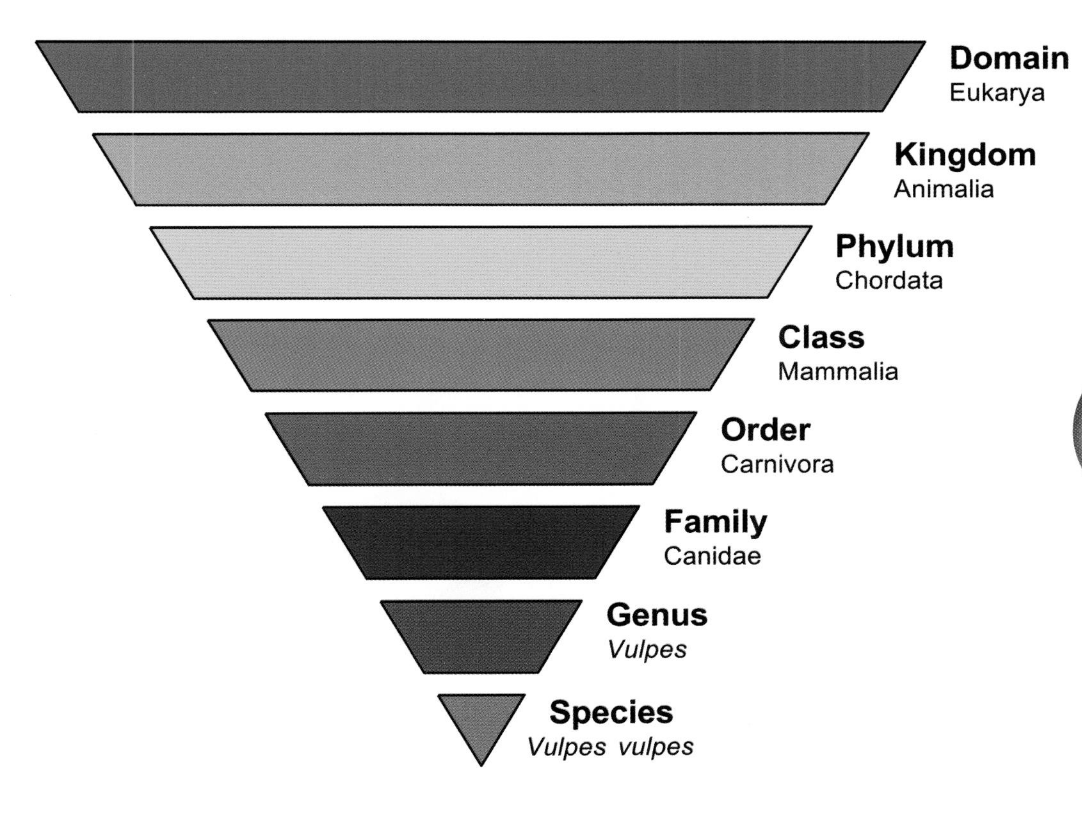

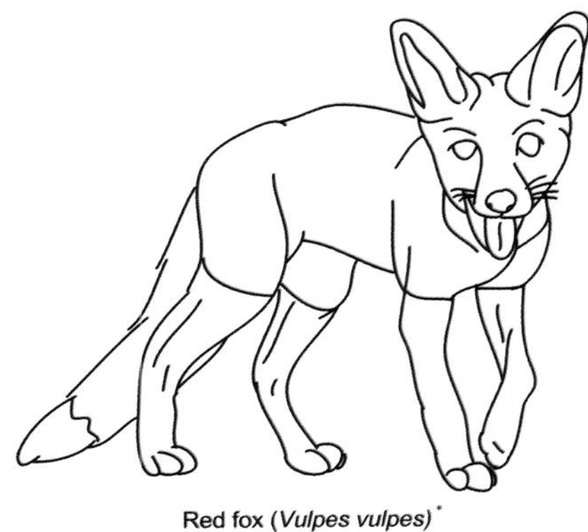

Red fox (*Vulpes vulpes*)*

*This is an example of the taxonomic rank for the red fox

Domains and kingdoms of organisms

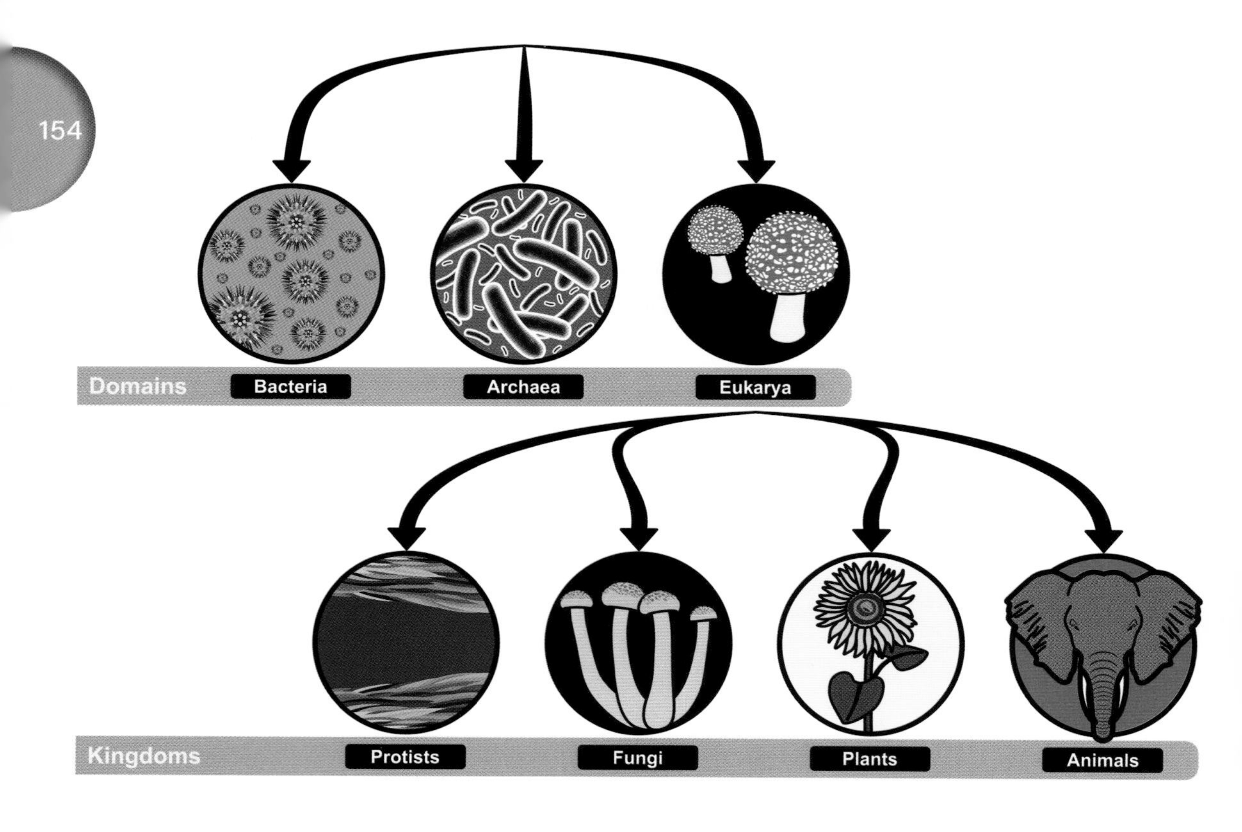

Animal kingdom

VERTEBRATES: ANIMALS WITH BACKBONE				
TYPE	BLOOD	PHYSICAL TRAITS	LIFE TRAITS	EXAMPLE
Amphibian	Cold-blooded	Smooth, moist skin (no scales). Breathe with gills and lungs.	Lay eggs. Spend part of their lives in water and part on land	
Bird	Warm-blooded	Have feathers, a beak and wings	Babies hatch from eggs	
Fish	Cold-blooded	Have gills to breathe, scales and fins on their bodies	Live in water	
Mammal	Warm-blooded	Have hair or fur	Drink milk when they are babies	
Reptile	Cold-blooded	Have scales and breathe with lungs	Usually lay eggs on land	

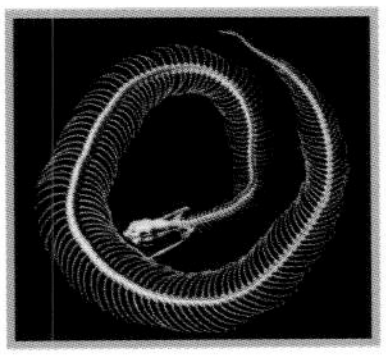

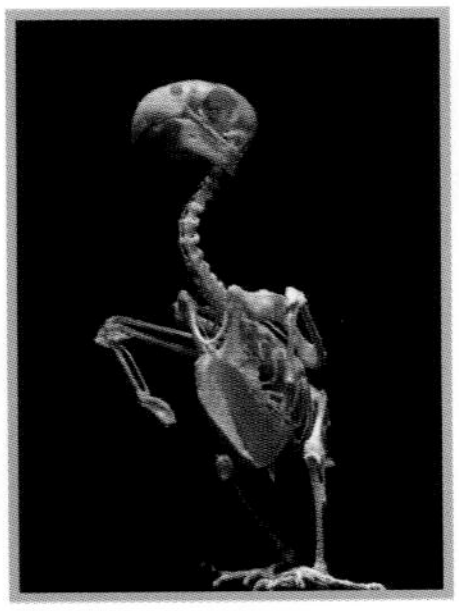

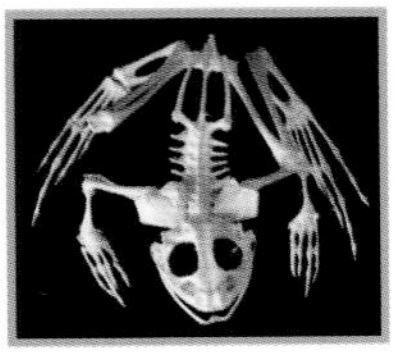

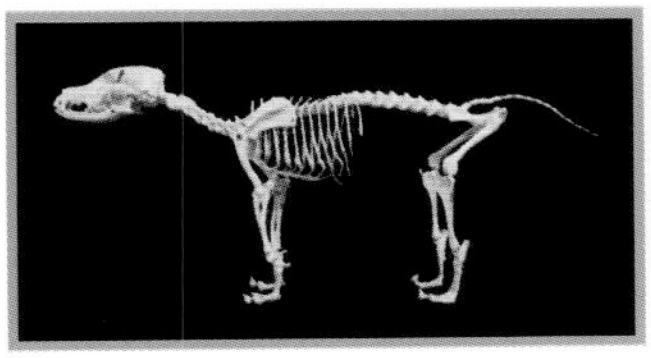

Clockwise from top left: snake skeleton; bird skeleton; fish skeleton; frog skeleton; dog skeleton

INVERTEBRATES: ANIMALS WITHOUT BACKBONE				
TYPE	PHYSICAL TRAITS	HABITAT	DIET	EXAMPLE
Worms	Soft, tube-shaped bodies and a distinct head	Some live inside other animals, some in water, some on land	Living organisms e.g. funghi, nematode, protozoan, rotifer, bacteria	
Anthropods	Have legs and some have wings	Live on land, in the water and in the air	Funghi, worms or other anthropods	
Cnidarians	Central opening surrounded by tentacles	Live in water	Take food in and eliminate waste through central opening	
Echino-derms	Covered in spikes or spines	Live in water	Central opening for taking in food	
Molluscs	Soft bodies with external or internal shells	Live on land or water	A muscular foot allows them to move and hunt food	
Sponges	The simplest invertebrates	Live in water	Filter food from water around them	

Crabs fall under the crustacean branch of anthropods

Animals and their habitats

VERTEBRATES: MAMMALS		
ANIMAL NAME	GROUP NAME	HABITAT
Ape	Shrewdness	Forests
Badger	Cete	Setts (networks of underground tunnels and chambers) below soft, well-drained soil e.g. Woodlands
Bat	Caludron, colony or camp	Woodlands, grasslands, farmlands
Bear	Sleuth or sloth	Mountain forests, ice fields, mountain woodland
Buffalo	Gang or obstinancy	Grassland
Cat	Clowder, pounce or glaring	Deserts, forests, urban environments
Cow	Drove or herd	Grasslands
Deer	Herd or bevy	Croplands, meadows, forested woodlots, brushy areas

A colony of bats flying at sunset

VERTEBRATES: MAMMALS		
ANIMAL NAME	GROUP NAME	HABITAT
Dog	Pack or cowardice	Prairies, deserts, grasslands, forests, rainforests, urban environment
Elephant	Parade	Deserts, Rainforests
Elk	Gang or herd	Rocky Mountains, forests
Ferret	Business	Prairies
Fox	Leash, skulk or earth	Forests, grasslands, mountains, deserts, urban environment
Giraffe	Tower	Open woodlands of savannas
Goat	Tribe or trip	Rugged mountains or deserts
Gorilla	Band	Forests, lowland swamps and marshes
Hippopotamus	Bloat or thunder	Swamplands, rivers
Horse	Team, stud, rag or string	Valleys, mountainsides, desert plateaus, grassy plains
Hyena	Cackle	Savannas, grasslands, woodlands, forest edges, deserts, mountains
Kangaroo	Troop or mob	Forests, grassy plains, savannas
Leopard	Leap	Forests, mountains, grassland and deserts
Lion	Pride or sawt	Savannah grasslands, scrub forests
Marten	Richness	Woodlands
Mole	Labour	Bogs, marshes, meadows, fields
Monkey	Troop or barrel	Grassland, high plains, mountains
Mule	Pack, span or barren	Mountain forests
Musk Ox	Team or yoke	Arctic
Otter	Romp, bevy, family or raft	Brackish habitats, rivers, lakes
Pig	Drift, drove (younger pigs), team, sounder (older pigs) or passel	Moist forests, swamps, shrublands
Porcupine	Prickle	Forests, deserts

VERTEBRATES: MAMMALS		
ANIMAL NAME	GROUP NAME	HABITAT
Rabbit	Colony, warren, nest (young), down and husk (hares) or herd (domestic)	Forests, grasslands, deserts, wetlands
Rhinoceros	Crash	Greenland, open savanna
Seal	Pod or herd	Arctic oceans
Sheep	Drive, flock or herd	Mountains, desert, grassland, tundra
Squirrel	Dray or scurry	Woodlands
Tiger	Ambush or streak	Swamps, grassland, forests
Whale	Pod, gam, school or herd	Oceans
Wolf	Pack, rout or route	Tundra, woodlands, forests, grasslands and deserts

A pack of wolves

VERTEBRATES: BIRDS		
ANIMAL NAME	**GROUP NAME**	**HABITAT**
Birds in general	Flight, flock, volary or brace	Grasslands, cypress swamp, pine woods, forests
Bittern	Sedge or seige	Reedbeds
Buzzard	Wake	Woodland edges, fields, meadows
Bobolink	Chain	Meadows, grasslands
Coot	Cover or raft	Marshlands
Cormorant	Gulp	Inland waters
Crane	Sedge or siege	Wetlands, marshlands
Crow	Murder, parcel, storytelling or horde	Woodlands, forests, farming sites
Dotterel	Trip	Freshwater lakes, freshwater marshes, coastlines saline lagoons and sandy beaches
Dove	Dule, bevy, cote, dole, paddling or pitying	Urban areas, farms, prairie, grassland, lightly wooded areas
Duck	Raft, Team, Paddling, Brace, badling, flock	Wetlands, marshes, ponds, rivers, lakes and oceans
Eagle	Convocation or aerie	Lakes, marshes, seacoasts, rivers
Finch	Charm	Grasslands, around barns and stables
Flamingo	Stand or flamboyance	Lakes, estuarine lagoons, mangrove swamps, tidal flats

A female bobolink perches in a meadow of prarie wildflowers

VERTEBRATES: BIRDS		
ANIMAL NAME	GROUP NAME	HABITAT
Goose	Flock, gaggle or skein	Lakes, rivers, marshes, bogs, sloughs
Grouse	Pack or covey	Woodlands
Gull	Colony or screech	Coastal environments
Hawk	Cast, kettle or boil	Scrublands, grasslands, fields, pastures, tropical rainforest
Heron	Sedge, hedge or siege	Wetlands
Jay	Party, band or scold	Woodlands with oaks and beeches
Mallard	Sord or brace	Grasslands, ponds, small lake, marshy areas
Magpie	Tiding, gulp, murder or charm	Moors, fields, parks, gardens, villages, towns
Nightingale	Watch	Forests and scrubs
Owl	Parliament or stare	Forests, mountains, deserts, plains, tundra
Parrot	Pandemonium or company	Tropical and sub-tropical forests
Partridge	Bevy, bew, covey, jugging, warren	Grasslands, woodlands, meadows
Peacock	Muster, pride or ostentation	Forests, rainforests
Penguin	Colony, muster, huddle, parcel or rookery	Continental Antarctica, equatorial Galapagos Islands
Pheasant	Nest, nide, nye or bouquet	Grasslands, idle fields, wetlands, croplands, shrublands
Plover	Wing, congregation	Coast on coastal marshes, estuaries, wetlands, agricultural land
Quail	Bevy or covey	Fields, grassland
Raven	Unkindness or storytelling	Forests, beaches, islands, chaparral, sagebrush, mountains, desert, grasslands, agricultural fields, tundra, ice floes

VERTEBRATES: BIRDS		
ANIMAL NAME	GROUP NAME	HABITAT
Snipe	Walk or wisp	Marshes, bogs, tundra, wet meadows
Sparrow	Host	Urban, rural settings
Stork	Mustering or muster	Wetlands, grasslands, tropical forests, savanna
Swallow	Flight or gulp	Fields, wetlands
Swan	Bevy, wedge, bank, herd or game	Freshwater marshes, shallow lakes coastal lagoons, estuaries, sheltered coastal bays
Turkey	Rafter, posse or gang	Woodlands
Wigeon	Company	Wetlands, lakes, ponds, brackish marshes
Woodcock	Fall	Trees and shrubs
Woodpecker	Descent	Forests, tree trunks

Macaw parrots licking clay for minerals in Brazil.

VERTEBRATES: REPTILES AND AMPHIBIANS		
ANIMAL NAME	GROUP NAME	HABITAT
Crocodile	Bask or float	Wetlands, ponds, coves, creeks, canals
Frog	Army, colony, knot	In or near ponds
Toad	Knot, knab or nest	Ponds
Turtle	Bale, turn, dole or nest	Ponds, bogs, large lakes, rivers
Snake, viper	Nest, den, pit, bed, knot	Bodies of water, forests, rainforests, deserts prairies

VERTEBRATES: FISH		
ANIMAL NAME	GROUP NAME	HABITAT
Tuna, Salmon, Tilapia, Pollock, Catfish, Cod, Carp, Mackerel, Herring, Barb, Sea bass, Bream, Bonito, Trout, Tetra, Eel and others	Nest, draft, shoal, school or hover	Bodies of water
Shark	Gam, herd, frenzy, school, shoal or shiver	Various aquatic habitats at various temperatures. Ranging from deep oceans to fresh, salt or brackish waters

A frenzy of hammerhead sharks in the Galapagos.

INVERTEBRATES		
ANIMAL NAME	GROUP NAME	HABITAT
Ant	Colony, army, swarm or nest	Every land habitat except the very coldest
Bee	Grist, hive or swarm	Forests, gardens, woodlands, orchards, meadows
Caterpillar	Army	Hedges and bushes
Clam	Bed	Salt water, mud, sand, shelly bottoms of creeks and rivers
Cockroach	Intrusion	They live in nearly every habitat, especially where it is warm and moist
Gnat	Cloud, swarm or horde	Moist environments
Grasshopper	Cloud	Forests, jungles, grasslands, dry environments
Jellyfish	Smack, bloom, brood or fluther	All oceans, deep sea and shallow saltwater lakes
Locust	Plague	Greenland, deserts
Oyster	Bed	Saltwater, marine and brackish habitats

Beehives

Popular cat breeds

Popular dog breeds – small

Popular dog breeds — medium

AUSTRALIAN CATTLE DOG

AUSTRALIAN SHEPHERD

BASSET HOUND

BORDER COLLIE

BOXER

BULLDOG

CHOW CHOW

DALMATION

LABRADOR RETRIEVER

PIT BULL TERRIER

SAMOYED

SHETLAND SHEEPDOG

SIBERIAN HUSKY

VIZSLA

WEIMARANER

Popular dog breeds — large

AKITA

ALASKAN MALAMUTE

BERNESE MOUNTAIN DOG

BLOODHOUND

BULLMASTIFF

CANE CORSO

ENGLISH MASTIFF

GERMAN SHEPHERD

GIANT SCHNAUZER

GOLDEN RETRIEVER

GREAT DANE

NEWFOUNDLAND

STANDARD POODLE

PYRENEAN SHEPHERD

ROTTWEILER

Famous gardens

NAME	LOCATION
Château de Versailles	Versailles, France
Royal Botanic Garden at Kew	Kew, Surrey, UK
Powerscourt Gardens	Enniskerry, County Wicklow, Ireland
Butchart Gardens	Vancouver Island, British Columbia
Villa d'Este	Tivoli, Italy
Dumbarton Oaks	Washington DC, USA
Gardens of the Villa Éphrussi de Rothschild	St Jean-Cap-Ferrat, France
Stourhead	Warminster, UK
The Master of Nets Garden	Suzhou, China
Sans Souci	Potsdam, Germany

Popular garden flowers

Popular indoor plants

CACTUS

CALATHEA WHITE STAR

FICUS MICROCARPA GINSENG

MONSTERA DELICIOSA

PEACE LILY

PHALAENOPSIS BLUME

SANSEVIERIA

SEDUM MOGANIANUM

ZZ PLANT

Entertainment

Highest grossing Oscar winners for Best Picture

1. Gone with the Wind (1939)

ORIGINAL GROSS	$189,523,031
ADJUSTED GROSS	$6,550,904,767

2. The Sound of Music (1965)

ORIGINAL GROSS	$163,214,286
ADJUSTED GROSS	$1,284,706,509

3. Ben-Hur (1959)

ORIGINAL GROSS	$73,000,000
ADJUSTED GROSS	$1,1137,941,176

4. Titanic (1997)

ORIGINAL GROSS	$600,788,188
ADJUSTED GROSS	$1,040,580,848

5. The Sting (1973)

ORIGINAL GROSS	$159,616,327
ADJUSTED GROSS	$716,920,790

6. Around the World in 80 Days (1956)

ORIGINAL GROSS	$42,000,000
ADJUSTED GROSS	$667,800,000

7. The Godfather (1972)

ORIGINAL GROSS	$134,966,411
ADJUSTED GROSS	$631,166,451

8. Forrest Gump (1994)

ORIGINAL GROSS	$329,694,499
ADJUSTED GROSS	$627,050,542

9. My Fair Lady (1964)

ORIGINAL GROSS	$72,000,000
ADJUSTED GROSS	$615,483,871

10. The Greatest Show on Earth (1952)

ORIGINAL GROSS	$36,000,000
ADJUSTED GROSS	$540,000,000

Lowest grossing Oscar winners for Best Picture

1. The Hurt Locker (2009)

ORIGINAL GROSS	$14,700,000
ADJUSTED GROSS	$15,582,000

2. All the King's Men (1949)

ORIGINAL GROSS	$3,500,000
ADJUSTED GROSS	$60,489,130

3. Hamlet (1948)

ORIGINAL GROSS	$3,075,000
ADJUSTED GROSS	$61,115,625

4. An American in Paris (1951)

ORIGINAL GROSS	$4,500,000
ADJUSTED GROSS	$67,500,000

5. Crash (2005)

ORIGINAL GROSS	$54,557,348
ADJUSTED GROSS	$67,664,729

6. Marty (1955)

ORIGINAL GROSS	$4,000,000
ADJUSTED GROSS	$70,666,666

7. No Country for Old Men (2007)

ORIGINAL GROSS	$74,273,505
ADJUSTED GROSS	$85,824,762

8. It Happened One Night (1934)

ORIGINAL GROSS	$2,500,000
ADJUSTED GROSS	$86,413,043

9. The Last Emperor (1987)

ORIGINAL GROSS	$43,984,000
ADJUSTED GROSS	$89,430,383

10. The Great Ziegfeld (1936)

ORIGINAL GROSS	$3,000,000
ADJUSTED GROSS	$95,400,000

Highest grossing movies of all time

RANK	TITLE	WORLDWIDE GROSS	YEAR
1	Avengers: Endgame	$2,797,800,564	2019
2	Avatar	$2,790,439,000	2009
3	Titanic	$2,194,439,542	1997
4	Star Wars: The Force Awakens	$2,068,223,624	2015
5	Avengers: Infinity War	$2,048,359,754	2018

RANK	TITLE	WORLDWIDE GROSS	YEAR
6	Jurassic World	$1,671,713,208	2015
7	The Lion King	$1,656,943,394	2019
8	The Avengers	$1,518,812,988	2012
9	Furious 7	$1,516,045,911	2015
10	Frozen II	$1,450,026,933	2019
11	Avengers: Age of Ultron	$1,402,805,868	2015
12	Black Panther	$1,346,913,161	2018
13	Harry Potter and the Deathly Hallows – Part 2	$1,341,932,398	2011
14	Star Wars: The Last Jedi	$1,332,539,889	2017
15	Jurassic World: Fallen Kingdom	$1,309,484,461	2018
16	Frozen	$1,290,000,000	2013
17	Beauty and the Beast	$1,263,521,126	2017
18	Incredibles 2	$1,242,805,359	2018
19	The Fate of the Furious	$1,238,764,765	2017
20	Iron Man 3	$1,214,811,252	2013

Multiple Oscar winners

ACTOR/ ACTRESS	TOTAL AWARDS	TOTAL NOMINATIONS	BEST ACTOR/ ACTRESS	BEST SUPPORTING ROLE
Katharine Hepburn	4	12	Morning Glory (1932); Guess Who's Coming to Dinner (1967); The Lion in Winter (1968); On Golden Pond (1981)	
Meryl Streep	3	17	Sophie's Choice (1982); The Iron Lady (2011)	Kramer vs. Kramer (1979)
Jack Nicholson	3	12	One Flew Over the Cuckoo's Nest (1975); As Good as It Gets (1997)	Terms of Endearment (1983)
Ingrid Bergman	3	7	Gaslight (1944); Anastasia (1956)	Murder on the Orient Express (1974)
Daniel Day-Lewis	3	5	My Left Foot (1989); There Will be Blood (2007); Lincoln (2012)	
Walter Brennan	3	4		Come and Get It (1936); Kentucky (1938); The Westerner (1940)
Olivia de Havilland	2	10	On the Waterfront (1954); The Godfather (1972)	

ACTOR/ ACTRESS	TOTAL AWARDS	TOTAL NOMINATIONS	BEST ACTOR/ ACTRESS	BEST SUPPORTING ROLE
Bette Davis	2	10	Dangerous (1935); Jezebel (1938)	
Spencer Tracy	2	9	Captains Courageous (1937); Boys Town (1938)	
Jack Lemmon	2	8	Save the Tiger (1973)	Mister Roberts (1955)
Jane Fonda	2	7	Klute (1971); Coming Home (1978)	
Dustin Hoffman	2	7	Kramer vs. Kramer (1979); Rain Man (1988)	
Cate Blanchett	2	6	Blue Jasmine (2013)	The Aviator (2004)
Michael Caine	2	6		Hannah and Her Sisters (1986); The Cider House Rules (1999)
Robert De Niro	2	6	Raging Bull (1980)	The Godfather Part II (1974)

ACTOR/ ACTRESS	TOTAL AWARDS	TOTAL NOMINATIONS	BEST ACTOR/ ACTRESS	BEST SUPPORTING ROLE
Jessica Lange	2	6	Blue Sky (1994)	Tootsie (1982)
Maggie Smith	2	6	The Prime of Miss Jean Brodie (1969)	California Suite (1978)
Gary Cooper	2	5	Sergeant York (1941); High Noon (1952)	
Olivia de Havilland	2	5	To Each His Own (1946); The Heiress (1949)	
Gene Hackman	2	5	The French Connection (1971)	Unforgiven (1992)
Tom Hanks	2	5	Philadelphia (1993); Forrest Gump (1994)	
Fredric March	2	5	Dr. Jekyll and Mr. Hyde (1941); The Best Years of Our Lives (1946)	
Sean Penn	2	5	Mystic River (2003); Milk (2008)	
Elizabeth Taylor	2	5	Butterfield 8 (1960); Who's Afraid of Virginia Woolf? (1966)	
Denzel Washington	2	5	Training Day (2001)	Glory (1989)
Jodie Foster	2	4	The Accused (1988); The Silence of the Lambs (1991)	
Glenda Jackson	2	4	Women in Love (1970); A Touch of Class (1973)	
Anthony Quinn	2	4		Viva Zapata! (1952); Lust for Life (1956)

ACTOR/ ACTRESS	TOTAL AWARDS	TOTAL NOMINATIONS	BEST ACTOR/ ACTRESS	BEST SUPPORTING ROLE
Shelley Winters	2	4		The Diary of Anne Frank (1959); A Patch of Blue (1965)
Melvyn Douglas	2	3		Hud (1963); Being There (1979)
Jason Robards	2	3		All the President's Men (1976); Julia (1977)
Peter Ustinov	2	3		Spartacus (1960); Topkapi (1964)
Dianne Wiest	2	3		Hannah and Her Sisters (1986); Bullets Over Broadway (1994)
Sally Field	2	2	Norma Rae (1979); Places in the Heart (1984)	
Helen Hayes	2	2	The Sin of Madelon Claudet (1931)	Airport (1970)
Vivien Leigh	2	2	Gone with the Wind (1939); A Streetcar Named Desire (1951)	
Luise Rainer	2	2	The Great Ziegfeld (1936); The Good Earth (1937)	
Kevin Spacey	2	2	American Beauty (1999)	The Usual Suspects (1995)
Hilary Swank	2	2	Boys Don't Cry (1999); Million Dollar Baby (2004)	
Christoph Waltz	2	2		Inglourious Basterds (2009); Django Unchained (2012)

James Bond films

FILM TITLE	JAMES BOND ACTOR	FILM DIRECTOR	BOX OFFICE (WORLDWIDE GROSS)
Dr. No (1962)	Sean Connery	Terence Young	$59.6 million
From Russia with Love (1963)	Sean Connery	Terence Young	$54.1 million
Goldfinger (1964)	Sean Connery	Guy Hamilton	$124.9 million
Thunderball (1965)	Sean Connery	Terence Young	$77.6 million
You Only Live Twice (1967)	Sean Connery	Lewis Gilbert	$68.5 million
On Her Majesty's Secret Service (1969)	George Lazenby	Peter R. Hunt	$59.2 million
Diamonds Are Forever (1971)	Sean Connery	Guy Hamilton	$116 million
Live and Let Die (1973)	Roger Moore	Guy Hamilton	$126.3 million
The Man with the Golden Gun (1974)	Roger Moore	Guy Hamilton	$97.6 million
The Spy Who Loved Me (1977)	Roger Moore	Lewis Gilbert	$185.4 million
Moonraker (1979)	Roger Moore	Lewis Gilbert	$140 million
For Your Eyes Only (1981)	Roger Moore	John Glen	$194.9 million
Octopussy (1983)	Roger Moore	John Glen	$119.6 million
Never Say Never Again (1983)	Sean Connery	Irvin Kershner	$138 million
A View to a Kill (1985)	Roger Moore	John Glen	$152.6 million
The Living Daylights (1987)	Timothy Dalton	John Glen	$191.2 million
Licence to Kill (1989)	Timothy Dalton	John Glen	$152.2 million

FILM TITLE	JAMES BOND ACTOR	FILM DIRECTOR	BOX OFFICE (WORLDWIDE GROSS)
Golden Eye (1995)	Pierce Brosnan	Martin Campbell	$352.1 million
Tomorrow Never Dies (1997)	Pierce Brosnan	Roger Spottiswoode	$221.3 million
The World Is Not Enough (1999)	Pierce Brosnan	Michael Apted	$361.8 million
Die Another Day (2002)	Pierce Brosnan	Lee Tamahori	$431.9 million
Casino Royale (2006)	Daniel Craig	Martin Campbell	$599 million
Quantum of Solace (2008)	Daniel Craig	Marc Forster	$586.1 million
Skyfall (2012)	Daniel Craig	Sam Mendes	$1.109 billion
Spectre (2015)	Daniel Craig	Sam Mendes	$880.7 million
No Time to Die (TBC)	Daniel Craig	Cary Joji Fukunaga	TBC

Grammy winners (record and song of the year)

YEAR	RECORD OF THE YEAR	SONG OF THE YEAR
1958	Nel Blu Dipinto Di Blu (Volare) by Domenico Modugno	Nel Blu Dipinto Di Blu (Volare)
1959	Mack The Knife by Bobby Darin	The Battle of New Orleans
1960	The Theme from A Summer Place by Percy Faith	Theme from Exodus
1961	Moon River by Henry Mancini	Moon River
1962	I Left My Heart In San Francisco by Tony Bennett	What Kind of Fool Am I
1963	Days of Wine And Roses bt Henry Mancini	Days of Wine And Roses
1964	The Girl from Ipanema by Stan Getz & Astrud Gilberto	Hello, Dolly!
1965	A Taste of Honey by Herb Alpert And The Tijuana Brass	The Shadow of Your Smile
1966	Strangers in The Night by Frank Sinatra	Michelle
1967	Up, Up and Away by 5th Dimension	Up, Up and Away
1968	Mrs. Robinson by Simon And Garfunkel	Little Green Apples
1969	Aquarius/Let the Sunshine In (The Flesh Failures) by 5th Dimension	Games People Play
1970	Bridge Over Troubled Water by Simon And Garfunkel	Bridge Over Troubled Water
1971	It's Too Late by Carole King	You've Got A Friend
1972	The First Time Ever I Saw Your Face by Roberta Flack	The First Time Ever I Saw Your Face

YEAR	RECORD OF THE YEAR	SONG OF THE YEAR
1973	Killing Me Softly with His Song by Roberta Flack	Killing Me Softly with His Song
1974	I Honestly Love You by Olivia Newton-John	The Way We Were
1975	Love Will Keep Us Together by Captain & Tennille	Send in The Clowns
1976	This Masquerade by George Benson	I Write the Songs
1977	Hotel California by Eagles	Love Theme from A Star Is Born
1978	Just the Way You Are by Billy Joel	Just the Way You Are
1979	What A Fool Believes by The Doobie Brothers	What A Fool Believes
1980	Sailing by Christopher Cross	Sailing
1981	Bette Davis Eyes by Kim Carnes	Bette Davis Eyes
1982	Rosanna by Toto	Always on My Mind
1983	Beat It by Michael Jackson	Every Breath You Take
1984	What's Love Got to Do With It by Tina Turner	What's Love Got to Do with It
1985	We Are the World by USA For Africa (Various Artists)	We Are the World
1986	Higher Love by Steve Winwood	That's What Friends Are For
1987	Graceland by Paul Simon	Somewhere Out There
1988	Don't Worry Be Happy by Bobby McFerrin	Don't Worry Be Happy
1989	Wind Beneath My Wings by Bette Midler	Wind Beneath My Wings
1990	Another Day in Paradise by Phil Collins	From A Distance
1991	Unforgettable by Natalie Cole (With Nat "King" Cole)	Unforgettable

YEAR	RECORD OF THE YEAR	SONG OF THE YEAR
1992	Tears in Heaven by Eric Clapton	Tears in Heaven
1993	I Will Always Love You by Whitney Houston	A Whole New World (Aladdin's Theme)
1994	All I Wanna Do by Sheryl Crow	Streets of Philadelphia
1995	Kiss from A Rose by Seal	Kiss from A Rose
1996	Change the World by Eric Clapton	Change the World
1997	Sunny Came Home by Shawn Colvin	Sunny Came Home
1998	My Heart Will Go on by Celine Dion	My Heart Will Go On
1999	Smooth by Santana Featuring Rob Thomas	Smooth
2000	Beautiful Day by U2	Beautiful Day
2001	Walk on by U2	Fallin'
2002	Don't Know Why by Norah Jones	Don't Know Why
2003	Clocks by Coldplay	Dance with My Father
2004	Here We Go Again by Ray Charles & Norah Jones	Daughters
2005	Boulevard of Broken Dreams by Green Day	Sometimes You Can't Make It on Your Own
2006	Not Ready to Make Nice by Dixie Chicks	Not Ready to Make Nice
2007	Rehab by Amy Winehouse	Rehab
2008	Please Read the Letter by Robert Plant & Alison Krauss	Viva La Vida
2009	Use Somebody by Kings of Leon	Single Ladies (Put A Ring on It)
2010	Need You Now by Lady Antebellum	Need You Now
2011	Rolling in The Deep by Adele	Rolling in The Deep
2012	Somebody That I Used to Know by Gotye Featuring Kimbra	We Are Young
2013	Get Lucky by Daft Punk Featuring Pharrell Williams & Nile Rodgers	Royals
2014	Stay with Me (Darkchild Version) by Sam Smith	Stay with Me (Darkchild Version)
2015	Uptown Funk by Mark Ronson Featuring Bruno Mars	Thinking Out Loud
2016	Hello by Adele	Hello
2017	24K Magic by Bruno Mars	That's What I Like
2018	This Is America by Childish Gambino	This Is America
2019	Bad Guy by Billie Eilish	Bad Guy

Shakespeare plays

COMEDIES
All's Well That Ends Well (1602)
As You Like It (1599)
Comedy of Errors (1589)
Love's Labour's Lost (1594)
Measure for Measure (1604)
Merchant of Venice (1596)
Merry Wives of Windsor (1600)
Midsummer Night's Dream (1595)
Much Ado about Nothing (1598)
Taming of the Shrew (1593)
Tempest (1611)
Twelfth Night (1599)
Two Gentlemen of Verona (1594)
Winter's Tale (1610)

TRAGEDIES
Antony and Cleopatra (1606)
Coriolanus (1607)
Cymbeline (1609)
Hamlet (1600)
Julius Caesar (1599)
King Lear (1605)
Macbeth (1605)
Othello (1604)
Romeo and Juliet (1594)
Timon of Athens (1607)
Titus Andronicus (1593)
Twelfth Night (1599)
Troilus and Cressida (1601)

HISTORIES
Henry IV, Part I (1597)
Henry IV, Part II (1597)
Henry V (1598)
Henry VI, Part I (1591)
Henry VI, Part II (1590)
Henry VI, Part III (1590)
Henry VIII (1612)
King John (1596)
Pericles (1608)
Richard II (1595)
Richard III (1592)

12 famous novels and their authors

BOOK	AUTHOR
Anna Karenina	Leo Tolstoy
To Kill a Mockingbird	Harper Lee
The Great Gatsby	F. Scott Fitzgerald
One Hundred Years of Solitude	Gabriel García Márquez
A Passage to India	E. M. Forster
Invisible Man	Ralph Ellison
Don Quixote	Miguel de Cervantes
Beloved	Toni Morrison
Mrs. Dalloway	Virginia Woolf
Things Fall Apart	Chinua Achebe
Jane Eyre	Charlotte Brontë
The Color Purple	Alice Walker

Leo Tolstoy
Harper Lee
F. Scott Fitzgerald
Gabriel Garcia Marquez
E. M. Forster
Ralph Ellison
Miguel de Cervantes
Toni Morrison
Virginia Woolf
Chinua Achebe
Charlotte Brontë
Alice Walker

Man Booker prize winners

YEAR	AUTHOR	TITLE
1969	P.H Newby	Something to Answer For
1970	Bernice Rubens	The Elected Member
1971	V.S Naipaul	In a Free State
1972	John Berger	G.
1973	J.G Farrell	The Siege of Krishnapur
1974	Nadine Gordimer	The Conservationist
1974	Stanley Middleton	Holiday
1975	Ruth Prawer Jhabvala	Heat and Dust
1976	David Storey	Saville
1977	Paul Scott	Staying On
1978	Iris Murdoch	The Sea, The Sea
1979	Penelope Fitzgerald	Offshore
1980	William Golding	Rites of Passage
1981	Salman Rushdie	Midnight's Children
1982	Thomas Keneally	Schindler's Ark
1983	J.M Coetzee	Life & Times of Michael K
1984	Anita Brookner	Hotel du Lac
1985	Keri Hulme	The Bone People

YEAR	AUTHOR	TITLE
1986	Kingsley Amis	The Old Devils
1987	Penelope Lively	Moon Tiger
1988	Peter Carey	Oscar and Lucinda
1989	Kazuo Ishiguro	The Remains of the Day
1990	A.S Byatt	Possession
1991	Ben Okri	The Famished Road
1992	Michael Ondaatje	The English Patient
1992	Barry Unsworth	Sacred Hunger
1993	Roddy Doyle	Paddy Clarke Ha Ha Ha
1994	James Kelman	How Late It Was, How Late
1995	Pat Barker	The Ghost Road
1996	Graham Swift	Last Orders
1997	Arundhati Roy	The God of Small Things
1998	Ian McEwan	Amsterdam
1999	J.M Coetzee	Disgrace
2000	Margaret Atwood	The Blind Assassin
2001	Peter Carey	True History of the Kelly Gang
2002	Yann Martel	Life of Pi
2003	DBC Pierre	Vernon God Little
2004	Alan Hollinghurst	The Line of Beauty
2005	John Banville	The Sea
2006	Kiran Desai	The Inheritance of Loss
2007	Anne Enright	The Gathering
2008	Aravind Adiga	The White Tiger
2009	Hilary Mantel	Wolf Hall
2010	Howard Jacobson	The Finkler Question
2011	Julian Barnes	The Sense of an Ending
2012	Hilary Mantel	Bring Up the Bodies
2013	Eleanor Catton	The Luminaries
2014	Richard Flanagan	The Narrow Road to the Deep North
2015	Marlon James	A Brief History of Seven Killings
2016	Paul Beatty	The Sellout
2017	George Saunders	Lincoln in the Bardo
2018	Anna Burns	Milkman
2019	Margaret Atwood / Bernardine Evaristo	The Testaments (Atwood) Girl, Woman, Other (Evaristo)

Pulitzer Prize winners: fiction, drama & poetry*

YEAR	FICTION	DRAMA	POETRY
1960	Advise and Consent, by Allen Drury	Fiorello!, by Jerome Weidman, George Abbott, Jerry Bock and Sheldon Harnick	Heart's Needle, by W. D. Snodgrass
1961	To Kill A Mockingbird, by Harper Lee	All the Way Home, by Tad Mosel	Times Three: Selected Verse from Three Decades, by Phyllis McGinley
1962	The Edge of Sadness, by Edwin O'Connor	How to Succeed in Business Without Really Trying, by Frank Loesser and Abe Burrows	Poems, by Alan Dugan
1963	The Reivers, by William Faulkner	No award given	Pictures from Brueghel, by William Carlos Williams
1964	No award given	No award given	At the End of The Open Road, by Louis Simpson
1965	The Keepers of The House, by Shirley Ann Grau	The Subject Was Roses, by Frank D. Gilroy	77 Dream Songs, by John Berryman
1966	Collected Stories, by Katherine Anne Porter	No award given	Selected Poems, by Richard Eberhart

*From 1960 onwards

YEAR	FICTION	DRAMA	POETRY
1967	The Fixer, by Bernard Malamud	A Delicate Balance, by Edward Albee	Live or Die, by Anne Sexton
1968	The Confessions of Nat Turner, by William Styron	No award given	The Hard Hours, by Anthony Hecht
1969	House Made of Dawn, by N. Scott Momaday	The Great White Hope, by Howard Sackler	Of Being Numerous, by George Oppen
1970	Collected Stories, by Jean Stafford	No Place to Be Somebody, by Charles Gordone	Untitled Subjects, by Richard Howard
1971	No award given	The Effect of Gamma Rays on Man-In-The-Moon Marigolds, by Paul Zindel	The Carrier of Ladders, by William S. Merwin
1972	Angle of Repose, by Wallace Stegner	No award given	Collected Poems, by James Wright
1973	The Optimist's Daughter, by Eudora Welty	That Championship Season, by Jason Miller	Up Country, by Maxine Kumin
1974	No award given	No award given	The Dolphin, by Robert Lowell
1975	The Killer Angels, by Michael Shaara	Seascape, by Edward Albee	Turtle Island, by Gary Snyder

Jospeh Pulitzer

YEAR	FICTION	DRAMA	POETRY
1976	Humboldt's Gift, by Saul Bellow	A Chorus Line, by Michael Bennett, James Kirkwood, Jr., Marvin Hamlisch, Nicholas Dante and Edward Kleban	Self-Portrait in a Convex Mirror, by John Ashbery
1977	No award given	The Shadow Box, by Michael Cristofer	Divine Comedies, by James Merrill
1978	Elbow Room, by James Alan McPherson	The Gin Game, by Donald L. Coburn	Collected Poems, by Howard Nemero
1979	The Stories of John Cheever, by John Cheever	Buried Child, by Sam Shepard	Now and Then, by Robert Penn Warren
1980	The Executioner's Song, by Norman Mailer	Talley's Folly, by Lanford Wilson	Selected Poems, by Donald Justice
1981	A Confederacy of Dunces, by John Kennedy Toole	Crimes of the Heart, by Beth Henley	The Morning of the Poem, by James Schuyler
1982	Rabbit Is Rich, by John Updike	A Soldier's Play, by Charles Fuller	The Collected Poems, by Sylvia Plath
1983	The Color Purple, by Alice Walker	Night, Mother, by Marsha Norman	Selected Poems, by Galway Kinnell
1984	Ironweed, by William Kennedy	Glengarry Glen Ross, by David Mamet	American Primitive, by Mary Oliver
1985	Foreign Affairs, by Alison Lurie	Sunday in the Park with George, by Stephen Sondheim and James Lapine	Yin, by Carolyn Kizer
1986	Lonesome Dove, by Larry McMurtry	No award given	The Flying Change, by Henry Taylor
1987	A Summons to Memphis, by Peter Taylor	Fences, by August Wilson	Thomas and Beulah, by Rita Dove
1988	Beloved, by Toni Morrison	Driving Miss Daisy, by Alfred Uhry	Partial Accounts: New and Selected Poems, by William Meredith

The grave of publisher Joseph Pulitzer, Woodlawn Cemetary, New York, USA

YEAR	FICTION	DRAMA	POETRY
1989	Breathing Lessons, by Anne Tyler	The Heidi Chronicles, by Wendy Wasserstein	New and Collected Poems, by Richard Wilbur
1990	The Mambo Kings Play Songs of Love, by Oscar Hijuelos	The Piano Lesson, by August Wilson	The World Doesn't End, by Charles Simic
1991	Rabbit at Rest, by John Updike	Lost in Yonkers, by Neil Simon	Near Changes, by Mona Van Duyn
1992	A Thousand Acres, by Jane Smiley	The Kentucky Cycle, by Robert Schenkkan	Selected Poems, by James Tate
1993	A Good Scent from a Strange Mountain, by Robert Olen Butler	Angels in America: Millennium Approaches, by Tony Kushner	The Wild Iris, by Louise Glück
1994	The Shipping News, by E. Annie Proulx	Three Tall Women, by Edward Albee	Neon Vernacular: New and Selected Poems, by Yusef Komunyakaa
1995	The Stone Diaries, by Carol Shields	The Young Man from Atlanta, by Horton Foote	The Simple Truth, by Philip Levine

YEAR	FICTION	DRAMA	POETRY
1996	Independence Day, by Richard Ford	Rent, by Jonathan Larson	The Dream of the Unified Field, by Jorie Graham
1997	Martin Dressler: The Tale of an American Dreamer, by Steven Millhauser	No award given	Alive Together: New and Selected Poems, by Lisel Mueller
1998	American Pastoral, by Philip Roth	How I Learned to Drive, by Paula Vogel	Black Zodiac, by Charles Wright
1999	The Hours, by Michael Cunningham	Wit, by Margaret Edson	Blizzard of One, by Mark Strand
2000	Interpreter of Maladies, by Jhumpa Lahiri	Dinner with Friends, by Donald Margulies	Repair, by C.K. Williams
2001	The Amazing Adventures of Kavalier & Clay, by Michael Chabon	Proof, by David Auburn	Different Hours, by Stephen Dunn
2002	Empire Falls, by Richard Russo	Topdog/Underdog, by Suzan-Lori Parks	Practical Gods, by Carl Dennis
2003	Middlesex, by Jeffrey Eugenides	Anna in the Tropics, by Nilo Cruz	Moy Sand and Gravel, by Paul Muldoon
2004	The Known World, by Edward P. Jones	I Am My Own Wife, by Doug Wright	Walking to Martha's Vineyard, by Franz Wright
2005	Gilead, by Marilynne Robinson	Doubt, a parable, by John Patrick Shanley	Delights & Shadows, by Ted Kooser
2006	March, by Geraldine Brooks	No award given	Late Wife, by Claudia Emerson
2007	The Road, by Cormac McCarthy	Rabbit Hole, by David Lindsay-Abaire	Native Guard, by Natasha Trethewey
2008	The Brief Wondrous Life of Oscar Wao, by Junot Diaz	August: Osage County, by Tracy Letts	Failure, by Philip Schultz; Time and Materials, by Robert Hass

YEAR	FICTION	DRAMA	POETRY
2009	Olive Kitteridge, by Elizabeth Strout	Ruined, by Lynn Nottage	The Shadow of Sirius, by W.S. Merwin
2010	Tinkers, by Paul Harding	Next to Normal, by Tom Kitt and Brian Yorkey	Versed, by Rae Armantrout
2011	A Visit from the Goon Squad, by Jennifer Egan	Clybourne Park, by Bruce Norris	The Best of It: New and Selected Poems, by Kay Ryan
2012	No award given	Water by the Spoonful, by Quiara Alegría Hudes	Life on Mars, by Tracy K. Smith
2013	The Orphan Master's Son, by Adam Johnson	Disgraced, by Ayad Akhtar	Stag's Leap, by Sharon Olds
2014	The Goldfinch, by Donna Tartt	The Flick, by Annie Baker	3 Sections, by Vijay Seshadri
2015	All the Light We Cannot See, by Anthony Doerr	Between Riverside and Crazy, by Stephen Adly Guirgis	Digest, by Gregory Pardlo
2016	The Sympathizer, by Viet Thanh Nguyen	Hamilton, by Lin-Manuel Miranda	Ozone Journal, by Peter Balakian
2017	The Underground Railroad, by Colson Whitehead	Sweat, by Lynn Nottage	Olio, by Tyehimba Jess
2018	Less, by Andrew Sean Greer	Cost of Living, by Martyna Majok	Half-light: Collected Poems 1965-2016, by Frank Bidart
2019	The Overstory by Richard Powers	Fairview by Jackie Sibblies Drury	Be With by Forrest Gander
2020	The Nickel Boys by Colson Whitehead	A Strange Loop by Michael R. Jackson	The Tradition by Jericho Brown

Nobel Prize winners: sciences*

YEAR	PHYSICS	CHEMISTRY	MEDICINE
1960	Donald Arthur Glaser	Willard Frank Libby	Frank Macfarlane Burnet; Peter Medawar
1961	Robert Hofstadter; Rudolf Ludwig Mössbauer	Melvin Calvin	Georg von Békésy
1962	Lev Davidovich Landau	Max Ferdinand Perutz; John Cowdery Kendrew	Francis Crick; James D. Watson; Maurice Wilkins
1963	Eugene Paul Wigner; Maria Goeppert Mayer; J. Hans D. Jensen	Karl Ziegler; Giulio Natta	Sir John Eccles; Alan Lloyd Hodgkin; Andrew Huxley
1964	Charles Hard Townes; Nikolay Gennadiyevich Basov; Alexandr Mikhailovich Prokhorov	Dorothy Crowfoot Hodgkin	Konrad Bloch; Feodor Felix Lynen
1965	Sin-Itiro Tomonaga; Julian Schwinger; Richard P. Feynman	Robert Burns Woodward	Francois Jacob; André Lwoff; Jacques Monod
1966	Alfred Kastler	Robert S. Mulliken	Peyton Rous; Charles Brenton Huggins
1967	Hans Albrecht Bethe	Manfred Eigen; Ronald George Wreyford Norrish; George Porter	Ragnar Granit; Haldan Keffer Hartline; George Wald
1968	Luis Walter Alvarez	Lars Onsager	Robert W. Holley; Har Gobind Khorana; Marshall W. Nirenberg

*From 1960 onwards

YEAR	PHYSICS	CHEMISTRY	MEDICINE
1969	Murray Gell-Mann	Derek H. R. Barton; Odd Hassel	Max Delbrück; Alfred Hershey; Salvador E. Luria
1970	Hannes Olof Alfvén; Louis Eugene Felix Néel	Luis F. Leloir	Julius Axelrod; Ulf von Euler; Sir Bernard Katz
1971	Dennis Gabor	Gerhard Herzberg	Earl W. Sutherland, Jr.
1972	John Bardeen; Leon Neil Cooper; John Robert Schrieffer	Christian B Anfinsen; Stanford Moore; William Howard Stein	Gerald Edelman; Rodney Robert Porter
1973	Leo Esaki; Ivar Giaever; Brian David Josephson	Ernst Otto Fischer; Geoffrey Wilkinson	Karl von Frisch; Konrad Lorenz Nikolaas Tinbergen
1974	Sir Martin Ryle; Antony Hewish	Paul J. Flory	Albert Claude; Christian de Duve; George Emil Palade
1975	Aage Niels Bohr; Ben Roy Mottelson; Leo James Rainwater	John Warcup Cornforth; Vladimir Prelog	David Baltimore; Renato Dulbecco; Howard Martin Temin
1976	Burton Richter; Samuel Chao Chung Ting	William N. Lipscomb	Baruch Samuel Blumberg; Daniel Carleton Gajudusek

Marie Curie (1867-1934), Polish-French physicist who won two Nobel Prizes, in 1903 for Physics and 1911 for Chemistry.

YEAR	PHYSICS	CHEMISTRY	MEDICINE
1977	Philip Warren Anderson; Sir Nevill Francis Mott; John Hasbrouck Van Vleck	Ilya Prigogine	Roger Guillemin; Andrew V. Schally; Rosalyn Yalow
1978	Pyotr Kapitsa; Arno Allan Penzias; Robert Woodrow Wilson	Peter D. Mitchell	Werner Arber; Daniel Nathans; Hamilton O. Smith
1979	Sheldon Lee Glashow; Abdus Salam; Steven Weinberg	Herbert C. Brown; Georg Witting	Allan McLeod Cormack; Godrey Hounsfield
1980	James Watson Cronin; Val Logsdon Fitch	Paul Berg; Walter Gilbert; Frederick Sanger	Baruj Benacerraf; Jean Dausset; George Davis Snell
1981	Nicolaas Bloembergen; Arthur Leonard Schawlow; Kai M Siegbahn	Kenichi Fukui; Roald Hoffmann	Roger Wolcott Sperry; David H. Hubel; Torsten Wiesel
1982	Kenneth G. Wilson	Aaron Klug	Sune Bergström; Bengt I. Samuelsson; John Vane
1983	Subramanyan Chandrasekhar; William Alfred Fowler	Henry Taube	Barbara McClintock
1984	Carlo Rubbia; Simon van der Meer	Robert Bruce Merrifeld	Niels K. Jerne; Georges J. F. Köhler; César Milstein
1985	Klaus von Klitzing	Herbert A. Hauptman; Jerome Karle	Michael Stuart Brown; Joseph L. Goldstein
1986	Ernst Ruska; Gerd Binnig; Heinrich Rohrer	Dudley R. Herschbach; Yuan T. Lee; John C. Polanyi	Stanley Cohen; Rita Levi-Montalcini
1987	J. Georg Bednorz; Karl Alexander Müller	Donald J. Cram; Jean-Marie Lehn; Charles J. Pedersen	Susumu Tonegawa
1988	Leon M Lederman; Melvin Schwartz; Jack Steinberger	Johann Deisenhofer; Robert Huber; Hartmut Michel	Sir James W. Black; Gertrude B. Elion; George H. Hitchings
1989	Norman F. Ramsay; Hans G. Dehmelt; Wolfgang Paul	Sidney Altman; Thomas R. Cech	J. Michael Bishop; Harold E. Varmus

Nobel Peace Center, Oslo, Norway

YEAR	PHYSICS	CHEMISTRY	MEDICINE
1990	Jerome I. Friedman; Henry W. Kendall; Richard E. Taylor	Elias James Corey	Joseph Murray; E. Donnall Thomas
1991	Pierre-Gilles de Gennes	Richard R. Ernst	Erwin Neher; Bert Sakmann
1992	Georges Charpak	Rudolph A. Marcus	Edmond H. Fischer; Edwin G. Krebs
1993	Russell Alan Hulse; Joseph Hooton Taylor Jr.	Kary B. Mullis; Michael Smith	Richard J. Roberts; Phillip Allen Sharp
1994	Bertram Brockhouse; Clifford G. Shull	George Andrew Olah	Alfred G Gilman; Martin Rodbell
1995	Martin Lewis Perl; Frederick Reines	Paul J. Crutzen; Mario J. Molina; Frank Sherwood Rowland	Edward B. Lewis; Christiana Nüsslein-Volhard; Eric Wieschaus
1996	David M Lee; Douglas D Osheroff; Robert Coleman Richardson	Robert F Curl Jr; Sir Harold W Kroto; Richard E Smalley	Peter C. Doherty; Rolf M. Zinkernagel

YEAR	PHYSICS	CHEMISTRY	MEDICINE
1997	Steven Chu; Claude Cohen-Tannoudji; William Daniel Phillips	Paul D. Boyer; John E. Walker; Jens Christian Skou	Stanley B. Prusiner
1998	Robert B Laughlin; Horst Ludwig Störmer; Daniel C. Tsui	Walter Kohn; John Pople	Robert F. Furchgott; Louis Ignarro; Ferid Murad
1999	Gerardus 't Hooft; Martinus J. G. Veltman	Ahmed H. Zewail	Günter Blobel
2000	Zhores I. Alferov; Herbert Kroemer; Jack Kilby	Alan J. Heeger; Alan MacDiarmid; Hideki Shirakawa	Arvid Carlsson; Paul Greengard; Eric Kandel
2001	Eric Allin Cornell; Wolfgang Ketterle; Carl E. Wieman	William Standish Knowles; Ryoji Noyori; Karl Barry Sharpless	Leland H. Hartwell; Tim Hunt; Sir Paul Nurse
2002	Raymond Davis Jr; Masatoshi Koshiba; Riccardo Giacconi;	John Fenn; Koichi Tanaka; Kurt Wüthrich	Sydney Brenner; H. Robert Horvitz; John Sulston
2003	Alexei Alexeyevich Abrikosov; Vitaly Ginzburg; Anthony James Leggett	Peter Agre; Roderick MacKinnon	Paul Lauterbur; Peter Mansfield
2004	David Gross; Hugh David Politzer; Frank Wilczek	Aaron Ciechanover; Avram Hershko; Irwin Rose	Richard Axel; Linda B. Buck
2005	Roy J. Glauber; John L. Hall; Theodor W. Hänsch	Yves Chauvin; Robert H. Grubbs; Richard R. Schrock	Barry Marshall; Robin Warren
2006	John C. Mather; George F. Smoot	Roger D. Kornberg	Andrew Fire; Craig Mello
2007	Albert Fert; Peter Grünberg	Gerhard Ertl	Mario Capecchi; Sir Martin Evans; Oliver Smithies
2008	Yoichiro Nambu; Makoto Kobayashi; Toshihide Maskawa	Osamu Shimomura; Martin Chalfie; Roger Y. Tsien	Harald zur Hausen; Francoise Barré-Sinoussi; Luc Montagnier
2009	Charles Kuen Kao; Willard S. Boyle; George E. Smith	Venkatraman Ramakrishnan; Thomas A. Steiz; Ada Yonath	Elizabeth Blackburn; Carol W. Greider; Jack W. Szostak

YEAR	PHYSICS	CHEMISTRY	MEDICINE
2010	Andre Geim; Konstantin Novoselov	Richard F. Heck; Ei-ichi Negishi; Akira Suzuki	Robert G. Edwards
2011	Saul Perlmutter; Adam G. Riess; Brian P. Schmidt	Dan Shechtman	Bruce Beutler; Jules A. Hoffmann; Ralph M. Steinman
2012	Serge Haroche; David J. Wineland	Brian K. Kobilka; Robert J. Lefkowitz	John B. Gurdon; Shinya Yamanaka
2013	Francois Englert; Peter W. Higgs	Martin Karplus; Michael Levitt; Arieh Warshel	James E. Rothman; Randy W. Schekman; Thomas Südhof
2014	Isamu Akasaki; Hiroshi Amano; Shuji Nakamura	Eric Betzig; Stefan Hell; William Moerner	John O'Keefe; May-Britt Moser; Edvard Moser
2015	Takaaki Kajita; Arthur B. McDonald	Tomas Lindahl, Paul Modrich; Aziz Sancar	William C. Campbell; Satoshi Ōmura; Tu Youyou
2016	David J. Thouless; F. Duncan M. Haldane; J. Michael Kosterlitz	Jean-Pierre Sauvage; Sir J. Fraser Stoddart; Bernard L. Feringa	Yoshinori Ohsumi
2017	Rainer Weiss; Barry C. Barish; Kip S. Thorne	Jacques Dubochet, Joachim Frank; Richard Henderson	Jeffrey C. Hall, Michael Rosbash; Michael W. Young
2018	Arthur Ashkin; Gérard Mourou; Donna Strickland	Frances H. Arnold; George P. Smith; Sir Gregory P. Winter	James P. Allison; Tasuku Honjo
2019	James Peebles; Michel Mayor;Didier Queloz	John B. Goodenough, M. Stanley Whittingham; Akira Yoshino	William G. Kaelin Jr, Sir Peter J. Ratcliffe; Gregg L. Semenza
2020	Roger Penrose; Reinhard Genzel; Andrea Ghez	Emmanuelle Charpentier; Jennifer A. Doudna	Harvey J. Alter, Michael Houghton; Charles M. Rice

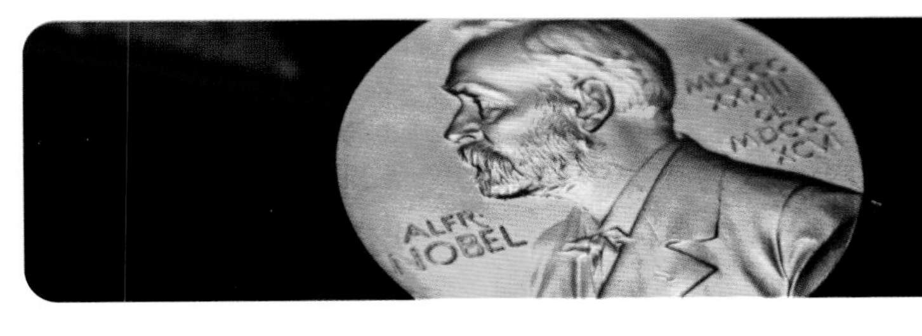

Nobel Prize winners: other*

YEAR	LITERATURE	PEACE	ECONOMICS
1960	Saint-John Perse	Albert John Lutuli	None
1961	Ivo Andrić	Dag Hjalmar Agne Carl Hammarskjöld	None
1962	John Steinbeck	Linus Pauling	None
1963	Giorgos Seferis	International Committee of the Red Cross; League of Red Cross Societies	None
1964	Jean-Paul Sartre	Martin Luther King Jr.	None
1965	Mikhail Sholokhov	United Nations Children's Fund (UNICEF)	None
1966	Shmuel Yosef Agnon; Nelly Sachs	None	None
1967	Miguel Ángel Asturias	None	None
1968	Yasunari Kawabata	René Cassin	None
1969	Samuel Beckett	International Labour Organization (I.L.O)	Ragnal Frisch; Jan Tinbergen
1970	Aleksandr Isayevich Solzhenitsyn	Norman E. Borlaug	Paul Samuelson
1971	Pablo Neruda	Willy Brandt	Simon Kuznets
1972	Heinrich Böll	None	John Hicks; Kenneth Arrow
1973	Patrick White	Henry Kissinger; Le Duc Tho	Wassily Leontief
1974	Eyvind Johnson; Harry Martinson	Seán MacBride; Eisaku Sato	Gunnar Myrdal; Friedrich Hayek
1975	Eugenio Montale	Andrei Sakharov	Leonid Kantorovich; Tjalling Koopmans

*From 1960 onwards

YEAR	LITERATURE	PEACE	ECONIMICS
1976	Saul Bellow	Betty Williams; Mairead Maguire	Milton Friedman
1977	Vincente Aleixandre	Amnesty International	Bertil Ohlin; James E. Meade
1978	Isaac Bashevis Singer	Mohamed Anwar al-Sadat; Menachem Begin	Herbert A. Simon
1979	Odysseas Elytis	Mother Teresa	Theodore Schultz; Arthur Lewis
1980	Czeslaw Milosz	Adolfo Pérez Esquivel	Lawrence Klein
1981	Elias Canetti	United Nations High Commissioner Refugees (UNHCR)	James Tobin
1982	Gabriel García Márquez	Alva Mydral; Alfonso Garcia Robles	George Stigler
1983	William Golding	Lech Walesa	Gérard Debreu
1984	Jaroslav Seifert	Desmond Mpilo Tutu	Richard Stone
1985	Claude Simon	International Physicians for the Prevention of Nuclear War	Franco Modigliani
1986	Wole Soyinka	Elie Wiesel	James M. Buchanan Jr.
1987	Joseph Brodsky	Oscar Arias Sanchez	Robert M. Solow
1988	Naguib Mahfouz	United Nations Peacekeeping Forces	Maurice Allais
1989	Camilo José Cela	The 14th Dalai Lama (Tenzin Gyatso)	Trygve Haavelmo

Youngest Nobel Laureate, Malala Yousafzai

YEAR	LITERATURE	PEACE	ECONOMICS
1990	Octavio Paz	Mikhail Gorbachev	Harry M. Markowitz; Merton H. Miller; William F. Sharpe
1991	Nadine Gordimer	Aung San Suu Kyi	Ronald Coarse
1992	Derek Walcott	Rigoberta Menchu Tum	Gary S. Becker
1993	Toni Morrison	Nelson Mandela; Frederik Willem de Klerk	Robert C. Fogel; Douglass C. North
1994	Kenzaburö Oe	Yasser Araft; Shimon Peres; Yitzhak Rabin	John Harsanyi; John Forbes Nash Jr; Reinhard Selten
1995	Seamus Heaney	Joseph Rotblat; Pugwash Conferences on Science and World Affairs	Robert Lucas Jr.
1996	Wislawa Szymborska	Carlos Filipe Ximenes Belo; José Ramos-Horta	James Mirrlees; William Vickrey
1997	Dario Fo	International Campaign to Ban Landmines (ICBL); Jody Williams	Robert C. Merton; Myron Scholes
1998	José Saramago	John Hume; David Trimble	Amartya Sen
1999	Günter Grass	Médecins Sans Frontières	Robert Mundell
2000	Gao Xingjian	Kim Dae-jung	James Heckman; Daniel McFadden
2001	Sir Vidiadhar Surajprasad Naipaul	United Nations (U.N); Kofi Annan	George Akerlof; Michael Spence; Joseph E. Stiglitz
2002	Imre Kertész	Jimmy Carter	Daniel Kahneman; Vernon L. Smith
2003	John M. Coetzee	Shirin Ebadi	Robert F. Engle III; Clive Granger
2004	Elfriede Jelinek	Wangari Muta Maathai	Finn E. Kydland; Edward C. Prescott
2005	Harold Pinter	International Atomic Energy Agency (IAEA); Mohamed ElBaradei	Robert Aumann; Thomas Schelling

YEAR	LITERATURE	PEACE	ECONOMICS
2006	Orhan Pamuk	Muhammad Yunus; Grameen Bank	Edmund Phelps
2007	Doris Lessing	Intergovernmental Panel on Climate Change (IPCC); Albert Arnold (Al) Gore Jr.	Leonid Hurwicz; Eric Maskin; Roger Myserson
2008	Jean-Marie Gustave Le Clézio	Martti Ahtisaari	Paul Krugman
2009	Herta Müller	Barack Obama	Elinor Ostrom; Oliver E. Williamson
2010	Mario Vargos Llosa	Liu Xiaobo	Peter A. Diamond; Dale T. Mortensen; Christopher A. Pissarides
2011	Tomas Tranströmer	Ellen Johnson Sirleaf; Leymah Gbowee; Tawakkol Karman	Thomas J. Sargent; Christopher A. Sims
2012	Mo Yan	European Union (EU)	Alvin E. Roth; Lloyd S. Shapley
2013	Alice Munro	Organisation for the Prohibition of Chemical Weapons (OPCW)	Eugene F. Fama, Lars Peter Hansen; Robert Shiller
2014	Patrick Modiano	Kailash Satyarthi; Malala Yousafzai	Jean Tirole
2015	Svetlana Alexievich	National Dialogue Quartet	Angus Deaton
2016	Bob Dylan	Juan Manuel Santos	Oliver Hart; Bengt Holmström
2017	Kazuo Ishiguro	International Campaign to Abolish Nuclear Weapons (ICAN)	Richard H. Thaler
2018	None	Denis Mukwege; Nadia Murad	William D. Nordhaus; Paul M. Romer
2019	Peter Handke	Abiy Ahmed Ali	Abhijit Banerjee, Esther Duflo; Michael Kremer
2020	Louise Glück	World Food Programme (WFP)	Paul R. Milgrom; Robert B. Wilson

Sports

Major sporting events

FIFA World Cup
Occurs every four years
Last held Russia, 2018

Grand National (UK)
Occurs annually

NBA Finals (US)
Occurs annually

Olympic Games
Occurs every four years
Last held Rio, Brazil, 2016

Superbowl (US)
Occurs annnually

The Masters (US)
Occurs annually

Tour de France (FR)
Occurs annually

Wimbledon (UK)
Occurs annually

World Series (US)
Occurs annually

Major tennis tournaments

TOURNAMENT	DATE	SURFACE	PRIZE	FIRST PLAYED
Australian Open (Melbourne)	Jan	Australian Open GreenSet	$55 million AUD (2018)	1905
French Open (Paris)	May - Jun	Red Clay	€39 million (2018)	1891
Wimbledon (London)	Jun - Jul	100% Perennial Ryegrass	£34 million (2018)	1877
US Open (New York)	Aug - Sept	Laykold Cushion Plus System	$53 million USD (2018)	1881

Australian Open

French Open

Wimbledon

US Open

Major rugby union tournaments

NAME	FREQUENCY	FIRST PLAYED
Asian 5 Nations	Annually	2008
European Nations Cup	Annually	2000
FIRA Women's European Championship	Annually	1988
Nations Cup	Annually	2006
Pacific Nations Cup	Annually	2006
Rugby World Cup	Every four years	1987
Six Nations Championship (formerly Five Nations)	Annually	2000 (1910)
The Rugby Championship	Annually	1996
Women's Rugby World Cup	Every four years	1991
Women's Six Nations Championship	Annually	1996

All Blacks, New Zealand's rugby union team

Football World Cup winners

YEAR	WINNER	SCORE
1930	Uruguay	Uruguay 4-2 Argentina
1934	Italy	Italy 2-1 Czechoslovakia
1938	Italy	Italy 4-2 Hungary
1950	Uruguay	Uruguay 2-1 Brazil
1954	Germany	Germany 3-2 Hungary
1958	Brazil	Brazil 5-2 Sweden
1962	Brazil	Brazil 3-1 Czechoslovakia
1966	England	England 4-2 Germany
1970	Brazil	Brazil 4-1 Italy
1974	Germany	Germany 2-1 Netherlands
1978	Argentina	Argentina 3-1 Netherlands
1982	Italy	Italy 3-1 Germany
1986	Argentina	Argentina 3-2 Germany
1990	Germany	Germany 1-0 Argentina
1994	Brazil	Brazil defeated Italy 3-2 in penalties
1998	France	France 3-0 Brazil
2002	Brazil	Brazil 2-0 Germany
2006	Italy	Italy defeated France 5-3 in penalties
2010	Spain	Spain 1-0 Netherlands
2014	Germany	Germany 1-0 Argentina
2018	France	France 4-2 Croatia

Host Olympic cities

WINTER GAMES	
YEAR	HOST CITY
1924	Chamonix, France
1928	Saint Moritz, Switzerland
1932	Lake Placid, US
1936	Garmisch-Partenkirchen, Germany
1948	Saint Moritz, Switzerland
1952	Oslo, Norway
1956	Cortina D'Ampezzo, Italy
1960	Squaw Valley, US
1964	Innsbruck, Austria
1968	Grenoble, France
1972	Sapporo, Japan
1976	Innsbruck, Austria
1980	Lake Placid, US
1984	Sarajevo, Bosnia & Herzegovina
1988	Calgary, Canada
1992	Albertville, France
1994	Lillehammer, Norway
1998	Nagano, Japan
2002	Salt Lake City, US
2006	Turin, Italy
2010	Vancouver, Canada
2014	Sochi, Russia
2018	Pyeongchang, South Korea
2022	Beijing, China
2026	Milano Cortina, Italy

Ice town, Sochi, Russia, 2014

Bobsled exhibit, Salt Lake City, US, 2002

Russia's Alina Zagitova performs at the 2018 Winter Olympics

Panathenaic Stadium, Athens, Greece, 1896

Stadium of the Olympiapark in Munich, Germany

North Sydney Olympic Swimming Pool

Tokyo, Japan

SUMMER GAMES

YEAR	HOST CITY
1896	Athens, Greece
1900	Paris, France
1904	St Louis, US
1908	London, UK
1912	Stockholm, Sweden
1920	Antwerp, Belgium
1924	Paris, France
1928	Amsterdam, Netherlands
1932	Los Angeles, US
1936	Berlin, Germany
1948	London, UK
1952	Helsinki, Finland
1956	Melbourne, Australia
1960	Rome, Italy
1964	Tokyo, Japan
1968	Mexico City, Mexico
1972	Munich, Germany
1976	Montreal, Canada
1980	Moscow, Russia
1984	Los Angeles, US
1988	Seoul, South Korea
1992	Barcelona, Spain
1996	Atlanta, US
2000	Sydney, Australia
2004	Athens, Greece
2008	Beijing, China
2012	London, UK
2016	Rio de Janeiro, Brazil
2021*	Tokyo, Japan
2024	Paris, France
2028	Los Angeles, US

*Due to the Covid-19 outbreak, the Olympic Games Tokyo 2020 were postponed and will be held July 2021.

3 highest Olympic medal winners

Michael Phelps

SPORT Swimming

YEARS 2000, 2004, 2008, 2012, 2016

Larisa Latynina

SPORT Gymnastics Artistic

YEARS 1956, 1960, 1964

Nikolai Andrianov

SPORT Gymnastics

YEARS 1972, 1976, 1980

US sports leagues and teams

American Football

AFC: American Football Conference

TEAMS
Baltimore Ravens
Buffalo Bills (New York)
Cincinnati Bengals
Cleveland Browns
Denver Broncos West
Houston Texans
Indianapolis Colts
Jacksonville Jaguars
Kansas City Chiefs
Los Angeles Chargers
Miami Dolphins
New England Patriots
New York Jets
Oakland Raiders
Pittsburgh Steelers
Tennessee Titans

American Football

NFC: National Football Conference

TEAMS
Arizona Cardinals
Atlanta Falcons
Carolina Panthers
Chicago Bears
Dallas Cowboys
Detroit Lions
Green Bay Packers
Los Angeles Rams
Minnesota Vikings
New Orleans Saints
New York Giants
Philadelphia Eagles
San Francisco 49ers
Seattle Seahawks
Tampa Bay Buccaneers
Washington Redskins

American Football

WFA: Western Conference (2020)

TEAMS
Arlington Impact
Austin Outlaws
Cali War (Torrance)
Capital Pioneers (Salem)
Dallas Elite
Gulf Coast Monarchy (Biloxi)
Houston Energy
Houston Power
Huntsville Tigers
Iowa Phoenix (Des Moines)
Kansas City Saints
Kern County Crusaders (Bakersfield)
Louisiana Bayou Storm Surge (Baton Rouge)
Memphis Sabercats
Midwest Mountain Lions (Kenosha/Racine)
Mile High Blaze (Denver)
Minnesota Vixen
Mississippi Royalty (Hattiesburg)
New Orleans Hurricanes
Nevada Storm (Reno)
Oklahoma City Force
Phoenix Phantomz
Portland Shockwave
Rio Grande Heat (Santa Fe)
Rocky Mountain Thunderkatz (Colorado Springs)
Sacramento Sirens
St Louis Slam
Seattle Spartans
Sin City Trojans (Las Vegas)
Southern Oregon Lady Gades
Sun City Stealth (El Paso)
Tulsa Threat
Waco Madbears

American Football

WFA: Eastern Conference (2020)

TEAMS
Baltimore Nighthawks
Boston Renegades
Capital City Savages (Lansing)
Carolina Phoenix (High Point)
Cincinnati Sizzle
Cleveland Fusion
Columbus Comets
Columbus Vanguards
(Western) Connecticut Hawks (Fairfield)
D.C. Divas (Washington D.C.)
Daytona Waverunners
Derby City Dynamite (Elizabethtown)
Detroit Dark Angels
Grand Rapids Tidal Waves
Jacksonville Dixie Blues
Knoxville Lightning
Maine Mayhem (Portland)
Miami Fury
Music City Mizfits (Nashville)
New York Knockout
New York Wolves
Ontario MIFA All-Stars
Orlando Anarchy
Pittsburgh Passion
Richmond Black Widows
Toledo Reign

Baseball

Major League Baseball: American League

TEAMS
Baltimore Orioles
Boston Red Sox
Chicago White Sox
Cleveland Indians
Detroit Tigers
Houston Astros
Kansas City Royals
Los Angeles Angels of Anaheim
Minnesota Twins
New York Yankees
Oakland Athletics
Seattle Mariners
Tampa Bay Rays
Texas Rangers
Toronto Blue Jays

Baseball

Major League Baseball: National League

TEAMS
Arizona Diamondbacks
Atlanta Braves
Chicago Cubs
Cincinnati Reds
Colorado Rockies
Los Angeles Dodgers
Miami Marlins
Milwaukee Brewers
New York Mets
Philadelphia Phillies
Pittsburgh Pirates
St. Louis Cardinals
San Diego Padres
San Francisco Giants
Washington Nationals

Basketball

NBA: Eastern Conference

TEAMS
Atlanta Hawks
Boston Celtics
Brooklyn Nets
Charlotte Hornets
Chicago Bulls
Cleveland Cavaliers
Detroit Pistons
Indiana Pacers
Milwaukee Bucks
Miami Heat
New York Knicks
Orlando Magic
Philadelphia 76ers
Toronto Raptors
Washington Wizards

Basketball

NBA: Western Conference

TEAMS
Dallas Mavericks
Denver Nuggets
Golden State Warriors (San Francisco)
Houston Rockets
Los Angeles Clippers
Los Angeles Lakers
Memphis Grizzlies
Minnesota Timberwolves
New Orleans Pelicans
Oklahoma City Thunder
Phoenix Suns
Portland Trail Blazers
Sacramento Kings
San Antonio Spurs
Utah Jazz

Basketball

WNBA: Eastern Conference

TEAMS
Atlanta Dream
Chicago Sky
Connecticut Sun
Indiana Fever
New York Liberty
Washington Mystics

Basketball

WNBA: Western Conference

TEAMS
Dallas Wings
Las Vegas Aces
Los Angeles Sparks
Minnesota Lynx
Phoenix Mercury
Seattle Storm

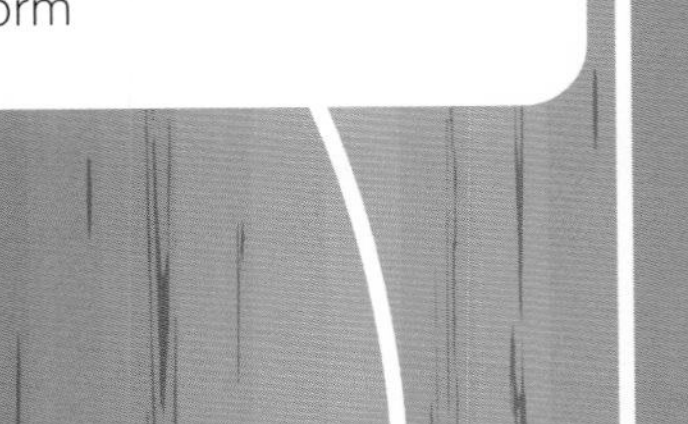

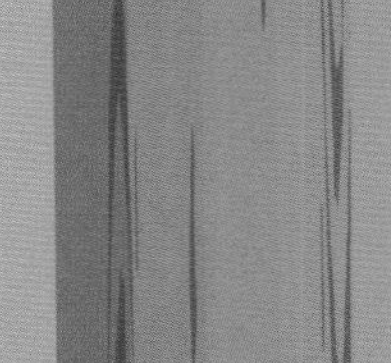

Ice Hockey

NHL: Western Conference

TEAMS
Anaheim Ducks
Arizona Coyotes
Calgary Flames
Chicago Blackhawks
Colorado Avalanche
Dallas Stars
Edmonton Oilers
Los Angeles Kings
Minnesota Wild
Nashville Predators
San Jose Sharks
St. Louis Blues
Vancouver Canucks
Vegas Golden Knights
Winnipeg Jets

Ice Hockey

NHL: Eastern Conference

TEAMS
Boston Bruins
Buffalo Sabres
Carolina Hurricanes
Columbus Blue Jackets
Detroit Red Wings
Florida Panthers
Montreal Canadiens
New Jersey Devils
New York Islanders
New York Rangers
Ottawa Senators
Philadelphia Flyers
Pittsburgh Penguins
Tampa Bay Lighting
Toronto Maple Leafs
Washington Capitals

Ice Hockey

National Women's Hockey League (NWHL)

TEAMS
Boston Pride
Buffalo Beauts (New York)
Connecticut Whale
Metropolitan Riveters (New Jersey)
Minnesota Whitecaps
Toronto Six

ICE HOCKEY

Soccer

MLS: Western Conference

TEAMS
Colorado Rapids
FC Dallas
Houston Dynamo
Los Angeles Galaxy
Los Angeles FC
Minnesota United FC
Portland Timbers
Real Salt Lake
San Jose Earthquakes
Seattle Sounders FC
Sporting Kansas City
Vancouver Whitecaps FC

Soccer

MLS: Eastern Conference

TEAMS
Atlanta United FC
Chicago Fire FC
Columbus Crew SC
FC Cincinnati
D.C. United
Inter Miami CF
Montreal Impact
Nashville SC
New England Revolution
New York City FC
New York Red Bulls
Orlando City SC
Philadelphia Union
Toronto FC

Soccer

National Women's Soccer League (NWSL)

TEAMS
Chicago Red Stars
Houston Dash
North Carolina Courage
OL Reign (Washington)
Orlando Pride
Portland Thorns FC
Sky Blue FC (New Jersey)
Utah Royals FC
Washington Spirit

US American football champions

American Football

AFC: American Football Conference

YEAR	CHAMPIONS
2004	New England Patriots
2005	Pittsburgh Steelers
2006	Indianapolis Colts
2007	New England Patriots
2008	Pittsburgh Steelers
2009	Indianapolis Colts
2010	Pittsburgh Steelers
2011	New England Patriots
2012	Baltimore Ravens
2013	Denver Broncos
2014	New England Patriots
2015	Denver Broncos
2016	New England Patriots
2017	New England Patriots
2018	New England Patriots
2019	Kansas City Chiefs

American Football

NFC: National Football Conference

YEAR	CHAMPIONS
2004	Philadelphia Eagles
2005	Seattle Seahawks
2006	Chicago Bears
2007	New York Giants
2008	Arizona Cardinals
2009	New Orleans Saints
2010	Green Bay Packers
2011	New York Giants
2012	San Francisco 49ers
2013	Seattle Seahawks
2014	Seattle Seahawks
2015	Carolina Panthers
2016	Atlanta Falcons
2017	Philadelphia Eagles
2018	Los Angeles Rams
2019	San Francisco 49ers

US baseball champions

Baseball

American League

YEAR	CHAMPIONS
2005	Chicago White Sox
2006	Detroit Tigers
2007	Boston Red Sox
2008	Tampa Bay Rays
2009	New York Yankees
2010	Texas Rangers
2011	Texas Rangers
2012	Detroit Tigers
2013	Boston Red Sox
2014	Kansas City Royals
2015	Kansas City Royals
2016	Cleveland Indians
2017	Houston Astros
2018	Boston Red Sox
2019	Houston Astros

Baseball

National League

YEAR	CHAMPIONS
2005	Houston AstrosC
2006	St. Louis Cardinals
2007	Colorado RockiesW
2008	Philadelphia Phillies
2009	Philadelphia Phillies
2010	San Francisco Giants
2011	St. Louis Cardinals
2012	San Francisco Giants
2013	St. Louis Cardinals
2014	San Francisco Giants
2015	New York Mets
2016	Chicago Cubs
2017	Los Angeles Dodgers
2018	Los Angeles Dodgers
2019	Washington Nationals

US basketball champions

Basketball

NBA Eastern Conference

YEAR	CHAMPIONS
2005	Detroit Pistons
2006	Miami Heat
2007	Cleveland Cavaliers
2008	Boston Celtics
2009	Orlando Magic
2010	Boston Celtics
2011	Miami Heat
2012	Miami Heat
2013	Miami Heat
2014	Miami Heat
2015	Cleveland Cavaliers
2016	Cleveland Cavaliers
2017	Cleveland Cavaliers
2018	Cleveland Cavaliers
2019	Toronto Raptors

Basketball

NBA Western Conference

YEAR	CHAMPIONS
2005	San Antonio Spurs
2006	Dallas Mavericks
2007	San Antonio Spurs
2008	Los Angeles Lakers
2009	Los Angeles Lakers
2010	Los Angeles Lakers
2011	Dallas Mavericks
2012	Oklahoma City Thunder
2013	San Antonio Spurs
2014	San Antonio Spurs
2015	Golden State Warriors
2016	Golden State Warriors
2017	Golden State Warriors
2018	Golden State Warriors
2019	Golden State Warriors

US ice hockey champions

Ice Hockey

NHL: Western Conference

YEAR	CHAMPIONS
2005	No Conference Finals played due to the lockout
2006	Edmonton Oilers
2007	Anaheim Ducks
2008	Detroit Red Wings
2009	Detroit Red Wings
2010	Chicago Blackhawks
2011	Vancouver Canucks
2012	Los Angeles Kings
2013	Chicago Blackhawks
2014	Los Angeles Kings
2015	Chicago Blackhawks
2016	San Jose Sharks
2017	Nashville Predators
2018	Vegas Golden Knights
2019	St. Louis Blues

Ice Hockey

NHL: Eastern Conference

YEAR	CHAMPIONS
2005	No Conference Finals played due to the lockout
2006	Carolina Hurricanes
2007	Ottawa Senators
2008	Pittsburgh Penguins
2009	Pittsburgh Penguins
2010	Philadelphia Flyers
2011	Boston Bruins
2012	New Jersey Devils
2013	Boston Bruins
2014	New York Rangers
2015	Tampa Bay Lightning
2016	Pittsburgh Penguins
2017	Pittsburgh Penguins
2018	Washington Capitals
2019	Boston Bruins

US soccer champions

Soccer

MLS: Western Conference

YEAR	CHAMPIONS
2008	New York Red Bulls
2009	LA Galaxy
2010	FC Dallas
2011	LA Galaxy
2012	LA Galaxy
2013	Real Salt Lake
2014	LA Galaxy
2015	Portland Timbers
2016	Seattle Sounders FC
2017	Seattle Sounders FC
2018	Portland Timbers
2019	Seattle Sounders FC

Soccer

MLS: Eastern Conference

YEAR	CHAMPIONS
2008	Columbus Crew SC
2009	Real Salt Lake (W)
2010	Colorado Rapids (W)
2011	Houston Dynamo (W)
2012	Houston Dynamo (W)
2013	Sporting Kansas City
2014	New England Revolution
2015	Columbus Crew SC
2016	Toronto FC
2017	Toronto FC
2018	Atlanta United FC
2019	Toronto FC

(W) – Western Conference team.

UK sports leagues

FOOTBALL
Premier League
Championship
League One
League Two
National League
FA Cup
EFL Cup
Scottish Football
Scottish Premiership
Scottish Championship
Scottish League One
Scottish League Two
Scottish Cup
Scottish League Cup
Scottish Challenge Cup
Welsh Football
Irish Football
Women's Football

RUGBY LEAGUE
1895 Cup
Challenge Cup
Championship
League 1
Super League

RUGBY UNION
Championship
Gallagher Premiership
Guinness PRO14
Super Rugby

CRICKET
County Championship
Royal London One - Day Cup
Vitality Blast

Popular European football leagues

LEAGUE	COUNTRY
Bundesliga	Germany
Eredivisie	The Netherlands
La Liga	Spain
Ligue 1	France
Premier League	England
Primeira Liga	Portugal
Serie A	Italy

Bundesliga champions

YEAR	CHAMPIONS
1993-94	Werder Bremen
1994-95	Bayern München
1995-96	Borussia Dortmund
1996-97	Borussia Dortmund
1997-98	Bayern München
1998-99	1. FC Kaiserslautern
1999-00	Bayern München
2000-01	Bayern München
2001-02	Bayern München
2002-03	Borussia Dortmund
2003-04	Bayern München
2004-05	Werder Bremen
2005-06	Bayern München
2006-07	Bayern München
2007-08	VfB Stuttgart
2008-09	Bayern München
2009-10	VfL Wolfsburg
2010-11	Bayern München
2011-12	Borussia Dortmund
2012-13	Borussia Dortmund
2013-14	Bayern München
2014-15	Bayern München
2015-16	Bayern München
2016-17	Bayern München
2017-18	Bayern München
2018-19	Bayern München
2019-20	Bayern München

Eredivisie champions

YEAR	CHAMPIONS
1993-94	AFC Ajax
1994-95	AFC Ajax
1995-96	AFC Ajax
1996-97	PSV Eindhoven
1997-98	AFC Ajax
1998-99	Feyenoord
1999-00	PSV Eindhoven
2000-01	PSV Eindhoven
2001-02	AFC Ajax
2002-03	PSV Eindhoven
2003-04	AFC Ajax
2004-05	PSV Eindhoven
2005-06	PSV Eindhoven
2006-07	PSV Eindhoven
2007-08	PSV Eindhoven
2008-09	AZ Alkmaar
2009-10	FC Twente
2010-11	AFC Ajax
2011-12	AFC Ajax
2012-13	AFC Ajax
2013-14	AFC Ajax
2014-15	PSV Eindhoven
2015-16	PSV Eindhoven
2016-17	Feyenoord
2017-18	PSV Eindhoven
2018-19	AFC Ajax
2019-20	No champions due to coronavirus pandemic

La Liga champions

YEAR	CHAMPIONS
1993-94	Barcelona
1994-95	Real Madrid
1995-96	Atlético Madrid
1996-97	Real Madrid
1997-98	Barcelona
1998-99	Barcelona
1999-00	Deportivo Coruña
2000-01	Real Madrid
2001-02	Valencia
2002-03	Real Madrid
2003-04	Valencia
2004-05	Barcelona
2005-06	Barcelona
2006-07	Real Madrid
2007-08	Real Madrid
2008-09	Barcelona
2009-10	Barcelona
2010-11	Barcelona
2011-12	Real Madrid
2012-13	Barcelona
2013-14	Atlético Madrid
2014-15	Barcelona
2015-16	Barcelona
2016-17	Real Madrid
2017-18	Barcelona
2018-19	Barcelona
2019-20	Real Madrid

Ligue 1 champions

YEAR	CHAMPIONS
1993-94	Paris Saint-Germain
1994-95	FC Nantes
1995-96	AJ Auxerre
1996-97	AS Monaco
1997-98	RC Lens
1998-99	Girondins Bordeaux
1999-00	AS Monaco
2000-01	FC Nantes
2001-02	Olympique Lyon
2002-03	Olympique Lyon
2003-04	Olympique Lyon
2004-05	Olympique Lyon
2005-06	Olympique Lyon
2006-07	Olympique Lyon
2007-08	Olympique Lyon
2008-09	Girondins Bordeaux
2009-10	Olympique Marseille
2010-11	Lille OSC
2011-12	Montpellier HSC
2012-13	Paris Saint-Germain
2013-14	Paris Saint-Germain
2014-15	Paris Saint-Germain
2015-16	Paris Saint-Germain
2016-17	AS Monaco
2017-18	Paris Saint-Germain
2018-19	Paris Saint-Germain
2019-20	Paris Saint-Germain

Premier League champions

YEAR	CHAMPIONS
1993-94	Manchester United
1994-95	Blackburn Rovers
1995-96	Manchester United
1996-97	Manchester United
1997-98	Arsenal
1998-99	Manchester United
1999-00	Manchester United
2000-01	Manchester United
2001-02	Arsenal
2002-03	Manchester United
2003-04	Arsenal
2004-05	Chelsea
2005-06	Chelsea
2006-07	Manchester United
2007-08	Manchester United
2008-09	Manchester United
2009-10	Chelsea
2010-11	Manchester United
2011-12	Manchester City
2012-13	Manchester United
2013-14	Manchester City
2014-15	Chelsea
2015-16	Leicester City
2016-17	Chelsea
2017-18	Manchester City
2018-19	Manchester City
2019-20	Liverpool FC

Primeira Liga champions

YEAR	CHAMPIONS
1993-94	FC Porto
1994-95	SL Benfica
1995-96	FC Porto
1996-97	FC Porto
1997-98	FC Porto
1998-99	FC Porto
1999-00	FC Porto
2000-01	Sporting CP
2001-02	Boavista
2002-03	Sporting CP
2003-04	FC Porto
2004-05	FC Porto
2005-06	SL Benfica
2006-07	FC Porto
2007-08	FC Porto
2008-09	FC Porto
2009-10	FC Porto
2010-11	SL Benfica
2011-12	FC Porto
2012-13	FC Porto
2013-14	FC Porto
2014-15	SL Benfica
2015-16	SL Benfica
2016-17	SL Benfica
2017-18	SL Benfica
2018-19	SL Benfica
2019-20	FC Porto

Serie A champions

YEAR	CHAMPIONS
1993-94	AC Milan
1994-95	AC Milan
1995-96	Juventus
1996-97	AC Milan
1997-98	Juventus
1998-99	Juventus
1999-00	AC Milan
2000-01	Lazio Roma
2001-02	AS Roma
2002-03	Juventus
2003-04	AC Milan
2004-05	No Champion
2005-06	Inter
2006-07	Inter
2007-08	Inter
2008-09	Inter
2009-10	Inter
2010-11	AC Milan
2011-12	Juventus
2012-13	Juventus
2013-14	Juventus
2014-15	Juventus
2015-16	Juventus
2016-17	Juventus
2017-18	Juventus
2018-19	Juventus
2019-20	Juventus

Grand Prix circuits

LOCATION	CIRCUIT	FIRST YEAR	TOTAL GRAND PRIX
Australia	Albert Park	1996	24
Bahrain	Bahrain International Circuit	2004	20
Italy	Autodromo Nazionale Monza	1950	76
Mexico	Autódromo Hermanos Rodríguez	1963	20
Brazil	Autódromo José Carlos Pace	1973	36
Azerbaijan	Baku City Circuit	2016	5
Bahrain	Bahrain International Circuit	2004	20
USA	Circuit of the Americas	2012	8
Spain	Circuit de Catalunya	1991	34
Canada	Circuit Gilles Villeneuve	1978	40
Monaco	Circuit de Monaco	1950	71
Germany	Hockenheimring	1970	40
Hungary	Hungaroring	1986	40
Singapore	Marina Bay Circuit	2008	14
France	Circuit Paul Ricard	2018	2
Austria	Red Bull Ring, Spielberg	1970	34
China	Shanghai International Circuit	2004	16
UK	Silverstone Circuit	1950	58
Russia	Sochi Autodrom	2014	8
Belgium	Spa-Francorchamps	1950	58
Japan	Suzuka Circuit	1987	31
UAE	Yas Marina Circuit	2009	16

Major horse races across the world

RACE	RACE TYPE	LOCATION	FESTIVAL	TIME OF YEAR
Breeders' Cup	Flat race	North America	Breeders' Cup World Championships	Late October or early November
Champion Hurdle	Hurdle	Cheltenham Racecourse	Cheltenham Festival	March
Cheltenham Gold Cup	Steeplechase	Cheltenham Racecourse	Cheltenham	March
Dubai World Cup	Flat race	Meydan Racecourse	Dubai World Cup Night	Last Saturday in March
Grand National	Steeplechase	Aintree Racecourse	Aintree	Early-mid April
Hennessy Gold Cup	Hurdle	Newbury	Newbury Festival	May
Kentucky Derby	Flat race	Churchill Downs	Kentucky Derby Festival	1st Saturday in May
Melbourne Cup	Flat race	Flemington Racecourse	Spring Carnival	1st Tuesday in November
Prix de l'Arc de Triomphe	Flat race	Longchamp Racecourse	Arc Weekend	1st Sunday in October
Epsom Derby	Flat race	Epsom Downs Racecourse	Investec Epsom Derby Festival	1st Saturday in June

UK racecourses

RACECOURSE	LOCATION	LEFT/RIGHT	COURSE TYPE	OPENED
Aintree	Liverpool	Left-handed	National Hunt	1939
Ascot	Ascot	Right-handed	Mixed	1711
Ayr	Ayr	Left-handed	Mixed	1907
Bangor on Dee	Wrexham	Left-handed	National Hunt	1859
Bath	Bath	Left-handed	Flat	1728
Beverley	Beverley	Right-handed	Flat	1767
Brighton	Brighton	Left-handed	Flat	1783
Carlisle	Carlisle	Right-handed	Mixed	1904
Cartmel	Grange-over-Sands	Left-handed	National Hunt	1856
Catterick Bridge	Richmond	Left-handed	Mixed	1783
Cheltenham	Cheltenham	Left-handed	National Hunt	1818
Chelmsford City	Chelmsford	Left-handed	Flat	2015
Chepstow	Chepstow	Left-handed	Mixed	1926
Chester	Chester	Left-handed	Flat	1539
Doncaster	Doncaster	Left-handed	Mixed	1614
Epsom Downs	Epsom	Left-handed	Flat	1661
Exeter	Exeter	Right-handed	National Hunt	1750
Fakenham	Fakenham	Left-handed	National Hunt	1905
Ffos Las	Trimsaran	Left-handed	Mixed	2009
Fontwell Park	Arundel	Left-handed	National Hunt	1924
Goodwood	Chichester	Right-handed	Flat	1802
Great Yarmouth	Great Yarmouth	Left-handed	Flat	1715
Hamilton Park	Hamilton	Right-handed	Flat	1782
Haydock Park	Newton-Le-Willows	Left-handed	Mixed	1899
Hereford	Hereford	Right-handed	National Hunt	1771
Hexham	Hexham	Left-handed	National Hunt	1720
Huntingdon	Huntington	Right-handed	National Hunt	1755

RACECOURSE	LOCATION	LEFT/RIGHT	COURSE TYPE	OPENED
Kelso	Kelso	Left-handed	National Hunt	1822
Kempton Park	Sunbury on Thames	Right-handed	Mixed	1878
Leicester	Leicester	Right-handed	Mixed	1833
Lingfied Park	Lingfield	Left-handed	Mixed	1890
Ludlow	Ludlow	Right-handed	National Hunt	1729
Market Rasen	Market Rasen	Right-handed	National Hunt	1800
Musselburgh	Musselburgh	Right-handed	Mixed	1816
Newbury	Newbury	Left-handed	Mixed	1905
Newcastle	Newcastle-Upon-Tyne	Left-handed	Mixed	1882
Newmarket	Newmarket	Right-handed	Flat	1667
Newton Abbot	Newton Abbot	Left-handed	National Hunt	1866
Nottingham	Nottingham	Right-handed	Flat	1892
Perth	Perth	Right-handed	National Hunt	1908
Plumpton	Plumpton	Left-handed	National Hunt	1884
Pontefact	Pontefact	Left-handed	Flat	1648
Redcar	Redcar	Left-handed	Flat	1875
Ripon	Ripon	Right-handed	Flat	1900
Salisbury	Salisbury	Right-handed	Flat	Mid 16C
Sandwon Park	Esher	Right-handed	Mixed	1875
Sedgefield	Sedgefield	Left-handed	National Hunt	1732
Southwell	Rolleston	Left-handed	Mixed	1898
Stratford-on-Avon	Stratford-upon-Avon	Left-handed	National Hunt	1755
Taunton	Somerset	Right-handed	National Hunt	1927
Thirsk	Thursk	Left-handed	Flat	1923
Towcester	Towcester	Right-handed	National Hunt	1928
Uttoxeter	Uttoxeter	Left-handed	National Hunt	1907
Warwick	Warwick	Left-handed	National Hunt	1700
Wetherby	Wetherby	Left-handed	Mixed	1891
Wincanton	Wincanton	Right-handed	National Hunt	1895
Windsor	Windsor	Right-handed	Flat	1866
Wolverhampton	Wolverhampton	Left-handed	Flat	1887
Worcester	Worcester	Left-handed	National Hunt	1718
York	York	Left-handed	Flat	1731

Epsom Derby winners

YEAR	WINNERS
1900	Diamond Jubilee
1901	Volodyovski
1902	Ard Patrick
1903	Rock Sand
1904	St. Amant
1905	Cicero
1906	Spearmint
1907	Orby
1908	Signorinetta
1909	Minoru
1910	Lemberg
1911	Sunstar
1912	Tagalie
1913	Aboyeur
1914	Durbar
1915	Pommern
1916	Fifinella
1917	Gay Crusader
1918	Gainsborough
1919	Grand Parade
1920	Spion Kop
1921	Humorist
1922	Captain Cuttle
1923	Papyrus
1924	Sansovino
1925	Manna
1926	Coronach
1927	Call Boy
1928	Felstead

YEAR	WINNERS
1929	Trigo
1930	Blenheim
1931	Cameronian
1932	April the Fifth
1933	Hyperion
1934	Windsor Lad
1935	Bahram
1936	Mahmoud
1937	Mid-day Sun
1938	Bois Roussel
1939	Blue Peter
1940	Pont l'Eveque
1941	Owen Tudor
1942	Watling Street
1943	Straight Deal
1944	Ocean Swell
1945	Dante
1946	Airborne
1947	Pearl Diver
1948	My Love
1949	Nimbus
1950	Galcador
1951	Arctic Prince
1952	Tulyar
1953	Pinza
1954	Never Say Die
1955	Phil Drake
1956	Lavandin
1957	Crepello

YEAR	WINNERS
1958	Hard Ridden
1959	Parthia
1960	St. Paddy
1961	Psidium
1962	Larkspur
1963	Relko
1964	Santa Claus
1965	Sea Bird Ii
1966	Charlottown
1967	Royal Palace
1968	Sir Ivor
1969	Blakeney
1970	Nijinsky
1971	Mill Reef
1972	Roberto
1973	Morston
1974	Snow Knight
1975	Grundy
1976	Empery
1977	The Minstrel
1978	Shirley Heights
1979	Troy
1980	Henbit
1981	Shergar
1982	Golden Fleece
1983	Teenoso
1984	Secreto
1985	Slip Anchor
1986	Shahrastani
1987	Reference Point
1988	Kahyasi
1989	Nashwan
1990	Quest for Fame
1991	Generous
1992	Dr Devious
1993	Commander in Chief

YEAR	WINNERS
1994	Erhaab
1995	Lammtarra
1996	Shaamit
1997	Benny the Dip
1998	High-Rise
1999	Oath
2000	Sinndar
2001	Galileo
2002	High Chaparral
2003	Kris Kin
2004	North Light
2005	Motivator
2006	Sir Percy
2007	Authorized
2008	New Approach
2009	Sea the Stars
2010	The Derby Workforce
2011	Pour Moi
2012	Camelot
2013	Ruler Of The World
2014	Australia
2015	Golden Horn
2016	Harzand
2017	Wings of Eagles
2018	Masar
2019	Anthony Van Dyck
2020	Serpentine

Grand National fence guide

FENCE	DESCRIPTION
2 (18): The Fan	4 ft 7 in
6 (22): Becher's Brook	4ft 10in on take off, there is a confusing drop on the landing side
7 (23): Foinavon	4 ft 6 in
8 (24): Canal Turn	5ft fence presents a dangerous challenge as many riders take it at an angle to minimise the 90-degree turn on the course, in an attempt to gain ground.
9 (25): Valentine's Brook	5 ft fence with a 5 ft 6 in wide brook
15: The Chair	5 ft 2 in high and preceded by open 6 ft ditch
16: The Water Jump	2 ft 6 in but requires a huge leap to clear the 12 ft 6 in expanse of water beyond

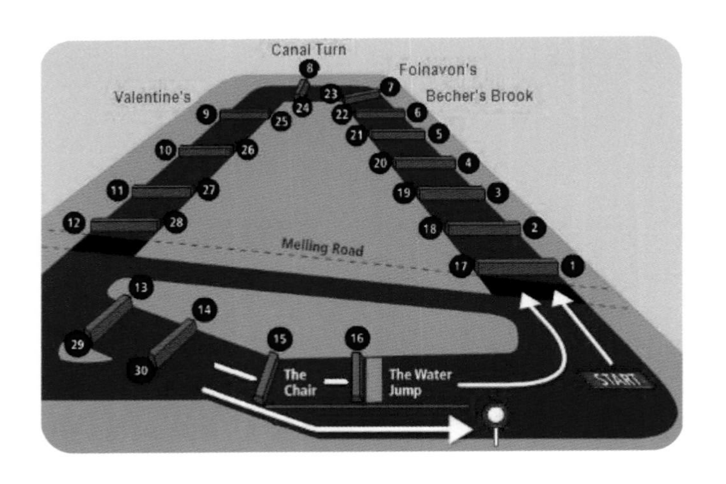

Gamebird and waterfowl open seasons

SPECIES	ENGLAND & WALES	SCOTLAND	N. IRELAND	ISLE OF MAN
Pheasant	Oct 1 – Feb 1	Oct 1 – Feb 1	Oct 1 – Jan 31	Oct 1 – Jan 31
Grey Partridge	Sep 1 – Feb 1	Sep 1 – Feb 1	Sep 1- Jan 31	Protected (ban in force)
Red-legged Partridge	Sep 1 – Feb 1	Sep 1 – Feb 1	Sep 1- Jan 31	Sep 13 – Jan 31
Red Grouse	Aug 12 – Dec 10	Aug 12 – Dec 10	Aug 12 – Nov 30	Aug 25 – Oct 31
Black Grouse	Aug 20 – Dec 10 (Somerset, Devon and New Forest: Sep 1 – Dec 10)	Aug 20 – Dec 10	–	–

A flying pheasant

SPECIES	ENGLAND & WALES	SCOTLAND	N. IRELAND	ISLE OF MAN
Ptarmigan	—	Aug 12 – Dec 10	—	—
Duck & Goose inland	Sep 1 – Jan 31	Sep 1 – Jan 31	Sep 1 – Jan 31	Sep 1 – Jan 31 – Ducks July 1 – Mar 31 – Geese
Duck & Goose below HWM (see below)	Sep 1 – Feb 20	Sep 1 – Feb 20	Sep 1 – Jan 31	Sep 1 – Jan 31- Ducks Jul 1 – Mar 31 – Geese
Common Snipe	Aug 12 – Jan 31	Aug 12 – Jan 31	Sep 1 – Jan 31	Sep 1 – Jan 31
Jack Snipe	Protected	Protected	Sep 1 – Jan 31	Protected
Woodcock	Oct 1 – Jan 31	Sep 1 – Jan 31	Oct 1 – Jan 31	Oct 1 – Jan 31
Golden Plover	Sep 1 – Jan 31	Sep 1 – Jan 31	Sep 1 – Jan 31	Protected
Coot/ Moorhen	Sep 1 – Jan 31	Sep 1 – Jan 31	Protected	Protected

Moorhen, Gallinula chloropus, Norfolk, UK.

Deer – open season

SPECIES	SEX	ENGLAND & WALES	SCOTLAND	N. IRELAND
Red	Stags	Aug 1st – April 30th	July 1st – Oct 20th	Aug 1st – April 30th
	Hinds	Nov 1st – Mar 31	Oct 21st – Feb 15th	Nov 1st – Mar 31
Sika	Stags	Aug 1st – April 30th	July 1st – Oct 20th	Aug 1st – April 30th
	Hinds	Nov 1st – Mar 31st	Oct 21st – Feb 15th	Nov 1st – Mar 31st
Red/Sika Hybrids	Stags	Aug 1st – April 30th	July 1st – Oct 20th	Aug 1st – April 30th
	Hinds	Nov 1st – Mar 31st	Oct 21st – Feb 15th	Nov 1st – Mar 31st
Fallow	Bucks	Aug 1st – April 30th	Aug 1st – April 30th	Aug 1st – April 30th
	Doe	Nov 1st – Mar 31st	Oct 21st – Feb 15th	Nov 1st – Mar 31st
Roe	Bucks	April 1st – Oct 31st	April 1st – Oct 20th	—
	Doe	Nov 1st – Mar 31st	Oct 21st – March 31st	—
Chinese Water Deer	Bucks	Nov 1st – Mar 31st	—	—
	Doe	Nov 1st – Mar 31st	—	—

General Knowledge

1-10 in most widely spoken languages

NO.	ENGLISH	MANDARIN	SPANISH	HINDUSTANI	ARABIC
1	One	Yī (一)	Uno	Ek	Wahid
2	Two	Èr (二)	Dos	Do	Thnan
3	Three	Sān (三)	Tres	Teen	Thalatha
4	Four	Sì (四)	Cuatro	Chaar	Arba'a
5	Five	Wǔ (五)	Cinco	Paanch	Khamsa
6	Six	Liù (六)	Seis	Chhah	Sitta
7	Seven	Qī (七)	Siete	Saat	Sab'a
8	Eight	Bā (八)	Ocho	Aaath	Thamaniya
9	Nine	Jiǔ (九)	Nueve	Nou	Tis'a
10	Ten	Shí (十)	Diez	Das	'Ashra

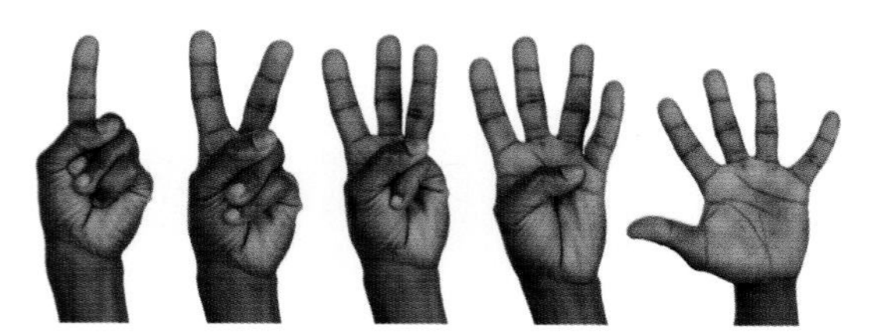

NO.	MALAY	RUSSIAN	BENGALI	PORTUGUESE	FRENCH
1	Satu	A-déen	Ek (এক)	Um	Un
2	Dua	Dva	Dui (দুই)	Dois	Deux
3	Tiga	Tré	Tin (তনি)	Três	Trois
4	Empat	Chee-tý-rye	Chā (চার)	Quatro	Quatre
5	Lima	Pyat	Pāṅch (পাঁচ)	Cinco	Conq
6	Enam	Shest	Chhɔẏ (ছয়)	Seis	Six
7	Tujah	Sem	Sāt (সাত)	Sete	Sept
8	Lapan	Vó-seem	Aṭh (আট)	Oito	Huit
9	Sembilan	Dyé-veet	Nɔẏ (নয়)	Nove	Neuf
10	Sepuluh	Dyé-seet	Dɔś (দশ)	Dez	Dix

Most commonly used Latin phrases

PHRASE	MEANING
Ad hoc	Formed or done for a particular purpose only
Alibi	Elsewhere
Bona fide	With good faith
Bonus	Good
Carpe diem	Seize the day
De facto	In fact; in reality
Exempli gratia (e.g.)	For example
Ego	First person pronoun, I
Ergo	Therefore
Et cetera	And so on
Extra	In addition to
Id est (i.e.)	That is
Impromptu	Spontaneous
Intro	Within
Multi	Many
Nota bene (N.B)	Note well
Per se	In itself/themselves
Pro bono (publico)	For the good (of the public)
Quid pro quo	Something for something
Re	About; concerning; regarding
Semi	Half
Status quo	Existing state of affairs
Verbatim	In exactly the same words
Versus; vs; v	Against
Vice versa	The other way round

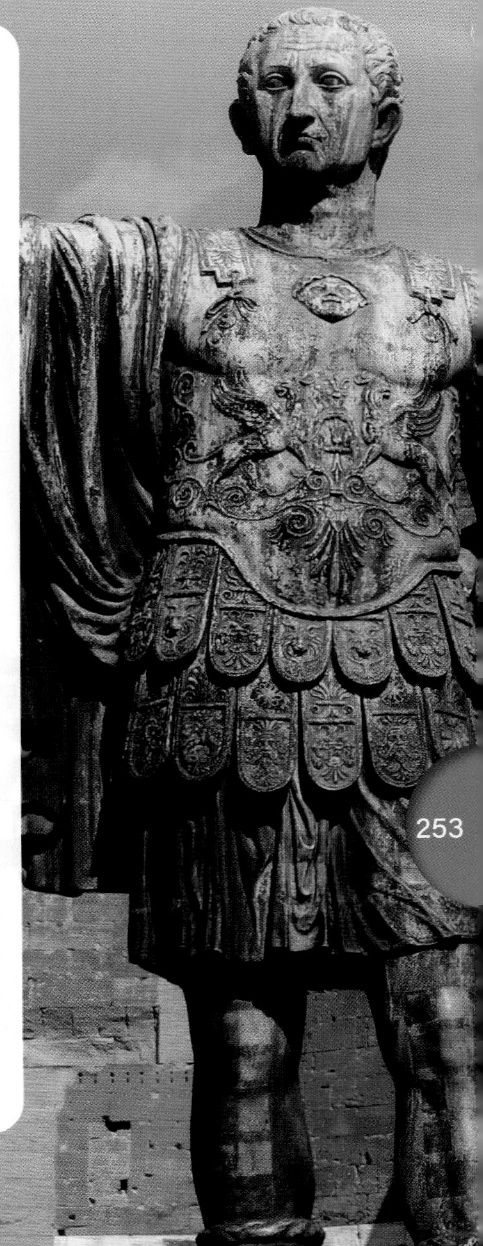

International morse code

A	•▬	N	▬•	1	•▬▬▬▬	.	•▬•▬•▬	=	▬•••▬
B	▬•••	O	▬▬▬	2	••▬▬▬	,	▬▬••▬▬	+	•▬•▬•
C	▬•▬•	P	•▬▬•	3	•••▬▬	?	••▬▬••	-	▬••••▬
D	▬••	Q	▬▬•▬	4	••••▬	!	▬•▬•▬▬	$	•••▬••▬
E	•	R	•▬•	5	•••••	'	•▬▬▬▬•	@	•▬▬•▬•
F	••▬•	S	•••	6	▬••••	"	•▬••▬•		
G	▬▬•	T	▬	7	▬▬•••	(	▬•▬▬•		
H	••••	U	••▬	8	▬▬▬••	)	▬•▬▬•▬		
I	••	V	•••▬	9	▬▬▬▬•	&	•▬•••		
J	•▬▬▬	W	•▬▬	0	▬▬▬▬▬	:	▬▬▬•••		
K	▬•▬	X	▬••▬			;	▬•▬•▬•		
L	•▬••	Y	▬•▬▬			/	▬••▬•		
M	▬▬	Z	▬▬••			_	••▬▬•▬		

UK phonetic alphabet

Alpha	Bravo	Charlie	Delta	Echo	Foxtrot
Golf	Hotel	India	Juliet	Kilo	Lima
Mike	November	Oscar	Papa	Quebec	Romeo
Sierra	Tango	Uniform	Victor	Whiskey	X-ray
		Yankee	Zulu		

Common acronyms used in business

ACRONYM	DESCRIPTION
AKA	Also known as
CAPTCHA	Completely automated public turing test to tell computers and humans apart
COB	Close of business
CST	Central standard time
DBA	Doing business as
DND	Do not disturb
EDS	Electronic data systems
EOD	End of day
EST	Eastern standard time
ETA	Estimated time of arrival
ETD	Estimated time of departure
FIO	For information only
FYI	For your information
FYO	For your opinion
GMT	Greenwich mean time
HR	Human resources
JIT	Just in time
MBA	Masters of business administration
OT	Overtime
POS	Point of service
PST	Pacific standard time
SWOT	Strengths, weaknesses, opportunities, threats
SMART Goals	Specific, measurable, attainable, realistic, time-bound goals
TBA	To be announced
TBC	To be confirmed
TBD	To be determined
TED (Talk)	Tell me, explain to me, describe to me, (Talk)
WST	Western standard time

Cuts of meat

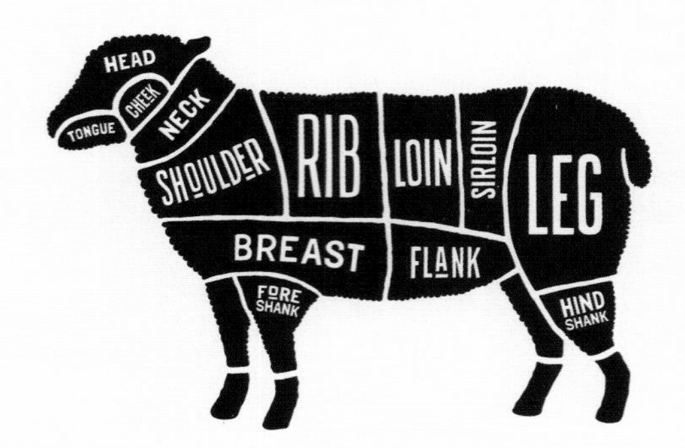
HEAD
TONGUE
CHEEK
NECK
SHOULDER
RIB
LOIN
SIRLOIN
LEG
BREAST
FLANK
FORE SHANK
HIND SHANK

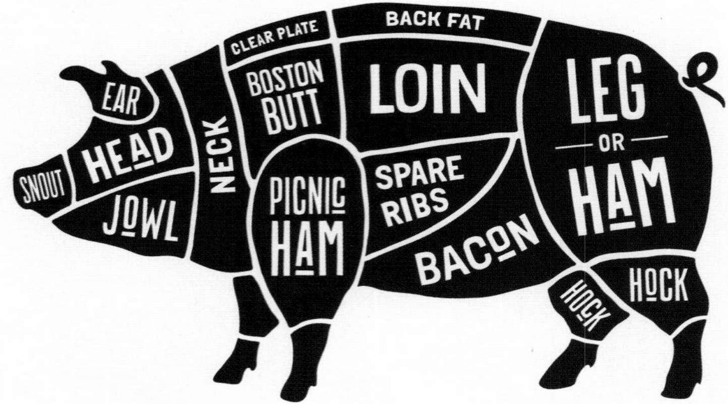
CLEAR PLATE
BACK FAT
EAR
BOSTON BUTT
LOIN
LEG OR HAM
SNOUT
HEAD
JOWL
NECK
PICNIC HAM
SPARE RIBS
BACON
HOCK
HOCK

HEAD
NECK
BACK
TAIL
TENDERLOIN
BREAST
WING
THIGH
DRUMSTICK

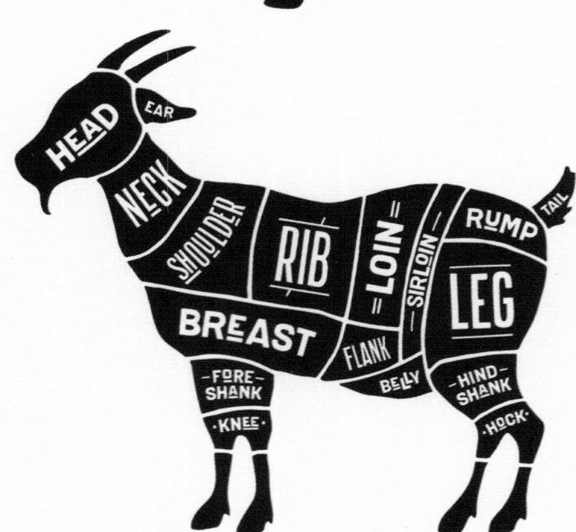
HEAD
EAR
NECK
SHOULDER
RIB
LOIN
SIRLOIN
RUMP
TAIL
LEG
BREAST
FLANK
BELLY
FORE-SHANK
HIND-SHANK
KNEE
HOCK

EAR
HEAD
NECK
CHUCK
RIB
SHORT SIRLOIN
SIRLOIN
RUMP
TAIL
BREAST
SHOULDER
SHORT RIBS
PLATE
FLANK
ROUND
FORE-SHANK
HIND-SHANK
HEAD
NECK
BACK
TAIL
DRUMETTE
WING
TIP
TENDERLOIN
BREAST
THIGH
DRUMSTICK
HEAD
NECK
BACK
TIP
TAIL
WINGETTE
DRUMETTE
TENDERLOIN
BREAST
THIGH
DRUMSTICK
HEAD
KAMA
BACK MEAT
ABDOMEN MEAT
TAIL MEAT
TAIL
CAVIAR
EAR
EAR
HEAD
NECK
SHOULDER
LOIN
HIP
RUMP
TAIL
HIND LEG
BELLY
RIB
FORE LEG
FOREFOOT
FOREFOOT
SHANK
SHANK
HINDFOOT
HINDFOOT
HEAD
EAR
NECK
SHOULDER
LOIN
TENDERLOIN
RUMP
TAIL
FORE LEG
RIBS
FLANK
SIRLOIN
TOP ROUND
BOTTOM ROUND
BRISKET
SHANK
SHANK
SHANK
HEAD
NECK
BACK
TENDERLOIN
BREAST
DRUMETTE
WINGETTE
TIP
TAIL
THIGH
DRUMSTICK

Cuts of beef

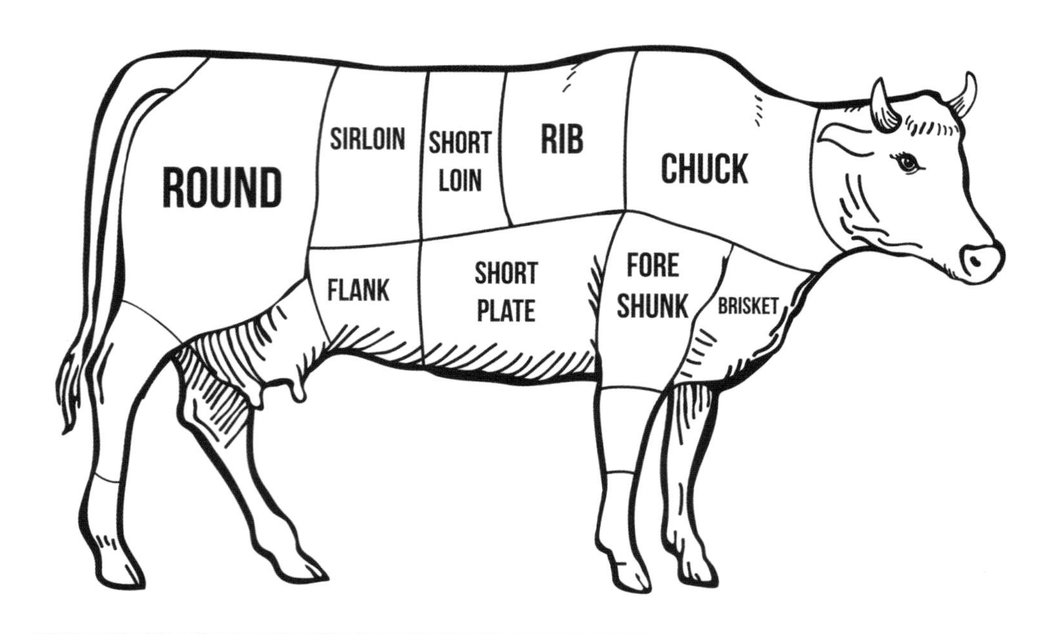

CHUCK

Boneless short ribs

Shoulder petite tender medallions

Shoulder petite tender

Shoulder pot roast boneless

Shoulder steak boneless

Shoulder centre ranch steak

Chuck eye steak boneless

Shoulder top blade steak

Shoulder top blade steak flatiron

Chuck steak boneless

Chuck bone 7 pot roast

Chuck boneless pot roast

ROUND

Eye round steak

Eye round roast

Round tip roast

Bottom round roast

Top round roast

Bottom round steak western griller

Round top steak

Sirloin top centre roast

Sirloin top centre steak

Sirloin top centre side steak

SHORT LOIN

Top loin steak boneless

Tender roast

Tenderloin steak (inc. fillet)

Top loin steak bone-in

T-bone steak

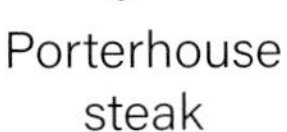
Porterhouse steak

SIRLOIN

Top sirloin steak boneless

Top steak

Top roast

RIB

Ribeye steak boneless

Back ribs

Ribeye roast boneless

Rib steak

Rib roast

FLANK

Flank steak

SHORT PLATE

Skirt steak

FORE SHUNK

Shank crosscut

BRISKET

Brisket flat cut

Bullet types and their abbreviations

ABBREVIATION	DESCRIPTION
A-BOND	Accu-Bond
A-FRAME	A-Frame
A-MAX	Hornady Match
B-TIP	Ballistic Tip
BK	Blitz King
BR	Bench Rest
BT	Boat Tail or Nosler Balistic Tip
BTSP	Boat Tail Spire Point
DEWC	Double End Wadcutter
DGX	Dangerous Game™ eXpanding
E-TIP	Expansion Tip Lead Free Bullet
ELD Match	Extremely Low Drag Match
ELD-X	Extremely Low Drag - eXpanding
FMC	Full Metal Case
FMJ	Full Metal Jacket
FMJ BT	Full Metal Jacket Boat Tail
FMJ FP	Full Metal Jacket Flat Point
FMJ HP	Full Metal Jacket Hollow Point
FMJ RN	Full Metal Jacket Round Nose
FMJ TC	Full Metal Jacket Truncated Cone
FN	Flat Nose
FNSP	Flat Nose Soft Point
FP	Flat Point

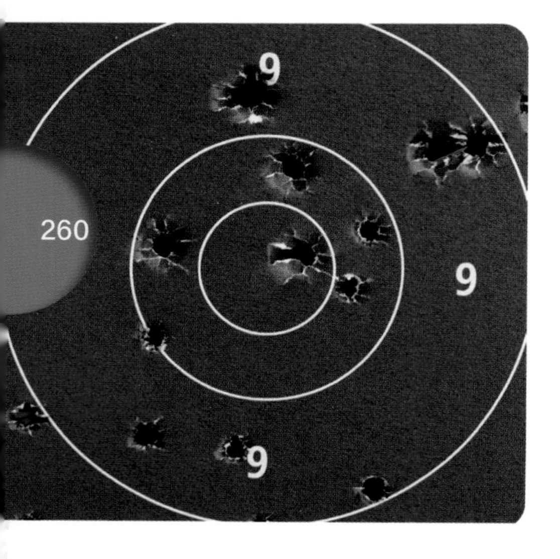

ABBREVIATION	DESCRIPTION
FP XTP	Flat Point eXtreme Terminal Performance
FPJ	Full Plated Jacket
FS	Fail Safe
FTX	Flex Tip
FTX ME	Flex Tip for Marlin Express
GC	Gas Check
GDHP	Gold Dot Hollow Point
GDSP	Gold Dot Soft Point
GK	Game King
GMX	Hornady GMX
GSAB	Golden Saber
GSLAM	Grand Slam
HAP	Hornady Action Pistol
HB	Hollow Base
HBFP	Hollow Base Flat Point
HBRN	Hollow Base Round Nose
HBRN TP	Hollow Base Round Nose Thick Plate
HBWC	Hollow Base Wadcutter
HC	Hollow Cavity
HORNET	HORNET
HP	Hollow Point
HPBT	Hollow Point Boat Tail
HPBT CC	Hollow Point Boat Tail Custom Competition
HPBT GK	Hollow Point Boat Tail Game King
HPBT MK	Hollow Point Boat Tail Match King
HSP	Hollow Soft Point
IB	Inter Bond
JFP	Jacketed Flat Point
JHC	Jacketed Hollow Cavity
JHP	Jacketed Hollow Point
JRN	Jacketed Round Nose
JSP	Jacketed Soft Point

ABBREVIATION	DESCRIPTION
JSWC	Jacketed Semi-Wadcutter
LBBWC	Lead Bevel Base Wadcutter
LCN	Lead Conical Nose
LFN	Lead Flat Nose
LFN GC	Lead Flat Nose w/ Gas Check
LFNPB	Lead Flat Nose Plain Base
LFP	Lead Flat Point
LHBWC	Lead Hollow Base Wadcutter
LRN	Lead Round Nose
LRNFP	Lead Round Nose Flat Point
LSWC	Lead Semi-Wadcutter
LWC	Lead Wadcutter
MC	Metal Case
Mega	Lapua Mega
MK	Match King
MRX	Maximum Range X Bullet
MT-SP	Mag Tip Soft Point
Naturalis	Lapua Naturalis
PART	Partition
PSPCL	Pointed Soft Point "Core Lokt"
RN	Round Nose
RNFP	Round Nose Flat Point
RNHB	Round Nose Hollow Base
RNSP	Round Nose Spire Point
SB	Solid Base
SBT	Spitzer Boat Tail
SBT GK	Spitzer Boat Tail Game King
SCENAR	Lapua Scenar
Scenar-L	Lapua Scenar L
SCIR	Scirocco
SFIR	Sinterfire

ABBREVIATION	DESCRIPTION
SJ	Short Jacket
SJSP	Semi-Jacketed Soft Point
SMP	Semi-Pointed
SP	Spire Point, Soft Point
SPBT	Soft Point Boat Tail
SPT	Spitzer
SPT PH	Pro Hunter Spitzer
SSP	Single Shot Pistol
SST	Super Shock Tip
ST	Silver Tip
SWC	Semi-Wadcutter
SX	Super Explosive
TAC-XP	M/LE TAC XP Pistol Bullets
TC	Truncated Cone
TMJ	Total Metal Jacket
TMJ FN	Total Metal Jacket Flat Nose
TMJ FP	Total Metal Jacket Flat Point
TMJ RN	Total Metal Jacket Round Nose
TMJ SWC	Total Metal Jacket Semi-Wadcutter
TNT	Varmint Bullet
TSX	Triple Shock X Bullet
TSX BT	Triple Shock X Bullet Boat Tail
TSX FB	Triple Shock X Bullet Flat Base
TTSX	Tipped Triple Shock X Bullet
TTSX BT	Tipped Triple Shock X Bullet Boat Tail
V-Max	Varmint Express
VG	Varmint Grenade
VG FB	Varmint Grenade Flat Base
VLD	Very Low Drag

ABBREVIATION	DESCRIPTION
W/GC	With Gas Check
WC	Wadcutter
X	X Bullet
XBT	X Boat Tail
XBTC	X Boat Tail Coated
XFB	X Flat Base Bullet
XLC	X Coated Bullet
XPB	X Pistol Bullet
XTP	eXtreme Terminal Performance
XTP MAG	eXtreme Terminal Performance — Magnum

Top 10 largest aircrafts

AIRCRAFT	LENGTH	WINGSPAN
HAV Airlander 10	92 meters	43.5 meters
Antonov An-225 Mriya	84 meters	88.4 meters
Boeing 747-8	76.3 meters	68.4 meters
Lockheed C-5 Galaxy	75.31 meters	67.89 meters
Stratolaunch	73 meters	117 meters
Airbus A380-800	72.72 meters	79.75 meters
Antonov An-124	68.96 meters	73.3 meters
Hughes H-4 Hercules	66.65 meters	97.54 meters
Tupolev Tu-160	54.1 meters	55.7 meters (spread)
Mil Mi-26	40 meters (with rotors turning)	32 meters

The Scaled Composites Stratolaunch aircraft, Mojave airport

Zodiac signs

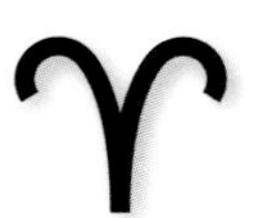

Aries
The Ram
Mar 21 - Apr 20

Taurus
The Bull
Apr 21 - May 30

Gemini
The Twins
May 31 -Jun 20

Cancer
The Crab
Jun 21 - Jul 21

Leo
The Lion
Jul 22 - Aug 22

Virgo
The Virgin
Aug 23 - Sept 21

Libra
The Scales
Sept 22 - Oct 21

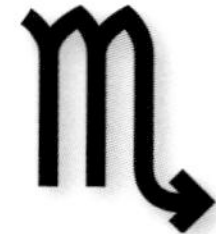

Scorpio
The Scorpion
Oct 22 - Nov 21

Sagittarius
The Archers
Nov 22 - Dec 21

Capricorn
The Sea-Goat
Dec 22 - Jan 20

Aquarius
The Water Bearer
Jan 21 - Feb 19

Pisces
The Fish
Feb 20 - Mar 20

Chinese zodiac

Rat
1924, 1936, 1948, 1960, 1972, 1984, 1996, 2008, 2020

Ox
1925, 1937, 1949, 1961, 1973, 1985, 1997, 2009, 2021

Tiger
1926, 1938, 1950, 1962, 1974, 1986, 1998, 2010, 2022

Rabbit
1927, 1939, 1951, 1963, 1975, 1987, 1999, 2011, 2023

Dragon
1928, 1940, 1952, 1964, 1976, 1988, 2000, 2012, 2024

Snake
1929, 1941, 1953, 1965, 1977, 1989, 2001, 2013, 2025

Horse
1930, 1942, 1954, 1966, 1978, 1990, 2002, 2014, 2026

Goat
1931, 1943, 1955, 1967, 1979, 1991, 2003, 2015, 2027

Monkey
1932, 1944, 1956, 1968, 1980, 1992, 2004, 2016, 2028

Rooster
1933, 1945, 1957, 1969, 1981, 1993, 2005, 2017, 2029

Dog
1934, 1946, 1958, 1970, 1982, 1994, 2006, 2018, 2030

Pig
1935, 1947, 1959, 1971, 1983, 1995, 2007, 2019, 2031

Boating knots

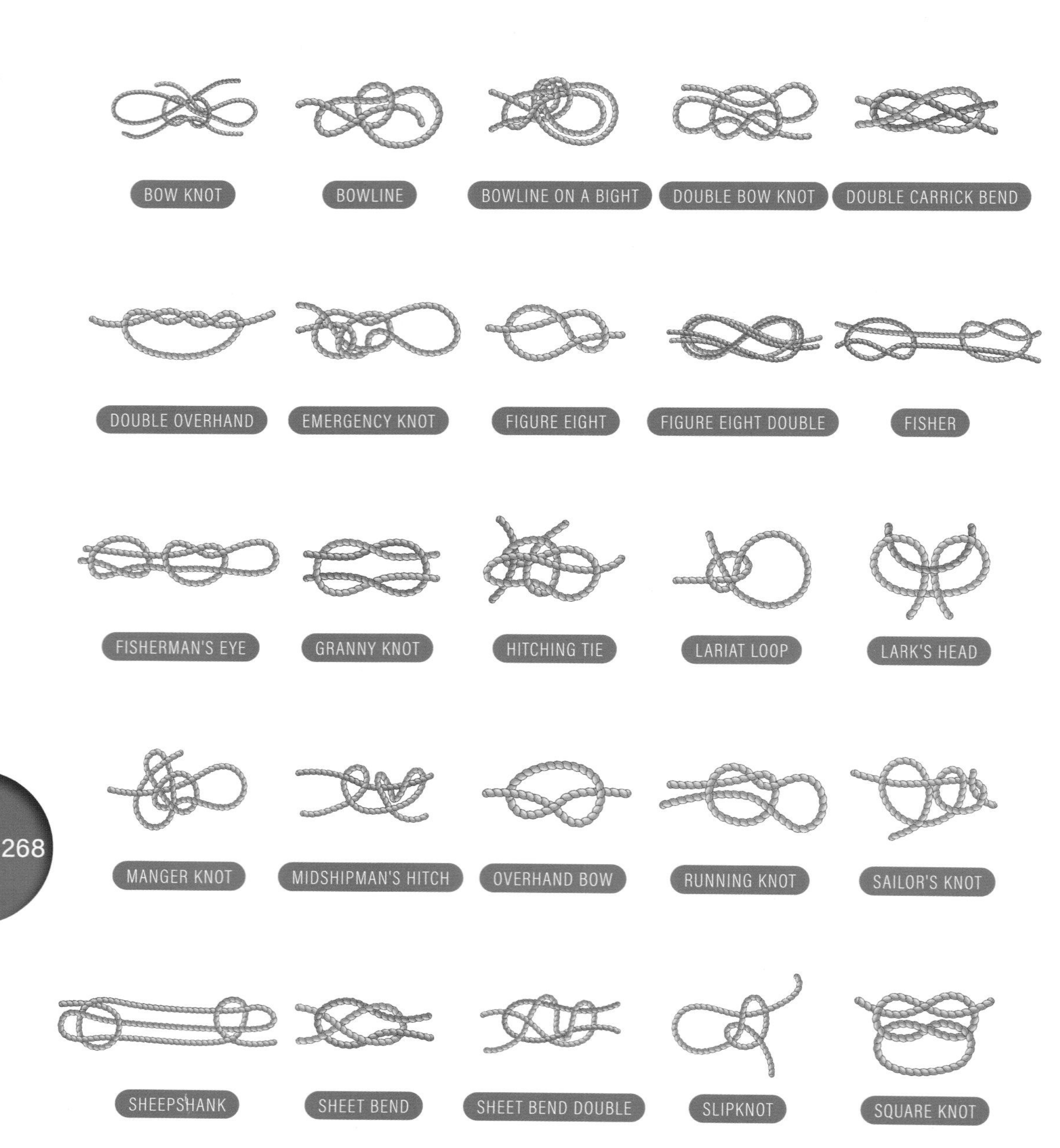

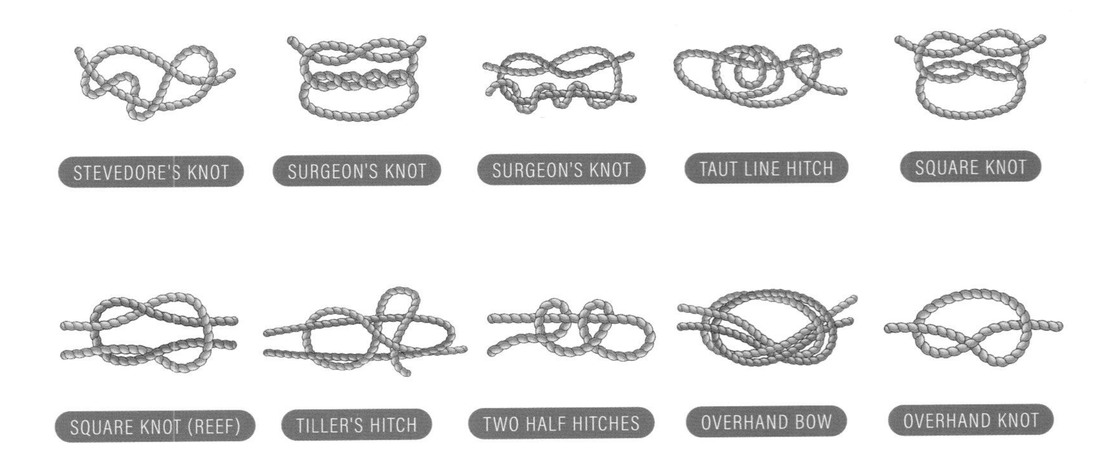
STEVEDORE'S KNOT
SURGEON'S KNOT
SURGEON'S KNOT
TAUT LINE HITCH
SQUARE KNOT
SQUARE KNOT (REEF)
TILLER'S HITCH
TWO HALF HITCHES
OVERHAND BOW
OVERHAND KNOT

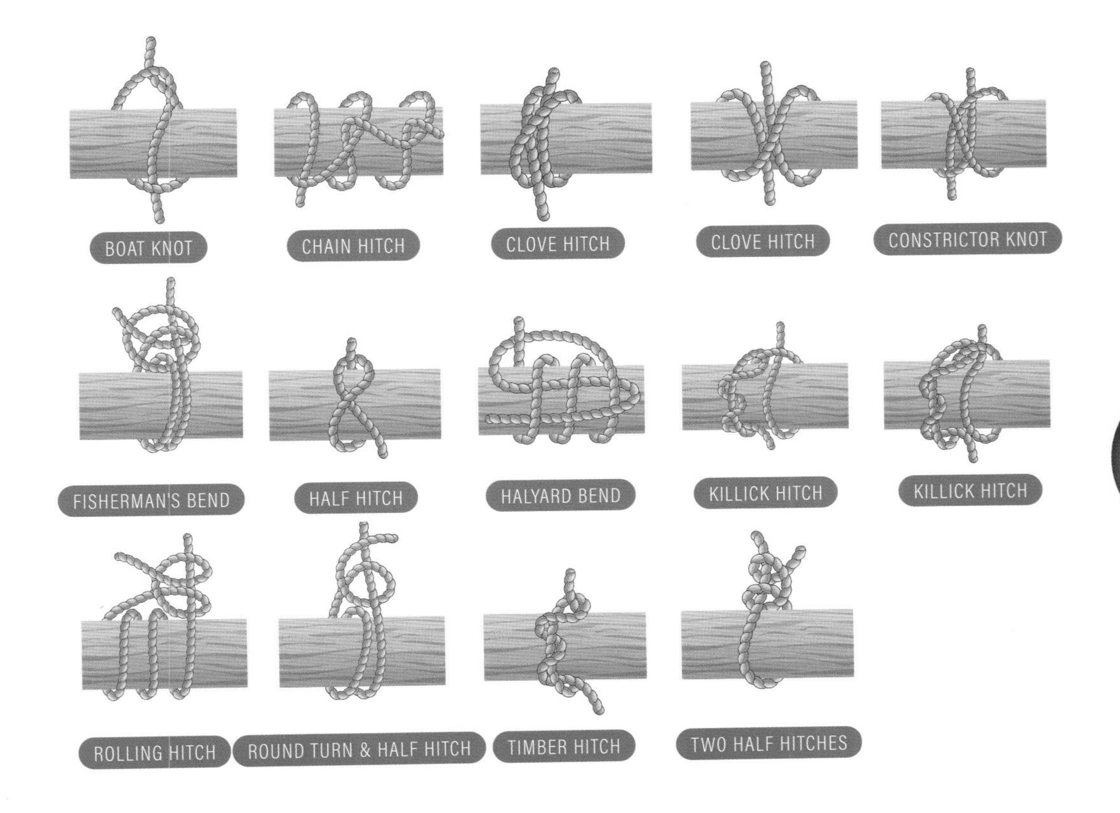
BOAT KNOT
CHAIN HITCH
CLOVE HITCH
CLOVE HITCH
CONSTRICTOR KNOT
FISHERMAN'S BEND
HALF HITCH
HALYARD BEND
KILLICK HITCH
KILLICK HITCH
ROLLING HITCH
ROUND TURN & HALF HITCH
TIMBER HITCH
TWO HALF HITCHES

Major worldwide stock exchanges*

STOCK EXCHANGE	LOCAL TRADING TIME	GMT TRADING TIME
Australian Securities Exchange (ASX)	10.00 - 16.00	00.00 - 06.00
Bombay Stock Exchange (BSE)	09.15 - 15.30	03.45 - 10.00
Brazil Stock Exchange (B3)	10.00 - 17.30	13.00 - 20.30
Euronext	09.00 - 17.30	08.00 - 16.30
Frankfurt Stock Exchange (FSX)	08.00 - 20.00	07.00 - 19.00
Hong Kong Stock Exchange (HKEX)	09.30 - 16.00	01.30 - 08.00
Johannesburg Stock Exchange (JSE)	09.00 - 17.00	07.00 - 15.00
Korea Exchange (KRX)	09.00 - 15.30	00.00 - 06.30
London Stock Exchange (LSE)	08.00 - 16.30	08.00 - 16.30
NASDAQ (National Association of Securities Dealers Automated Quotations)	09.30 - 16.00	14.30 - 21.00
New York Stock Exchange (NYSE)	09.30 - 16.00	14.30 - 21.00
Shanghai Stock Exchange (SSX)	09.30 - 15.00	01.30 - 07.00
Swiss Stock Exchange (SIX)	09.00 - 17.30	08.00 - 16.30
Tokyo Stock Exchange (TSE)	09.00 - 15.00	00.00 - 06.00
Toronto Stock Exchange (TSX)	09.30 - 16.00	14.30 - 21.00

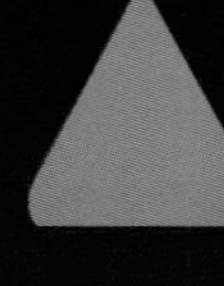

*and their opening times

Stock market abbreviations

ABBREVIATION	DESCRIPTION
ADTV	Average Daily Trading Volume
AMEX	American Stock Exchange
CB	Current Bid
CMP	Current Market Price
FTSE	Financial Times Stock Exchange
DJIA	Dow Jones Industrial Average
IPO	Initial Public Offering
IRA	Individual Retirement Account
NASDAQ	National Association of Securities Dealers Automated Quotation
NIKKEI 225	Stock market index for the Tokyo Stock Exchange
PFD	Preferred stock
QTE	Quote

References

GEOGRAPHY

www.europa.eu
www.gateway-africa.com
www.bbc.co.uk
www.britannica.com
www.nationsonline.org
www.livescience.com
www.county-wise.org.uk
www.canada.ca
www.australia.com
www.media.newzealand.com
www.telegraph.co.uk
www.worldatlas.com
www.earthnworld.com
www.worldlistmania.com
www.statista.com
www.wwf.org.uk
www.metoffice.gov.uk
www.shutterstock.com

HISTORY

www.britannica.com
www.history.com
www.ancient.eu
www.history.org.uk
www.ancient-origins.net
www.chinaeducenter.com
www.greekgodsandgoddesses.net
www.historic-uk.com
www.newadvent.org
www.salamina.gr
www.south-pole.com
www.telegraph.co.uk
www.maryceleste.net
www.bbc.co.uk
www.modelshipmaster.com
www.rmg.co.uk
www.coolantarctica.com
www.study.com
www.marineinsight.com
www.liverpoolmuseums.org.uk
www.wrecksite.eu
www.battlefields.org
www.shipwreckworld.com
www.answersafrica.com
www.nalakagunawardene.com
www.britainirelandcastles.com
www.royaltymonarchy.com
www.sport-histoire.fr
www.metmuseum.org
www.gov.uk
www.care.org.uk
www.thecultureconcept.com
www.parliament.uk
www.britainexpress.com
www.vam.ac.uk
www.placesjournal.org
www.westminster-abbey.org
www.identifythisart.com
www.shutterstock.com

SCIENCE & NATURE

www.theplanetstoday.com
www.nasa.gov
www.sciencenews.org
www.shutterstock.com
www.history.com
www.thoughtco.com
www.britannica.com
www.chemistry.tutorvista.com
www.worldatlas.com
www.mnn.com
www.nationalgeographic.com
www.telegraph.co.uk

ENTERTAINMENT

www.businessinsider.com
www.theatlantic.com
www.imdb.com
www.grammy.com
www.opensourceshakespeare.org
www.britannica.com
www.themanbookerprize.com
www.pulitzer.org
www.nobelprize.org
www.shutterstock.com

SPORTS

www.nationalgeographic.com
www.tennis.com.au
www.rugbyworld.com
www.britannica.com
www.olympic.org
www.skysports.com
www.bbc.co.uk
www.premierleague.com
www.eurosport.com
www.worldfootball.net
www.f1mix.com
www.britishhorseracing.com
www.racingbetter.co.uk
www.grand-national.me.uk
www.basc.org.uk
www.shutterstock.com

GENERAL KNOWLEDGE

www.worldatlas.com
www.inklyo.com
www.shutterstock.com
www.abbreviations.yourdictionary.com
www.shootersreference.com
www.edition.cnn.com
www.chinesenewyear.net
www.shutterstock.com

Other publications from Lounge Lizard Languages (available on Spotify™ and iTunes™)

This series seeks to teach the most common 100 words in each language - enough for you to understand and be understood at a basic level.

Whether you are learning a language for travel, business, pleasure or to further your career, vocabulary underpins the formation of understanding

The learn words series concentrates solely on vocabulary, building a solid foundation for learning another language with native speakers. Specific areas include; numbers, colours, food and drink, conversation, directions, rooms, verbs etc.

Nearly a hundred useful phrases are also included to help you put together the words learned.

There is no easy way to learn vocabulary - so we hope you find these useful!